Also by

MIDTOWN PUBLISHING CORP.

SOME THINGS I WISH WE WOULDN'T FORGET
(and others I wish we could)

The hilarities and tragedies of life as seen through newspaper columns and writings of a true Southern traditionalist.

By Jim Minter

Jim Minter is a master of subtle humor. He is a shrewd observer of suburban living, and his weekly newspaper articles are a treat. Now this belated selection provides everyone an opportunity to enjoy his columns.

Jesse Outlar, retired *Atlanta Constitution* sports editor.

I've known Jim Minter for more than 30 years. When he writes, I read every work because they're magic.

Ludlow Porch
Radio Talk Show Host

MURDER IN THE PEACH STATE

Infamous Murders Of Georgia's Past

Another Book By

Midtown Publishing Corp.

Also by

MIDTOWN PUBLISHING CORP.

DEATH UNEXPECTED

*Solved and unsolved murders in
Fayette County, Georgia.*

By Bruce L. Jordan

"*Death Unexpected* kept me up most of the night. It is a carefully researched, well written account of murder, solved and unsolved..."

Celestine Sibley
Atlanta Journal-Constitution

"Bruce Jordan is a policeman's policeman and a writer's writer. *Death Unexpected* is a good read for those of us who love a good mystery..."

Ludlow Porch
Radio Talk Show Host

MURDER IN THE PEACH STATE

Infamous Murders Of Georgia's Past

Best Wishes

By

Bruce L. Jordan

Bruce L. Jordan

Published by MIDTOWN PUBLISHING CORPORATION
1349 West Peachtree Street Suite 1250
Atlanta Georgia, 30309

Library of Congress Cataloging-in-Publication data

Jordan, Bruce L.
Murder in the Peach State

Printed in the United States of America

First printing in 2000

ISBN 0-9660768-3-4

This book was printed by McNaughton & Gunn
Saline, Michigan

Legal Consultant
William J. McKennney, Esq.
Atlanta, Georgia 30309

Cover design by Ken Rose
Cover photo by Annette Chambers

To Celestine

Actual names and locations appear throughout this publication, however some names have been changed for privacy reasons and are designated with the following symbol †.

CONTENTS

Author's note

It was December, 1997 when I drove up the winding driveway of the white-columned, brick plantation style home. Jim Minter was on a tractor in the front pasture. Although I knew he was once the editor of the largest newspaper in Georgia, on that day he looked like a farmer who had wandered his Massey-Ferguson onto the grounds of a Southern mansion. I'm sure he wouldn't call it a mansion, but I would.

He invited me inside to sign some books intended as presents for his friends. He escorted me into an immaculate, white-carpeted living room, decorated with freshly cut flowers and a grand piano. The room was decorated for Christmas; I felt like I had stepped into a *Southern Living* magazine.

Jim was ....well, filthy. Wearing blue jeans and a ball cap, he was sweaty and grimy from what obviously had been a long day working in the pasture on that tractor. From his appearance he looked like he was more comfortable on that Massey-Ferguson than in that living room.

I had just met him, but I knew his wife, Anne. I also knew a little bit about their relationship by reading his column. I surmised that he probably had very little to do with the decoration of their home, and I also knew he probably wouldn't be sitting on that white sofa if Anne was home.

I was well aware of how fortunate I was to have his attention for the 20 minutes I spent there. He said to me, "Well Bruce, I think you ought to do for Georgia what you've done for Fayette County. There are some very interesting murders in Georgia's history, too."

He went on to tell me about trials he thought would make interesting stories. He warned me: "I wouldn't mention it to Celestine, though. She covered most of those trials, and she could probably write that book from memory if she wanted to." He was talking about Atlanta Journal-Constitution columnist Celestine Sibley. I assumed he knew that Celestine and I had been spending some time together at some of the bookstores. He walked me back out to my Jeep and said goodbye. He probably never gave our conversation another thought.

It was only a few weeks later that I was with Celestine at a book-signing. I tried to pick her memory about some of the old murders Jim had mentioned to me. The fact that she was in her 80s didn't prevent her from running intellectual rings around me while I sat there thinking I was being coy. I had begun asking what I thought were innocent, curious questions about some of the trials she had covered when she asked me, "Bruce, are you planning to write about those murders?" She was too sharp for anything but honesty.

I went on to tell her about the project I was considering: Jim Minter's idea of re-creating some of the more interesting stories about murders in Georgia's history. She told me: "I've always wanted to write a book like that, Bruce, but I just never got around to it. If you decide to do it, I'll give you all that I have on those cases." She went on to invite me to her home to plan the project.

There was nothing left to decide. I felt that two of the state's elite journalists had placed a golden egg in my lap and it would be foolish to drop it. Three years later, this is the result of their ideas and my development of them. Let me be the first to admit, it pales in comparison to what it would be if either of them had written it.

To my sorrow, and to the sorrow of hundreds of thousands of others as well, Celestine didn't live to see the final product. It is a painful realization that she will never see what became of that day we sat by the fire at Sweet Apple and talked about life and death in Georgia.

1

THE MURDERS OF MARY PHAGAN AND LEO FRANK
1913-1915

Her name was Mary Phagan. A pretty face with dimples and deep strawberry blonde hair made her appear older than her true age of 13. She would have turned 14 the following month had fate, or her killer, allowed it. She lived in a time which required her to be older than the child she truly was. She worked in a pencil factory in Atlanta, Georgia. She was born on a farm and raised with traditional Southern values but she worked in a city in moral decline. Her death would spark rebellion against the changes taking place in what was once a proud South. Her story and its aftermath became the epitome of injustice.

It was 1913. The newly-elected governor of Georgia was John M. Slaton. The president of the nation, also in his first year of office, was Woodrow Wilson. The 28th president of the United States was winning praise for his "New Freedom" program. He also would introduce the new Federal Income Tax, the first federal tax since the Civil War.

It had been only 12 months since Fredrick Fleet and Reginald Lee stood in a crow's nest high above the North Atlantic Ocean and realized that what first appeared as a haze on the horizon was actually a mountain of ice. Fleet's cry, "Iceberg right ahead!" came too late, and the impending collision led to the worst disaster in maritime history. Having seen the collision from a bird's-eye view and realizing the danger, Fleet had boarded one of the first lifeboats to leave the ship and survived the disaster. More than 1,500 others did not. After extensive studies of the sinking of the *Titanic*, the U.S. Coast Guard was announcing in the nation's newspapers that the first International Ice Patrols would now begin, one year after the tragedy.

It was known as the Progressive Era. But what was progress to the nation was change and destruction of the quality of life to the South. Most Southerners wished to remain an agrarian society, but industrialists from the North would not allow it. Industry was forcing its way into Southern cities — the Industrialist — the obvious culprit. The feeling was widespread that these Industrialists from the North were getting rich at the expense of entire families of Southerners living a squalid life. Because many of the Industrialists were Jewish, anti-Semitism was prevalent.

The laborers used in the factories were mostly ex-tenant farmers and their families, forced into the city by poverty and declining profits from tenant farming. Farmers who had already suffered the humiliation of defeat on the farm then were forced to face the humiliation of sending their entire families to work in the factories. Child labor was prevalent. Some children worked for salaries as low as 22 cents a week with 12-hour-a-day work schedules.

Living conditions in Atlanta were deplorable for the factory workers forced to live in the slums. A third of the city was without sewers or running water. More than half the children of the city suffered from malnutrition and anemia.

The death of her father had forced Mary Phagan into labor work in a factory. Once her mother remarried she no longer had to work. But she had come to enjoy the social life otherwise unknown to her outside the workplace, so she continued — a decision which cost her her life.

It was April 26, 1913 — Confederate Memorial Day. The city woke with the excited anticipation of the parade that would take place that day in Atlanta. There would be bands and more than 200 Confederate veterans marching through the streets of Atlanta to Five Points: a proud but beaten South commemorating the veterans of a lost war.

The front page of The Atlanta Journal led with a picture of a large floral arrangement donated by the Atlanta Lodge of Elks in commemoration of the heroism of the Confederate soldier. Also pictured was Dr. Charles E. Lee, who was to be the "Orator" for the day.

There was news in the daily papers about probes into corruption in Atlanta. The April 26, 1913, Atlanta Journal reported on a Grand Jury probe of what was known as "The Tower"— The Fulton County Jail. The probe involved punishment being handed out in a cell known as "slick nine"— so named, the article reported, because the floor was so slick prisoners could not remain standing in the cell.

There was also news on baseball. The Atlanta Crackers were 11 and 3 and ranked second in the Southern League. The Atlanta Journal had "snapped" a picture in the stands at Friday's game, placed an arrow beside the face of one of the fans and reported, "if you happen to be lucky enough to have the arrow pointing to you, bring the picture to The Atlanta Journal and receive a ticket to Monday's game."

Readers were told that a Detroit Tigers baseball player from Royston, Georgia, named Tyrus "Ty" Cobb was being reinstated to baseball by the American League after a long holdout over a salary dispute, a move no one knew would change baseball history for more than half of the remaining century. The only mention of crime on the front page that day was a small report of a feud in the Tennessee mountains that had left two people dead. It would be the last Saturday paper that Mary Phagan could have read. It was also the last Saturday paper for months that did not contain her name.

She put on her finest dress, lavender and lace, complimented her ensemble with her new, brightly-colored umbrella used for blocking the sun, and sat down to what would be her last meal — cabbage and bread.

She was due a dollar and twenty cents from her job and intended to pick it up while on her trip. She walked from her home in Marietta to English Avenue and caught the streetcar to Atlanta. She got off at the intersection of Broad and Hunter Street and began her walk towards 38 Forsyth Street and the factory which had laid her off earlier in the week. She entered the front doors of the National Pencil Company, climbed the stairs to the second floor, and made her way to her boss' office near the front corner of the building.

His name was Leo Frank, a Jewish industrialist from the North. She told him her payroll number, he checked the books and paid her the $1.20 she was due. As she began to leave she turned to ask her boss one last question, the last words ever recorded as having been spoken by her. "Has the metal come in yet?" The question related to the reason she had been laid off earlier in the week. Mary's job in the factory was placing metal on the ends of pencils. The factory was out of metal and another shipment would have to arrive before Mary could return to work. Her boss later told police he answered simply "no" and continued his task as he listened to her footsteps walking away towards the staircase.

There was another teenage worker in the pencil factory that Saturday — a 13-year-old boy. He saw Mary after she left Frank's office. She, however, did not see him — she was already dead and in the arms of her probable killer. The likely killer glared down at the frightened young boy and growled, "If you ever mention this, I'll kill you!" The threat was taken very seriously. The teenage office boy ran home and told his mother of the horrible sight and the resulting warning. His mother told him to do as he was told and tell no one. For sixty-nine years he heeded her admonishment.

Mary Phagan. Reprinted with the permission of The Atlanta Constitution.

Mary Phagan never made it back to her Marietta home that night. Her mother paced the floor and worried all night. The following day a mother's worst fears came true.

Newt Lee was the night-watchman for the pencil factory. He worked that Saturday night on into the early morning hours of the following Sunday. At 3 a.m., he went to the basement of the factory to use a "negro toilet" located there. The light from his lantern fell upon what appeared to be a body on the basement floor. He hoped the crumpled mass he first caught a glimpse of was someone's idea of a joke — but it wasn't. It was the body of a small child covered with sawdust and, upon closer review, dried blood.

The night watchman, in an obvious panic, quickly summoned police. Responding police found a sight too horrible to endure — slashes across the child's face, eyes bruised and swollen from a beating. Her underwear and a fiber rope were wrapped around her neck. The struggle had been violent. She was found with disjointed fingers and a dent in her skull caused by a blow from a blunt object. She was difficult to identify. Police had to check beneath her clothing to determine her race due to the grime covering her skin. One of the police called to the scene, had a relative who worked in the factory. The relative was asked to come and view the body for purposes of identification. "Oh my God!" she exclaimed, "that's Mary Phagan. Oh poor Mary!" An autopsy would reveal she had been strangled, beaten and sexually assaulted.

Important clues were found during those first hours of investigation by Atlanta police. Some would prove valuable, some ignored, and, unfortunately, some would be lost. The most controversial pieces of evidence were two notes left near the body.

The notes read as follows:

Mam that negro hire down here did this   i went to make water and he push me down that hole   a long tall negro black that hoo it wase   long sleam tall negro   i wright while play with me.

he said he wood love me land down play like the night witch did it but that long tall black negro did buy his slef.

Criticisms of the handling of the Mary Phagan crime scene were almost immediate, and some mistakes do appear to be the result of blatant incompetence. Most notably a wooden board said to contain bloody fingerprints was sawed off and taken into evidence, then reportedly lost. That one piece of evidence may have been the key to solving the entire mystery.

Investigating a murder is the most difficult work a police detective ever encounters.   In almost every homicide ever investigated, someone can — and almost always will — come behind investigators and offer alternative theories as to how an investigation could or should have been handled. In a period of hours detectives must perform work that will, for years if not decades, be scrutinized to the most minute detail. Nowhere in American history is this more true than in the murder of Mary Phagan.

The first newspaper report of the murder came from The Atlanta Constitution. According to later published reports, a fluke allowed the Constitution to scoop the other papers in town. Constitution reporter Britt Craig was reported to have been sleeping off a night of drinking in one of the police patrol wagons when he found himself transported to the scene of one of the most infamous murders in

Atlanta's history.

There were three major newspapers in Atlanta in 1913. The Atlanta Journal, The Atlanta Constitution and The Atlanta Georgian. Competition was fierce. The Atlanta Journal had been the most popular of the three papers until the previous year. In 1912, William Randolph Hearst purchased The Georgian. Hearst already owned papers in New York, Chicago and San Francisco. His aim was to shock his readers with alarmist headlines and inflammatory stories. In a year's time, the Georgian had surpassed the Journal in popularity.

The Georgian believed the murder of Mary Phagan to be the biggest news story the South had ever known. Sensational headlines about the murder ran with every issue. Each time a new angle to the story could be found another "extra" hit the street. The Georgian tripled its circulation, and became the largest daily circulation in the South for that year. The other Atlanta papers followed suit, and adopted similar policies of shocking headlines to grab the reader. Unfortunately for Atlanta, the papers appeared more interested in sensationalism than truth.

The night watchman's demeanor, and the references to the "night witch" in the letters, caused his arrest that night. Police began "sweating" Newt Lee for information. "Sweating" was a term used by police which meant a grueling interrogation. Leo Frank was summoned to police headquarters, reportedly to assist in the interrogation of Lee.

Police initially were arresting suspects for the slightest of reasons. Jim M. Gantt, a bookkeeper who had recently been discharged from the pencil factory, was arrested as he stepped from a train in Marietta and charged with the murder. Arthur Mullinax, a streetcar conductor, was arrested on a tentative charge of suspicion after a grocery clerk swore he saw Mullinax with Mary Phagan at midnight Saturday night at Forsyth and Hunter streets.

11

Mullinax denied the charge. Police later learned he had been in Atlanta with a woman named Pearl Robinson. At the time. Miss Robinson was wearing the same kind of dress as Phagan and was the same size and appearance as the murdered teenager.

Because police believed the elevator was used to transport the body, Gordon Lee, who was described by The Atlanta Journal as "a negro elevator boy at the pencil factory," also was arrested. Including Lee, there were a total of four persons under arrest for the murder by Monday afternoon.

Superintendent Leo Frank was questioned by police, but two days after the murder The Atlanta Journal reported that he was at police headquarters to aid police in solving the mystery. It was reported that he assisted police in the questioning of the night watchman. He also was shown Arthur Mullinax and asked if he had ever seen Mullinax at the pencil factory. Frank told police he had not. After several hours Frank, who was represented by an attorney, was allowed to leave while the four others arrested were held in jail in solitary confinement.

It was in the early morning hours after initially finding the body that police had met Frank. Frank, the pencil factory superintendent, came to the factory upon learning of the murder and, according to police, appeared nervous and shaken when told of the murder. Frank hired the Pinkerton National Detective Agency to represent the factory's interest in the murder. It would prove to be a costly mistake for Frank. In a lawsuit filed in 1915, lawyers for the National Pencil Company complained that Pinkerton detectives had concentrated their efforts on framing Frank.

A picture in Tuesday's Atlanta Journal portrayed a smiling, well dressed Leo Frank on his way to police headquarters for more questioning. The caption read "Talking to Police."

By Tuesday afternoon police and the public began to turn their attention to Frank. Chief of Detectives Newport Lanford announced

12

that Frank was back at police headquarters and was now going to be detained until the Coroner's Inquest. Frank's wife, Lucile Selig Frank, stood in the hallway of police headquarters in tears as the announcement was made. Police told reporters that Frank would not be placed in a jail cell but would have the run of police headquarters under the watch of a police guard.

Leo Frank, reprinted with permission of the Atlanta Constitution.

On Monday, April 28, Coroner Paul Donehoo conducted a Coroner's Inquest. On the coroner's jury, chosen by the coroner, were seven men: J.C. Hood, Clarence Langford, Glenn Dewberry, Homer C. Ashford, John Miller and C.Y. Sheets. Mr. Ashford was named foreman. They met at Bloomfield's Undertaking Chapel, and their first official act was the gruesome task of examining Mary Phagan's young, mutilated body. The purpose of a Coroner's Inquest was usually to determine if a police investigation was needed. If the death was ruled a murder, the jury was charged with deciding if the assailant could be immediately identified. If not, it was the coroner's duty to insure that a proper police investigation was conducted.

After examining the body the men excused the witnesses that had been summoned to testify and no testimony was heard that day. The jurors decided instead to visit the crime scene. They had to elbow their way through a crowd of people reported to number more than 500 — curious onlookers who had hoped to hear testimony and details of what was already the biggest news story of the young century.

Jury members examined the basement where the body was found. Lanterns had been used to mark the spot where the body was found and where Newt Lee was standing when he claimed to have first seen the body. The jury also examined a machine room on the second floor where stains were found on the floor which were believed to be blood. Strands of hair were found on a machine in the same room. The jury adjourned that Monday with no findings but agreed to meet again the following Wednesday.

Newspapers were running blow-by-blow accounts of every step of the investigation. Police were not only telling reporters everything they knew about the investigation but reporters also were being allowed to view and photograph police evidence. On April 28, 1913, The Atlanta Journal ran photographs of the notes found near the body alongside photographs of samples of watchman Lee's handwriting, which police had asked him to produce. Within hours of the body having been found, newspaper reporters were being allowed to scour the crime scene themselves. They reported numerous different angles and opinions of where the murder may have occurred and how the body might have been moved to the basement. No one believed Mary Phagan had been killed where her body was found.

It had been a tragic twist of fate for Mary. Had her family had a telephone she might never have been killed. Police learned that on the Friday before the murder, Mary's foreman, L.A. Quinn, had attempted to phone Mary and three of her working companions to request they pick up their paychecks on Friday since the normal payday, Saturday, was a holiday. Quinn was never able to reach Mary. She had arrived Saturday to a closed and almost empty factory.

The intense excitement and unrest surrounding the investigation caused the assistant superintendent to shut down the factory the following Monday. In spite of the fact that it put the women factory workers out of work, The Atlanta Journal reported that the women "lost no time in getting into their wraps and hats and leaving the scene of the mysterious tragedy."

Prior to the second meeting of the coroner's jury, news reports continued to implicate the night watchman, Newt Lee, as the murderer. When police returned him to the crime scene, people yelled at him with threats of lynching. Both the Journal and the Georgian proclaimed Lee as the murderer. The mayor of Atlanta cautioned police about releasing so much information to the news media which was, in turn, inflaming the public with exaggerations and misstatements. The governor placed the state militia on alert in order to protect both Lee and Frank.

At the second meeting of the coroner's jury held on Wednesday, April 30, a pattern of incriminating innuendo began to emerge against Leo Frank. A young man named George Epps testified that he rode into town with Mary Phagan on the day of the murder. Epps claimed that he had been told that day by Mary that she was afraid of her boss, Leo Frank, because he was too familiar with her and made advances towards her. Epps had been interviewed by an Atlanta Georgian reporter a few days earlier and had said only that he sometimes rode to town with her. During that interview Epps said nothing of having ridden to town with her the day she was killed.

Numerous former employees testified that Frank flirted and acted improperly with his female workers. No solid connection was made between Leo Frank and Mary Phagan, but the picture painted of Frank was that of a womanizing employer with a habit of taking advantage of his female employees. That picture was the worst nightmare of every husband and father who ever sent their women to work in a factory. The coroner's jury ordered that both Frank and

Lee remain in jail.

On May 23, the Atlanta police announced they were in possession of an affidavit given by a rooming house operator named Nina Formby. Mrs. Formby claimed in her affidavit that on the day of the murder, Leo Frank had telephoned her repeatedly asking for a room for himself and a young girl. The police indicated to the press that Frank had become their main suspect. On the following day, a grand jury indicted Leo Frank for the murder of Mary Phagan.

The grand jury that indicted Frank was not told about another suspect who had been arrested just two days after the murder — a suspect who would become a central figure in the case and eventual trial. Jim Conley was described by the press as a "negro sweeper" for the National Pencil Company. He was arrested after a foreman at the factory told police he had seen Conley washing what appeared to be blood from his shirt. On the same day Frank was indicted, Conley admitted to having written one of the notes found beside Mary's body. The grand jury was not told this before their indictment of Frank.

Conley was telling the incredible story that he had been summoned to Leo Frank's office the day before the murder and ordered to write one of the notes. Conley claimed in this first affidavit that while writing the note for his boss, Frank mumbled what Conley believed to be, "Why should I hang?" Conley also initially claimed that he was not even in the factory on the day of the murder.

Jim Conley was a 27-year-old, short, stocky, "ginger-colored" black male — the opposite of the long, tall, black negro described as the killer in the note Conley now admitted to having written.

Conley was no stranger to Atlanta's jail, having several previous arrests for theft and disorderly conduct. Unlike Frank, Conley was from the South — born and raised a black man in a South riddled with prejudices. Prejudices he could manipulate to steer suspicion away

16

from himself by stating that his Jewish, Industrialist, Northern boss had asked him to pen letters claiming to be from a young girl, identifying a "long tall negro black" as her killer.

It was a ludicrous story. Leo Frank was an intelligent man, a graduate of Cornell University. It is difficult to believe that he could have arranged for the crude letters to be written or that he would have expected people of average intelligence to believe they were written by Mary. Under normal circumstances Conley's story would never be given any credibility. But these were not normal circumstances. Public opinion was already running strong against Frank. The chief of detectives for Atlanta, Newport Lanford, who learned earlier that the mayor had declared "find this murderer fast, or be fired!", told the press that Frank was the murderer and would be convicted.

Detectives assigned to Phagan investigation. Reprinted with the permission of The Atlanta Journal-Constitution.

17

Detective Lanford was under tremendous community pressure. Even before the murder of Mary Phagan, the City of Atlanta had been engulfed in turmoil as the city tried to enforce local prohibition laws while the sensational-styled press pointed fingers at the Atlanta police as being part of the alleged "vice problems of the city." There were scores of accusations of police corruption and indifference to the law prohibiting the sale of illegal alcohol.

After newspapers reported that uniformed police officers were patronizing a "blind tiger" on Auburn Ave., Police Chief John Beavers ordered plain-clothes detectives to place a surveillance on the Auburn Ave. location.

These detectives observed three uniformed police officers enter the rear of 127 Auburn Ave. which the press described as a "negro" boarding house "generally believed to be a blind tiger." Blind tiger was the term for a house people could go to for whiskey shots. The detectives approached the window and observed the proprietor, Ola Bradley, described by the press as a "negro woman," pour and serve three shots of whiskey. A detailed account of the incident appeared in the following morning paper. It was reported that the three officers had been suspended immediately by Chief Beavers.

Other articles reported numerous officers were being indicted for various vice charges. All of the conduct surrounded the alleged blind tiger on Auburn Avenue. In the middle of the Phagan investigation, the controversy over the city's vice problems caught up with Lanford. Atlanta attorney Thomas B. Felder wrote a letter and distributed it to all of the Atlanta papers. It said, "An investigation of vice conditions by the grand jury would show abundantly (Lanford's) criminal connection therewith in all of its hideous deformity."

Already facing pressure from the mayor to solve the Phagan case, Lanford was accused in the Atlanta paper of being behind the alleged vice conditions in the city. When he tried to defend himself against "Colonel" Felder's attacks in the press, the pressure worsened for

18

him. When he wrote back to the paper defending himself and attacking attorney Felder, the grand jury decided to take up the matter. On June 26 of that year, the grand jury indicted both Felder and Lanford charging them with criminal libel. Lanford was required to post a $500 bond. He declared to the press that he could substantiate every charge he had ever made against Mr. Felder.

Although Lanford expressed confidence that Leo Frank was guilty, the press was not so convinced.

The Georgian pointed out that Frank had answered all questions put to him during the coroner's inquest "in a straight forward, unwavering manner, never once being trapped in a lie or misstatement." Conley, the paper pointed out, had lied continuously.

When confronted with the inconsistencies in his story, Conley changed it. During police questioning, Conley admitted he was at the factory on the date of the murder and that he helped dispose of the body. In his second statement, Conley claimed that Frank called him to Frank's second floor office. Conley said Frank told him he had let a girl fall against a machine in the metal room and that he wanted Conley to remove her.

Conley claimed he went to the metal room, found that the girl was dead and informed Frank. Conley told police that Frank ordered him to carry the body to the elevator. From there she was taken to the basement and disposed of in a sawdust-covered corner.

A key part of Conley's second statement was Conley's claim that he and Frank used the elevator to transport the body. When police first arrived on the crime scene, they observed what appeared to be human feces at the bottom of the elevator shaft. Conley later admitted he had defecated there earlier in the day, before the murder. No one had used the elevator until Leo Frank arrived at the factory. At that time the elevator was used for the first time since police had been called to the scene. When the elevator was lowered to the basement it disturbed the feces, creating a terrible smell that caused investigators to clear the basement. Had the killer used the elevator to lower the body to the basement, the feces would have been disturbed prior to police's arrival.

One of the notes found beside Mary Phagan's body made reference to a "hole." Part of the note read, "I went to make water and he push me down that hole." The "hole" may have been referring to a chute on the ground floor which led to the basement. "Make water" is a term used to describe relieving one's self.

Mary Phagan's body was found not far from the bottom of that chute, at the opposite end of the basement from the elevator. Conley eventually confessed to writing both notes found beside the body. The statement in the note, "he push me down that hole" was not consistent with Conley's current story.

Newspapers were continuously pointing out inconsistencies in Conley's story. Many began to believe that Conley was the killer. In July, Frank's attorneys released an affidavit they had obtained from an insurance agent. The insurance agent had come forward early in the investigation and told police and factory officials that on the day of the murder he tried to sell Conley insurance. Conley allegedly brushed him off with an incriminating statement: "I've killed a girl today; I don't want to kill nobody else." At the time the agent came forward, factory officials did not know that any negroes had been in the factory on that day.

It was reported that the foreman of the grand jury wanted to call the jurors into session and indict Conley. Solicitor Dorsey reportedly refused and the foreman threatened to take the action without the solicitor's involvement. The grand jury was called in to discuss the possibility of indicting Conley. The Atlanta press reported this to be the first time in the history of the county a grand jury had ever been convened over the protest of the solicitor. Solicitor Dorsey spent an hour and a half reportedly pleading with the jurors not to indict Conley, telling them it would hurt the criminal case against Leo

Frank. Newspapers reported he succeeded, but not without a difficult fight.

The Franks, who had initially remained silent in the papers, became vocal after the family cook, Minola McKnight, was arrested, held for 24 hours without a warrant, and forced to sign an affidavit containing incriminating statements against Frank. As soon as she was released, she recanted the affidavit she claimed she had been forced to sign. Mrs. Frank wrote a letter to all three Atlanta papers chastising the authorities for their treatment of the cook and their methods for gathering statements. The letter details what Mrs. Frank termed the torture of her cook until that cook gave statements against her husband. The letter also clearly illustrates to the city that Mrs. Frank no longer blames Chief Detective Lanford for her husband's plight. It shifts the blame to the prosecutor, Hugh Dorsey. Mrs. Frank also used the opportunity to try and quell rumors that she believed her husband was guilty and was going to divorce him. The letter began:

> Dear Sir: The action of the solicitor general in arresting and imprisoning our family cook because she would not voluntarily make a false statement against my innocent husband brings a limit to patience. This wrong is not chargeable to a detective acting under the necessity of shielding his own reputation against attacks in newspaper but of an intelligent, trained lawyer whose sworn duty is as much to protect the innocent, as to punish the guilty. My information is that this solicitor has admitted that no crime is charged against this cook and that he had no legal right to have her arrested and imprisoned.

After quoting several newspaper articles about the incident Mrs.

Frank wrote:

> Where will this end? My husband and my family and myself are the innocent sufferers now, but who will be the next to suffer? I suppose the witnesses tortured will be confined to the class who are not able to employ lawyers to relieve them from the torture in time to prevent their being forced to give false affidavits, but the lives sworn away may come from any class.
>
> It will be noted that the plan is to apply the torture until the desired affidavit is wrung from the sufferer. Then it ends but not before.
>
> It is to be hoped that no person can be convicted of murder in any civilized country on evidence wrung from witnesses by torture. Why, then does the solicitor continue to apply the third degree to produce testimony? How does he hope to get the jury to believe it? He can have only one hope, and that is to keep the jury from knowing the methods to which he has resorted.
>
> Of course, if he can torture witnesses into giving the kind of evidence he wants against my innocent husband in this case, he can torture them into giving evidence against any other man in the community in either this or any other case.

Mrs. Frank ended the letter by proclaiming her belief that her husband was innocent. "I know my husband is innocent," she wrote. "No man could make the good husband to a woman that he has been to me and be a criminal."

All of the Atlanta papers printed Mrs. Frank's letter in its entirety.

The city now knew that Leo Frank's chief pursuer and accuser was not a detective on the defense, but the city's prosecutor on the offense.

Forty-two-year-old Hugh Manson Dorsey had been appointed Solicitor General of the Atlanta Judicial Circuit in 1910 by then-Governor Joseph M. Brown. Dorsey was born in the small town of Fayetteville, 30 miles south of Atlanta. His family had lived in a white-columned home just off the courthouse square on what is now known as Lanier Avenue. The home was a historical landmark built by John Styles Holliday, uncle to infamous gunslinger Doc Holliday.

On the same day Mrs. Frank's letters were released to the press, the residents of the farming community which was Dorsey's hometown had learned in that day's Atlanta newspaper of President Woodrow Wilson's latest nomination. President Wilson had sent popular Fayetteville attorney A.O. Blalock's name to the Senate, nominating him to be the next Internal Revenue Collector of Georgia. They also learned on that same front page that another hometown attorney had just taken center stage in the prosecution of Leo Frank. Mrs. Frank was telling everyone who would listen that it was now Dorsey who was unjustifiably pursuing her husband's case.

Almost every edition of every paper in the first few weeks of June contained a front page article on the progress of the Phagan investigation. There was, however, news of other things going on in Atlanta.

The new governor, John M. Slaton, came to Atlanta for what was termed his "simple inauguration" after which he and his wife took possession of the governor's mansion in Ansley Park.

There were reports of Serbian conflict in Yugoslavia to which many people probably paid little attention. Few would know this conflict so far away would be the spark that would eventually ignite the planet's first World War.

There were problems at the new Atlanta Zoo at Grant Park. Zoo attendants were complaining that "certain types of persons" were teasing the lions in a deadly game of "get the hat." The culprits were said to be dangling their hats just inside the bars of the cages. The lions would approach slowly, as though they didn't notice the tease. Then suddenly the lions would lurch forward swinging their large paws outside the bars — swiping at their teaser — mauling many hats and endangering the hands that held them. The practice came to a head in a shocking manner in June. Zookeepers reported to the police and the press that they caught what was reported to be a "young Negress in the charge of a white infant from a prominent Grant Park family" teasing the lions with the infant as others with her watched and laughed. Zookeepers claimed she would hold the infant close to the bars drawing the lions near and then back away quickly with the child. The police were called, the woman was arrested, and the shocked mother of the infant was summoned to come get her baby. Zookeepers told the Atlanta press it was all they could do to prevent violence between the mother and the "Negress" when the mother arrived.

There were also indications that the mood in Georgia was moving away from capital punishment. The Atlanta Journal reported:

> It is quite evident from the annual report just compiled by the state prison commission that Georgia juries and judges are not partial to capital punishment even in cases of persons convicted of murder. Only a

24

very small percentage of the convicted murderers are hanged; the vast majority are given penitentiary sentences which in most instances are for life.

The Journal also reported that Sumter County Superior Court Judge Z.A. Littlejohn had convened a special grand jury to investigate the lynching death of "negro William Redding" after he was thought to have shot the chief of police in Americus. The press reported that a hundred witnesses were being forced to testify, including clergymen who attempted to interfere with the crowd and who were thought to know the identities of the lynchmen.

There was, however, no shortage of citizens championing the death penalty in Atlanta during the Mary Phagan investigation and things appeared ominous for Leo Frank. His family had retained attorney Luther Z. Rosser. The Atlanta press called him "the best all-around lawyer in Atlanta." In the first few weeks he worked quietly and avoided the press, but the press was becoming one of Leo Frank's biggest problems as the on-going banter between attorney Felder and Chief Detective Lanford began to affect the Frank case. Both Lanford and Felder accused each other of helping Frank. Rosser worried that in his attempt to prove Felder wrong Lanford would pursue Frank even more vigorously.

Rosser realized his case was being tried in the press and that he had no choice but to defend his client in that same venue. On June 10, 1913, attorney Rosser broke his silence and released a well-written letter to the Atlanta press stating Frank's case. In that letter Rosser wrote:

> Lanford, as soon as Felder charged him with favoring Frank, settled in his mind the guilt of Frank and from that moment has spent every energy of his department, not in finding the murderer, but in trying

25

to prove to the public that Felder was wrong in charging him with trying to shield Frank.

His department has exhausted itself in an effort to fix upon Frank an immoral life on the theory that a violator of the seventh commandment was likewise a murderer. This effort has failed. No man in Atlanta has had his moral character subjected to such a test and there is not in the whole city of Atlanta a half-dozen men who could have more successfully stood the test.

Speaking of the woman police said identified Frank as having called to try and secure a room on the day of the murder Rosser wrote:

This woman was not unknown to Lanford. She did not entrap him by appearing under the guise of a truthful, sober, virtuous woman. But so absorbed was he, either in trying to disprove Felder's charge or in the foolish pride of opinion that he accepted without doubt or fair investigation the drivel and nonsense of this woman.

About Jim Conley, Rosser wrote:

Conley is a very ordinary, ignorant, brutal negro, not unacquainted with the stockade. His actions immediately after the crime were suspicious. So much so that they attracted the attention of the employees of the factory and occasioned general comment. In spite of these facts, Conley was not taken into custody until several days after the crime and not then until the employees of the factory caught him suspiciously washing a shirt and as a result reported him to the police. He was not brought before the coroner's jury and practically no notice was taken of him in that investigation. So swiftly was Lanford and his associates pursuing Frank that they ran over this negro, standing in their path with the marks of guilt clearing upon him.

By now it was clear in the articles of The Georgian that its reporters also did not believe Leo Frank was guilty. The Georgian also realized that the rumors — and extensive reporting of them — had muddied the waters of rational opinion. One reporter wrote: "The public has not *yet* become convinced — and may never become convinced — that Leo Frank is innocent of the crime for which he has been indicted."

Others began to speculate that the officers of the court would find difficulty seating a jury that could view the evidence without prejudice. Those predictions, right or wrong, were not apparent on the first day of the trial — July 28, 1913. A 12 man jury was seated in just three hours. Attorneys for both sides had swiftly sifted through eight panels of jury members. The final juror chosen was the last man on the last panel. Among them were a bank teller, a bookkeeper, a real estate agent, a manufacturer, a contractor, an optician, a claim agent, a mailing clerk, two salesmen and two machinists. All were white, all but one were married. None were Jewish.

Twelve very ordinary men who would suddenly be thrust into notoriety. The top half of the front page of the July 29 edition of the Atlanta Journal was dedicated entirely to photographs of the jurors. Now more than ever these jurors found themselves the center of attention in the South. Their deliberation and ultimate decision would be watched by everyone they had ever known in the town in which they lived.

Leo Frank with his wife, Lucile, seated behind him.
Reprinted with the permission of The Atlanta Constitution.

Testimony in the Frank trial would begin within the first day of the proceedings. The atmosphere surrounding the courthouse was reported as ugly and 20 officers had been ordered to stand guard. The Atlanta Constitution would name it the "Greatest Legal Battle in the History of Dixie." Solicitor General Hugh Dorsey with assistance from Frank Hooper for the prosecution. Luther Z. Rosser and Reuben R. Arnold for the defense.

During the choosing of his jury, Leo Frank sat smiling and confident. His wife sat to his right, his mother to his left. A photograph was taken of the courtroom on the first day of the trial and ran on the first page of the following day's paper. The picture depicts more than 50 people seated in straight-back chairs. Most were men, but in the back, a few women's hats can be seen. Seated behind Leo Frank was his wife, Lucile, wearing a tall decorative hat. Every seat was filled. A few men were allowed to stand, probably courtroom security officers. Most of the crowd had not been allowed inside the courtroom. A photograph which ran in the Monday afternoon edition of The Atlanta Journal showed a much larger crowd outside.

The first witness called to the stand was Mrs. J.W. Coleman. The first question: What relation were you to Mary Phagan? "Her mother," she responded. Mrs. Coleman went on to testify that she had not seen her daughter since "April 26, Memorial Day."

Mrs. Coleman testified her daughter left their home at 146 Lindsay St., Marietta, Georgia, and was never seen again. She described her daughter as "fair, heavy set, very pretty, and with dimples in each cheek." Mrs. Coleman also described the lavender and lace dress she last saw her daughter wearing. After she described the dress, Solicitor Dorsey handed a suitcase to Newt Garner, a deputy in the solicitor's office. Garner approached Mrs. Coleman and pulled a bloodstained dress from the suitcase. Garner began to arrange the dress at Mrs. Coleman's feet. Mrs. Coleman raised a fan in front of her face and began to sob audibly. Leo Frank's mother, Rhea Frank raised her own hands in front of her face and bowed her head. The Atlanta Journal reported of the incident: "Many spectators in the court were affected." Deputy Plennie Minor offered a glass of ice water to Mrs. Coleman. She sipped it but continued sobbing. Dorsey cut his questioning short and turned to defense attorney Rosser. "The witness is with you," Dorsey said.

Rosser also kept his questions brief. Rosser asked Mrs. Coleman to identify Mary's hat and confirm that a ribbon was missing from the hat. He then attempted to elicit confirmation from Mrs. Coleman of a statement she was said to have made a month after the murder about George Epps, the boy who claimed to have ridden on the train with Mary on the day of her murder. "Did you on May 2 say to L.D. Whitfield that Mary detested Epps?" Mrs. Coleman did not remember having made the statement, and she was excused without further questioning.

The next witness was Epps. He entered the courtroom barefooted and took the stand. Epps was a 15-year-old "news boy." Epps testified that he had known Mary Phagan for a year before the murder. He testified that he met her on the streetcar on the morning of the murder and rode with her to Forsyth and Marietta streets and left her there around 12:10 p.m. Epps claimed he had made an appointment to meet Mary at Elkin-Watson's drug store at 2 o'clock. Epps testified that he went there and sold papers for two hours and that Mary never arrived. Epps impressed the reporters in the courtroom. One of them wrote, "He made a good impression by his straightforward answers." Defense Attorney Rosser asked the young witness, "How did you know what time it was when you got off the car?" "I looked at the sun," the boy answered. Rosser asked Epps why he had not told the coroner's jury the same story he was now testifying to. Epps responded, "Maybe I didn't tell about it, but it was there."

Jury selection had been calm as well as the testimony and cross-examination of the first two witnesses. There was little disagreement between the prosecution and defense. The atmosphere immediately changed with the introduction of the state's third witness. The photograph taken in the courtroom on the first day depicted a very nervous witness shortly after he took the stand — night watchman Newt Lee. It was apparently one of several photographs taken just after Lee took the stand, all at one time. The Atlanta Journal described it in the following manner: "A battery of half a dozen cameras flashed in the court startling everyone and the Negro in particular."

Defense attorneys grilled Lee for three hours and attempted to tie him to the notes found near the body. Lee gave a detailed description of how his night went up until the time around 3 a.m. when he found Mary Phagan's body.

The night watchman testified that he would normally report at 5 p.m. on Saturdays but that on Friday, April 25, Mr. Frank had instructed him to come at 4 p.m. because it was a holiday and Mr. Frank expressed a desire to leave early. The watchman further testified that when he arrived on Saturday at 4 p.m., he found the front doors unlocked, but a second set of inside doors on the stairs were found to be locked, forcing him to use his key. Lee testified that when he entered the pencil factory, he went upstairs to a small desk in the hallway and called for Mr. Frank. Lee testified that Frank "came bustin out of the office rubbing his hands." Lee testified that at that point Mr. Frank told him to "go out and have a good time" and come back at 6 p.m. Lee testified that when he told Frank that he would rather sleep, Frank insisted that Lee leave and return later.

When Dorsey pressed Lee to say that Frank appeared nervous, Lee would not come right out and say he appeared nervous but his words indicated nervous behavior. Lee told defense attorney Rosser that he could not see Frank's face but he could see him wringing his hands.

Lee testified that when he returned at a few minutes before 6 p.m., it took Frank twice as long to "fix the [time] slip" as he fumbled with it.

Lee was asked about the lighting in the factory when he arrived. Lee testified he usually lit the gaslights on the street level floor at 5:00 p.m. When he arrived back at 6 p.m. on April 26, he found the street level lights already lit. When asked about the lighting in the basement Lee testified that it was a rule that the light in the basement should remain lit at all times. Lee said that on April 26, he found the light in the basement barely burning. Lee explained to Solicitor Dorsey that there were two little chains on the light. Pulling one of the chains would make the light burn full blast. By pulling the other, the light would grow very dim and eventually go out. Lee testified that he found the basement light as dim as it could get without going out.

The courtroom grew quiet — all whispers ceasing as the aging night watchman spoke about finding the body of the child. "I looked around and saw something over by the bend. I thought, it being a holiday, some of those boys had put something there to scare me. I went over a little farther and looked, and then I left." Solicitor Dorsey pressed him for more detail. "Tell us all about it. How did you get up the ladder? Tell us everything." Lee responded, "I don't know boss. The next thing I remember I was calling the police over the telephone. I told them what I'd found. After I got the police, I tried to call Mr. Frank but I couldn't get him, and I kept on calling until the officers came. I guess it was about eight minutes." He testified that he was handcuffed immediately after the police arrived by an officer who declared, "You done this," and had been locked up ever since.

The statements made by the aging negro watchman to the press immediately following his testimony reflected the frustration of being the man who found the body of Mary Phagan. His statement, printed in The Atlanta Journal on July 29, 1913, read exactly as follows;

> All I wanted was a chew of 'bacca. Yes sir, dat was all. I can't say I was tired. Naw, sir not 'zactly' that. I jes needed the bacca. Soon as I left the stand, the first thing I did was to ask for a chew, and I felt all right.
>
> Mr. Rosser was putty terrible, wasn't he? Sorter wants you to say things jes his way. But I was there to tell the truf and I told it.
>
> Lawyers and detectives are sorter alike when they comes to askin' questions. I'd 'bout as soon be talked to by one as another. Lawyers though, don't 'buse you'n like detectives, that's a fact.
>
> But when folks don't do you right you jes know

32

they hurtin' they souls and ain't doin' you any real harm. That's the way to look at things.

Naw sir, i didn't get mad when Mr. Rosser kept tryin to make me say what he wanted said. Court's a place where you 'spect to be questioned and there ain't nothin to do but jes answer the best you kin. They certainly worked on me but all I needed was a little bit of 'bacca'.

The Atlanta Journal said of Lee's testimony:

When he was pressed hard about the truthfulness of his story, he sometimes became argumentative and proved his questioners wrong. At times he thought that attorneys were interfering with his story by their questions. "Now, Newt," asked Solicitor Dorsey, "what did he say?" "Well, if you'll just wait a minute." Answered Newt. "I'll tell you."

Later on when Solicitor Dorsey had given in discussing one incident, and drew his conclusions from them, Newt sighed and leaned back. "Yes sir," he said with humor which he may or may not have meant, "now you got it right."

The first day of testimony ended with Newt Lee still on the witness stand. The trial was proving to be the spectacle everyone had expected. The story was on the front page of the newspapers in every large city in the South. A reporter with The Atlanta Constitution complained the New York papers were paying little attention to the case. The case would eventually attract the attention of Northern papers and when it did, people in the South weren't very happy.

As the city waited for the second day of testimony, employees from the pencil factory declared to the press that Frank was innocent. The Atlanta Journal reported that "thirty girls and men are waiting to appear as character witnesses." The evening paper quoted factory employee Rebekah Carson:

> Every girl employed at the factory believes that Mr. Frank is innocent. He was as kind as an employer could be. There never was a time when he wasn't considerate of everyone employed at the factory.
>
> Everyone employed at the factory believes as I do. Everyone knows that Mr. Frank was kind and gentle and that he was honest and straight in everything that he did. You won't find an employee of the factory who doesn't really believe that and who isn't ready to testify to it before a jury.

In spite of the apparent loyalty of many of the employees, Solicitor Dorsey was still successful in finding employees who would testify for the prosecution. The state was seeking to establish that the murder occurred on the second floor in a metal workroom across from Frank's office.

National Pencil Company machinist R. P. Barrett testified in the second day of the trial that he found a large spot of blood surrounded by several smaller spots of blood at the water cooler near the dressing room on the second floor of the factory. He also testified that he found a broom nearby which appeared to have been used to smear the large blood spot over with a white substance. Barrett testified that on the same morning he found strands of hair on the lathe he used in the machine room. Employee Mell Stanford reinforced Barrett's testimony.

One of the key factory employees to testify against Frank was Monteen Stover. She testified that she came to the factory at 12:05

34

p.m. on the day of the murder to collect her pay. Stover testified she did not find Frank in his office at that time and, after waiting five minutes to no avail, left without her pay. In one of Frank's early statements, he told police that Mary Phagan had been in his office at 12:05 p.m. and that he never left his office between 12 p.m. and 12:30 p.m. on that day. The prosecution made it clear on the second day that they believed that Leo Frank was in the machine room committing the murder when Monteen Stover arrived in his office that Saturday.

As the trial progressed through the week there was nothing, other than innuendo, to directly link Leo Frank to Mary Phagan's murder. It became apparent that the state's case against Frank would depend entirely on the testimony of the man The Atlanta Journal described as "the negro sweeper," Jim Conley. When he finally entered the courtroom for his turn to testify, jurors observed a different Jim Conley than Leo Frank knew.

Conley, according to published reports, usually presented "a rather shabby if not down right filthy appearance." He appeared in court that day with his face "scrubbed" clean, his hair cut and combed and his clothes clean and new. The Journal reported that his testimony had a rehearsed air. Rehearsed or not, the testimony was devastating to Leo Frank.

Conley testified that he arrived at the factory that morning at 8:30 a.m. and spoke with Frank. Conley claimed that at that time, Frank revealed that he was expecting a young girl to visit the factory that day to "chat." Conley explained that he had on previous occasions acted as a lookout for Frank when other girls had visited him at the factory. Conley told the jury that Frank would give a signal by stomping his foot which was said to be Conley's cue to lock the front door of the factory. Conley would then wait to hear a whistle which was the signal for Conley to unlock the front door.

Jim Conley, reprinted with the permission of
The Atlanta Journal-Constitution.

Conley testified that he saw Mary Phagan arrive that day and proceed upstairs toward Leo Frank's office. Conley claimed he heard footsteps walking in the direction of the metal room. Up to this point Conley had said nothing about Frank stomping his foot or otherwise signaling to lock the front door. Conley testified that he heard a girl scream and then saw Monteen Stover enter the factory and go upstairs. He told the jury that Stover stayed awhile and then came back down stairs and left. Conley said he dozed off listening to steps move back and forth from the office to the metal room.

Conley testified he was awakened by someone stomping the floor. He told the jury he got up and locked the front door. Conley claimed that a few minutes later he heard a whistle, unlocked the front door, and went upstairs to Frank's office.

The following is Conley's testimony of what happened next:

Mr. Frank was standing up there at the top of the
steps and shivering and trembling and rubbing his

hands... He had a little rope in his hands — a long wide piece of cord. His eyes were large and they looked right funny. He looked funny out of his eyes. His face was red. Yes, he had a cord in his hands just like this here cord. After I got up to the top of the steps, he asked me, "Did you see that little girl who passed here just a while ago?" And I told him I saw one come along there and she come back again, and then I saw another one come along there and she hasn't come back down, and he says, "Well that one you say didn't come back down, she came into my office awhile ago and wanted to know something about her work in my office and I went back there to see if the little girl's work had come, and I wanted to be with the little girl, and she refused me, and I struck her and I guess I struck her too hard and she fell and hit her head against something, and I don't know how bad she got hurt. Of course you know I ain't built like other men."

The reason he said that was, I had seen him in a position I haven't seen any other man that has got children. I have seen him in the office two or three times before Thanksgiving and a lady was in his office, and she was sitting down in a chair and she had her clothes up to here, and he was down on his knees, and she had her hands on Mr. Frank.

I have seen him another time there in the packing room with a young lady lying on the table, she was on the edge of the table when I saw her. He asked me if I wouldn't go back there and bring her up so that he could put her somewhere, and he said to hurry, that there would be money in it for me.

37

When I came back there, I found the lady lying flat
on her back with a rope around her neck. The cloth
was also tied around her neck and part of it was under
her head like to catch blood... She was dead when I
went back there and I came back and told Mr. Frank
the girl was dead and he said, "shhh!" He told me to
go back there by the cotton box, get a piece of cloth,
put it around her and bring her up.

Conley went on to testify that he bundled the girl up in the cloth
and tried unsuccessfully to lift the body to his shoulders. Conley told
the jury that Frank had to help him carry the body to the elevator
where Conley claimed that he and Frank took the body to the
basement and left it, returning to the second floor again by using the
elevator.

Conley testified that, after hiding in a closet upon hearing
footsteps on the stairs, he again joined Frank in the superintendent's
office. At that time Conley claimed that Frank asked him if he could
write. Conley said he answered, "Yes sir, a little bit." Conley
testified that Frank told him he wanted him to "fix up some notes."
Conley told the jury:

I was willing to do anything to help Mr. Frank
because he was a white man and my superintendent...
I sat down at the table and Mr. Frank dictated the
notes to me. Whatever it was it didn't seem to suit
him, and he told me to turn over and write again, and
I turned the paper and wrote again, and when I done
that he told me to turn over again and I turned over
again and I wrote on the next page there, and he
looked at that and kind of like it and he said that was
all right.

38

Conley alleged that after writing the notes Frank gave him $200 and then told him, "you go down there in the basement and you take a lot of trash and burn that package that's in front of the furnace." Conley testified that when he told Frank he was afraid to go down to the basement by himself and was not willing to burn the body Frank took the $200 back that he had given Conley. Conley stated that he told Frank, "Mr. Frank you are a white man and you done it, and I am not going down there and burn that myself."

During this testimony Conley added details he had failed to mention in the numerous earlier statements he had made to police. After Frank allegedly took the money back Conley described the exchange that he said took place between him and his former boss:

> I said, "Is this the way you do things?" and he said, "You keep your mouth shut, that is all right." And Mr. Frank turned around in his chair and looked at the money and he looked back at me and folded his hands and looked up and said "Why should I hang? I have wealthy people in Brooklyn," and he looked down when he said that, and I looked up at him, and he was looking up at the ceiling and I said, "Mr. Frank, what about me?" and he said, "That's all right, don't you worry about this thing, you just come back to work Monday like you don't know anything, and keep your mouth shut, if you get caught I will get you out on bond and send you away," and he said, "Can you come back this evening and do it?" and I said, "Yes, that I was coming to get my money." He said, "Well, I am going home to get dinner and you come back here in about forty minutes and I will fix the money."

Conley told the jury that he did not return to the factory that night but instead went to a beer saloon, ate and drank, and then went home and went to sleep.

Conley's testimony gripped the interest of everyone in the courtroom. The content of his testimony was considered extremely lewd by 1913 standards. Presiding Judge Leonard S. Roan thought the testimony too offensive to be heard by ears he deemed delicate and ordered that women and children be barred from the courtroom for the remainder of Conley's testimony.

During cross-examination Conley admitted he had lied on several occasions and that his previous affidavits contained only "partial truths." Conley also admitted to having selective memory while being questioned by Solicitor Dorsey only remembering answers to questions the solicitor wanted answered.

Conley also admitted during cross-examination that he had defecated at the bottom of the elevator shaft on the morning of the murder. His testimony, which spanned the course of three days, lasted more than 16 hours.

Defense attorneys made what many considered a tactical error while questioning Conley. Rosser grilled him extensively about other alleged liasons between Frank and other females in the factory. After failing to shake Conley in his stories the defense then sought to strike the damaging testimony but was unsuccessful. The press thought it significantly damaging to Frank that the defense attempted to have the testimony stricken. Solicitor Dorsey vehemently argued that the testimony should stand because it was solicited by the defense. The Constitution wrote: "By asking that the testimony be eliminated (the defense) virtually admit their failure to break down Conley." The morning paper also wrote that the miscalculation "made Frank's road to acquittal a thousand times harder to journey."

When Judge Roan made the ruling that the testimony would

remain on the record, the courtroom erupted as though the home team had scored the winning touchdown. It was reported that the courtroom "broke out in a wild uproar like a bloodthirsty mob at a bull fight." Judge Roan demanded order, announcing that he would not tolerate further outbreaks. Defense attorney Ruben Arnold rose from his chair and said, "If that happens again I shall move for a mistrial." The following morning's Constitution headline read **"SPONTANEOUS APPLAUSE GREETS DORSEY'S VICTORY."**

Solicitor Dorsey rested his case shortly after Conley's testimony and not every publication believed he had done so victoriously. The only evidence linking Leo Frank to Mary Phagan had been the uncollaborated testimony of Jim Conley. The editors of Frost's Magazine spoke out against Solicitor Dorsey and Chief Lanford, reporting that the magazine had withheld comment on the case because Dorsey and Lanford had assured the public that they possessed evidence which would insure Frank's conviction. The editors wrote that the state had:

> [m]isled the public. We cannot conceive that at the close of the prosecution, before the defense has presented one single witness, that it could be possible for any juryman to vote for the conviction of Leo M. Frank.

Addressing Conley's testimony the magazine wrote:

> He did not adhere to his original story. He was shown by the cross-examination of attorney Rosser to be absolutely unreliable in veracity and memory. One thing the negro did was to reply that "he did not remember" to everything that did not tend toward the

guilt of Frank, and would always fall back to his invented story.

Of Solicitor Dorsey, *Frost's Magazine* wrote, "It is evident that he has sought self-aggrandizement in his ruthless effort to make out a case where he knew beforehand that he had no case."

Attorneys for the defense believed they presented a good case. There were several witnesses, most of whom were white, who gave Frank alibis for times when Conley swore to have been with him.

Leo Frank ended the defense's case by spending four hours on the stand defending himself. The Georgian wrote of Frank's testimony: "Frank was far away the very best witness the defense has put forward." The Constitution reported his testimony "carried the ring of truth in every sentence."

More than 100 witnesses testified as to Frank's good character. Numerous other witnesses testified that Conley could never be believed under oath.

Dorsey took advantage of the character witnesses to insert ideas into the juror's minds about Frank's alleged sexual behavior during his cross examination. He insinuated that Frank was a homosexual by asking an office boy if Frank had made improper advances toward him. The office boy denied it but the rumor spread through the courtroom and the crowd outside. He asked witnesses questions such as had they ever heard of Frank "kissing girls and playing with their nipples on their breasts..." Regardless of how the witnesses answered the seed was already planted in the minds of the jurors. Mrs. Rhea Frank, Leo's mother, tired quickly of Dorsey's sleazy tactics. Dorsey asked a witness had he ever heard of "Frank taking a little girl to Druid Hills, setting her on his lap and playing with her?" Mrs. Frank jumped to her feet and yelled at Dorsey, "No, nor you either — you dog!"

The testimony continued to be extremely controversial for the times. Newspapers reported that much of the testimony was "unprintable."

The trial was finally winding down after four sensational weeks of testimony which had captured the attention of every major city in the South. One of the more obscure witnesses was then 14-year-old Alonzo Mann, the teenage factory worker who had walked up on the probable killer carrying the limp body of Mary Phagan. He said nothing about what he had seen, and his brief testimony was inconsequential.

To the crowds outside the courthouse, Solicitor Dorsey had become a hero. He was leaving the courthouse each day to thunderous applause from an admiring crowd. All three Atlanta newspapers were concerned that if the jury were to return a verdict on a Saturday, there would be a riot in the city that Saturday night. The town was full of people from the rural areas who were in town showing great interest in the case.

Judge Roan conferred with the chief of police and the colonel of the Fifth Georgia Regiment as to how they would handle the crowds. The conference took place in the presence of the jury and it would later be argued that the conference placed pressure on the jurors that the city would riot if the verdict was not guilty. The conference interrupted Dorsey's final argument, which Judge Roan did not allow to continue until the following Monday.

The Augusta Chronicle described the feeling in the city the following way:

> The last day of the criminal trial which has absorbed the city's attention for four weeks was marked by an impatience which was evident in every move of the public. There was a nervous tension apparent in the very atmosphere today. Wherever two or three persons were gathered there was a discussion

43

of the probable outcome, of the time the jury would be out ... and more than all else— of the possibility of "something happening" in the case of acquittal.

That is the black shadow which has hung over Atlanta for a month — the unspoken fear of "trouble" — of violence. Nobody will admit there was such a danger — but the feeling was there. There was a fear of the same element which brought about the great Atlanta riot of 1907 — the lower element; the people of the back streets and the alleys; the near-beer saloons and the pool rooms.

That is recognized as the real reason the trial of Leo Frank was abruptly adjourned Saturday and a recess taken until today. The Saturday night crowd in Atlanta, beer-drinking , blind-tiger frequenting, is not an assemblage loving law and order. A verdict which displeased these sans-culottes of Marietta Street might well result in trouble should it be published in flaring extras after dark.

The report that state troops have been given some kind of warning to be ready will not down. There was vigorous denial that any steps had been contemplated — but still the rumors persisted, and even yet it still persists.

The Atlanta papers have been wiser than in the days before the riot when the headlines of at least one paper inflamed the mob to action. There has been no word of the fear of violence, no mention of troops or riot; a careful avoidance of stirring up passion except in the printing of the court record, with its inflammatory speeches. Atlanta wants no more trouble of the kind which brought a reign of terror in 1907.

44

During his first closing argument Dorsey told the jury he believed Frank to be a "Dr. Jekyll and Mr. Hyde." Because the state bears the burden of proof, the prosecution is allowed two closing arguments, one before and one after the defense's closing. The only way the defense could have avoided this would have been to have not presented any evidence in defense. It is only under those conditions that the court would have allowed the defense the last say in closing.

During defense attorney Arnold's closing he suggested to the jury "...if Frank hadn't been a Jew there would never have been any prosecution against him" and that the case was the "greatest frame-up in the history of the state."

In his final closing, Dorsey capitalized on the drama of the emotional crowd and the tension in the courtroom. When he entered the courtroom he was greeted with noisy enthusiasm which annoyed Judge Roan. The judge ordered the sheriff to quell the crowd and threatened to clear the courtroom if it occurred again. The sheriff responded "Your Honor. That is the only way it can be stopped."

Dorsey contributed little to calming the crowd during his closing argument. He pointed at Frank and told the jury that the child had lost her life to him defending her honor. This elicited piercing screams from Mary Phagan's mother. The press reported that many in the courtroom were in tears. Dorsey timed the end of his closing perfectly to coincide with the chiming of the noon hour of a nearby Catholic Church clocktower. With each punctuation of the bell, he repeated the word "Guilty!"

While the jury was out, Judge Roan made a controversial decision. He summoned Frank's attorneys to the bench and recommended that neither they nor Frank attend the announcement of the verdict. The attorneys agreed without consulting Frank. They also consented to not bring up the issue of Frank not being present during the reading of the verdict as an issue during appeal, again without consulting Frank. It was an issue that would haunt the Frank case to the end and probably was the main reason for the failure of many of Frank's appeals.

The jury took less than four hours to reach a verdict, but according to one reporting of the incident it did not appear that the jurors were happy about having to make the decision. The observer wrote:

> It took no student of human nature to read the verdict. On the face of each juror was the drawn look of men who had been compelled through duty to do an awful thing — to consign a fellow creature to the gallows. There was no mistaking that look. The strongest of the men shook as if some strange ailment had stricken them.

The foreman announced the verdict of guilty. The courtroom had reportedly been thinned out during the announcing of the verdict with only newspaper reporters and Frank's family in the courtroom. As Judge Roan attempted to poll the jury individually, a reporter stuck his head out the window and announced the awaited verdict to the crowd. The resulting uproar forced Judge Roan to order the windows shut in the hot and humid courtroom, and the polling continued. All twelve men said "guilty" when it came their time to announce. A crowd the Constitution described as "thousands strong" went wild with joy in the streets below. Judge Roan opted to pass sentence at a later date, due to the crowds.

When Solicitor Dorsey exited the courthouse and reached the sidewalk, he was physically lifted into the air by the cheering crowd and passed across the street to his office with tears rolling down his cheeks, his hat raised over his head, his feet never touching the ground until he reached his office. One newspaper wrote of the event: "Few will live to see another such demonstration."

Meanwhile, a shocked Leo Frank received the news in his jail cell where he was met by his wife and a small group of friends. Frank had fully expected to be acquitted. "My God!" he exclaimed, "Even the jury was influenced by mob law."

The following day Judge Roan quietly and secretively assembled Frank and the attorneys for both sides and sentenced Frank to hang. After the sentencing, Frank's attorneys condemned the trial stating in part: "The temper of the public mind invaded the courtroom and invaded the streets and made itself manifest at every turn the jury made; and it was just as impossible for the just to escape the effects of this public feeling..." The attorneys immediately announced their intention to appeal the case. Jim Conley plead guilty to a lesser charge of aiding Frank and received a minor sentence and served one year in the chain gang.

In the months following the trial, Frank's attorneys would come under scrutiny and criticism by many of Frank's supporters for what were viewed as crucial mistakes in the trial. One of the most glaring to outside observers was the fact that they had failed to request a change of venue in such an emotionally charged trial. Another was the fact that they allowed Conley to testify for hours without ever breaking his story and then attempting to have part of the testimony stricken. Some in the Jewish community believed that lawyers should have been brought in from New York or Chicago.

The case had attracted little attention in the North before the trial but after Frank's conviction the story spread through the cities of the most influential Jewish communities in America. A division was forming between Jews and Gentiles over the Georgia trial. The Macon Daily Telegraph reported the situation as follows:

>...the long case and its bitterness has hurt the city greatly in that it has opened a seemingly impassible chasm between the people of the Jewish race and the Gentiles. It has broken friendships of years, has divided the races, brought about bitterness deeply regretted by all factions. The friends who rallied to the defense of Leo Frank feel that racial prejudice has much to do with the verdict. They are convinced that Frank was not prosecuted but persecuted. They refuse to believe he had a fair trial.

The Atlanta Journal discovered a short time after the trial that the state biologist had issued a report to Solicitor Dorsey shortly after Mary Phagan's murder. After having examined with a microscope the hair found on a lathe in the metal room, the biologist concluded in his report that the hair was not Mary Phagan's. The hair had been a crucial piece of evidence which Dorsey had used to convince the jury that the murder had been committed in the room near Frank's office. The Journal confronted Dorsey about withholding the biologist's report from the jury. Dorsey told the Journal that he had relied on "other witnesses" who had testified the hair was Mary Phagan's.

Other papers throughout the country were reporting that key witnesses were giving statements which conflicted with their testimony at trial. An editorial in The Atlanta Journal demanded a new trial for Frank.

Just when it seemed the situation could not be more complicated, politics became a factor in the Frank case. Hoke Smith was the senior senator for Georgia in the United States Congress. He was also the former owner of the Journal. Although he had relinquished ownership and control of the paper years earlier, many in Georgia believed the Journal was Smith's political organ. Smith was running for reelection. There was another powerful politician, Tom Watson, who had his own candidate in mind for Smith's senatorial seat.

Watson was outraged at the Journal's demand for a new trial believing it was Smith's way of bringing the Frank trial into the election. Watson had his own newspaper, The Jeffersonian, which he used as his own political organ. The newspaper had made Watson a powerful figure in the rural areas of Georgia. In many of the communities, The Jeffersonian was the only contact many farmers had with the outside world. His word, to them, was the gospel.

Watson was a hero even in Solicitor Dorsey's hometown of Fayetteville. At the turn of the century there had been a trial in Fayetteville involving one the town's most prominent citizens accused of killing a local school teacher. Dorsey, 28 and an attorney in Atlanta at the time, undoubtedly followed the trial in his hometown with great interest. The trial shocked the town and gripped the attention of its citizens. The Atlanta lawyer who went to Fayetteville to defend the accused was Col. Tom Watson, hailed by local papers as one of the best legal talents in the state.

By the time of the Mary Phagan murder in 1913, Watson had become a powerful force in politics in Georgia, often determining the outcome of statewide elections by his writings in his paper, as well as in his monthly magazine, The Watson.

At this point in his career, later writings reported that Watson had become a bitter racist and anti-Semite. His influence among rural voters was so pervasive that it was nearly impossible to win the governorship without his support.

His editorials, one of which acknowledged that it was *either* Frank or Conley who committed the murder, began to enrage rural farmers

49

against Leo Frank. These were the same farmers who Watson had already convinced, through his writings, that the North was holding the South in economic bondage. In one of his editorials he asked his readers, "Does a Jew expect extraordinary favors and immunities *because* of his race?" and "Who is paying for all this?"

As Watson's editorials against Leo Frank intensified, the Frank case became more than just a conflict between the Jews and Gentiles. Southerners came to believe it was once again the North against the South.

Many people in the North believed that most Southern rural cotton farmers were illiterate. Referring to them as "crackers," many in the North thought that most in Georgia had to have Watson's newspapers read to them by others and that they followed Watson's writings with blind ignorance.

It is more likely Watson's following wasn't motivated by blind ignorance but by a strong sense of moral values — values of decency Southerners didn't believe Northerners possessed. Since the papers didn't print the specifics of testimony which dealt with the alleged promiscuous conduct of Leo Frank, those outside the city didn't know that the real evidence of misconduct and perversion was weak. Watson's writings inflamed Southerner's instincts to protect women and children from what some considered were "Northern vandals" as they read about "the little factory girl who held to her innocence."

Some Jewish writers believed that Watson "thrived upon the ignorance and prejudices of rural Georgians." The reality may have been that he thrived upon his ability to rally righteous Southerners against what he believed was an evil North. The truth, if it could have been found, would not have been a popular position for him to take. Watson was a politician, and this battle was his politics.

Some of Watson's criticisms of the defense's handling of the case were accurate and damaging. On the matter of Frank's defense not filing for a change of venue, Watson wrote: "No case can come under 'mob' influence, unless the defendant and his lawyers are entirely negligent."

The New York Times wanted to support Frank, but Northern Jews with influence over the Times recognized the need to temper their articles so as not to "arouse the sensitivities of the Southern people and engender the feeling that the North is criticizing the courts and the people of Georgia." Their attempts were to no avail. Anything which appeared in Northern papers in support of Frank was viewed as an attack on the South.

Northern Jews finally realized the danger Frank faced and rallied behind him, raising funds and recruiting the best talents they could find and bring to the cause. One such talent was attorney Henry Alexander.

Alexander was the first to point out that the notes left near the body of Mary Phagan were written on order forms with the date printed 190_. These forms were more than four years old and had been used by an employee who no longer worked for the company. Conley had stated that the notes were written in Frank's office on paper found there, but these forms were stored in the basement near where the body was found.

Alexander was also the first to discover that the words "play like the night witch did it," may have contained a deeper meaning than first thought. Up until that time everyone had assumed that "night witch" was a misspelling of the word night-watchman. Alexander presented the theory that, although there were misspellings in the note, none of them involved mispronunciation.

Alexander had learned that there was a character in a negro superstition referred to as "the night witch." The superstition, which was found to be well known by Southern negroes, was that when children call out in the night, the night witch is riding them. If they are not immediately awakened they would be found the following morning, strangled by the night witch with a cord around their neck, exactly the way Mary Phagan's body was found. It was not a superstition that Leo Frank would likely have ever heard.

Frank's attorneys began preparing motions for a new trial. A 1906 Constitutional Amendment prevented the attorneys from appealing on the basis of Frank's guilt or innocence. They could only ask for a new trial based on legal errors in the trial. There would not be another review of Frank's guilt unless a new trial could be won.

The defense prepared motions listing what they believed were legal mistakes in the trial and the state solicitors countered that the trial was proper. The first appeal was denied by Judge Roan, but the judge's writing during his ruling created even more doubt as to Frank's guilt. Judge Roan wrote:

> I have thought about this case more than any other I have tried. I am not certain of the man's guilt. With all the thought I have put on this case, I am not thoroughly convinced that Frank is guilty or innocent. The jury was convinced. There is no room to doubt that. I feel it is my duty to order that the motion for a new trial be overruled.

Judge Roan's ruling gave defense attorneys optimism that the Supreme Court would overrule the conviction because of previous overturnings when the trial judge doubted the guilt of the defendant.

Six weeks later, the Georgia Supreme Court heard the appeal of Leo Frank. Rosser and Arnold argued for Frank. Georgia Attorney

General Thomas Felder and Solicitor Dorsey argued for the state. Both sides were allowed two hours instead of the usual one hour to present their case because of the unusual case and its long written record. The court ruled 4-2 to deny Frank a new trial.

Addressing the defense's argument that a new trial should be granted because of the emotion of the crowd during the trial, Justice Samuel C. Atkinson wrote "the conduct of a spectator during the trial of a case will not be grounds for a reversal of the judgment, unless a ruling upon such conduct is invoked from the judge at the time it occurs." The court believed that if the conduct was prejudicial the judge would or should have ruled such at the time and declared a mistrial. This was an unrealistic view considering what Judge Roan knew to be the mood of the crowds and the city and what would likely have happened had he done so.

The Georgia Supreme Court ruling was a devastating setback for Frank's supporters. Attorneys began to prepare further appeals. By now virtually every newspaper in the country was writing stories about Leo Frank. This was mainly due to efforts by the Jewish community to get the word out about Frank. The majority of stories in the press, particularly outside of Georgia, were critical of Georgia justice.

One of the more disastrous moves of defense attorneys was the hiring of a nationally known investigator, William J. Burns. Burns' arrogance immediately offended the people of Atlanta. Upon arrival he confidently announced his attention to resolve the crime. Atlantans thought the crime was already solved. He told the press on more than one occasion, "I am utterly confident of success." Six weeks later Burns made the following statement to the press:

> I know who is the murderer of Mary Phagan. In time I will let the public know, and I will show conclusive proof. There will not be a single ground

for the public to contradict me. The Phagan mystery is no longer a mystery. We have cleared it. I was confident from the outset that we would have success. It was no difficult task and our work was simple — merely the following of the criminal trend of mind which left so many manifestations in the Phagan tragedy.

Burns' conceited assertions gave Northerners who supported Frank false hope that Burns was going to produce some sort of strong evidence such as a confession from the real killer or some other strong direct evidence. One of Frank's attorneys secretly wrote at the time, "...if he does not do something like that, it will hurt us and may do the case more harm than if he had not entered it at all."

Anger towards Burns by the people of Mary Phagan's hometown of Marietta revealed itself when Burns found himself stranded in the middle of the city when his car broke down. An angry crowd followed the arrogant investigator back to his hotel. A crowd of more than 200 reportedly shouted threats such as "Lynch him!" "Shoot him!" "Mob him!" The mayor of the town pleaded with the crowd to disperse, to no avail. A respected judge was summoned for assistance. The judge asked the mob to let Burns leave town. The crowd appeared to yield, but as Burns was rushed into a car to be hurried from town the car was pelted with eggs by the angry crowd.

Burns' work was not, however, without some moderate success. Burns had publicly offered a reward of $1,000, a huge sum of money at the time, for anyone who could provide solid proof that Frank was perverted. Initially, Chief Detective Lanford confidently told the press, "I'll certainly furnish him with what I believe to be convincing proof." But when Burns arrived at Lanford's office with a leading rabbi and Frank's defense attorney, Lanford reportedly backed off of his position. Lanford stated publicly, "The state does not contend, and never has contended, that Frank is a pervert. The perversion charge was injected into the case by the attorneys for the defense, not by those for the state."

Lanford's statement to the press angered Frank, who shot back in the paper a few days later, "Is there a man in Atlanta who would deny that the charge of perversion was the chief cause of my conviction, or deny that the case without that charge, would be an entirely different question?"

Burns also succeeded in proving the sweeper Jim Conley *did* have a perverted side. Burns did this by exposing the Annie Maude Carter letters. Annie Maude Carter claimed to be Conley's confidant and someone for whom Conley deeply lusted. The letters she produced — which she claimed were written by Conley — were, according to The Atlanta Constitution, "so vile and vulgar that their publication is impossible." Conley denied writing the notes but experts at the time confirmed that the notes were consistent with Conley's other writings. When it came to damaging information against Conley, the notes were not the worst of it. Annie Maude Carter had a much stronger and more startling revelation. She claimed that Conley had confessed to her.

Carter gave a sworn affidavit that Conley told her that he had summoned Mary Phagan over after she left Leo Frank's office. Carter further swore that Conley had stated that when Mary approached, Conley knocked her over the head, choked her, and then pushed her down a scuttle hole in the back of the building. According to Carter, Conley then went down into the basement, wrote the murder notes and left them near the body hoping the notes would implicate Newt Lee. Carter further swore that Conley then broke the bolt on the basement's back door and left the factory. Carter's statement was consistent with several known facts in the case but received little attention from the press at the time.

After hearing of Carter's affidavit, Dorsey immediately went before the courts and requested a subpoena for Carter which would order Carter to come to Atlanta from her current home in New Orleans. Upon her arrival Dorsey had her arrested. After a few days in jail, she signed an affidavit for Dorsey stating that Conley had confessed no crime to her.

Frank's attorneys were now gearing up for their appeals in the federal courts which would eventually lead them to the U.S. Supreme Court. Luther Rosser and Reuben Arnold were no longer a part of the defense team. The new team consisted of the Haas brothers, Herbert and Leonard; Henry Alexander; and the firm of Tye, Peeples and Jordan. The Atlanta attorneys' work was closely monitored and supervised by Louis Marshall, who remained in New York.

The main focus of the appeal now was the constitutional argument that Rosser and Arnold did not have the right to waive Frank's presence in the courtroom when the jury returned their verdict. At the time, the defense was responding to a request from Judge Roan that for fear of mob violence neither they nor Frank be present in the courtroom during the reading of the verdict. Rosser and Arnold agreed without consulting Frank. They also agreed not to raise the issue of their absence in future appeals. Because of this, in their initial appeal this issue was not raised.

The new defense team intended this to be their main focus before the U.S. Supreme Court. They initially petitioned U.S. Supreme Court Justice Joseph R. Lamar for a writ of error. Justice Lamar denied the petition. Attorneys then petitioned to Supreme Court Justice Oliver Wendell Holmes. Holmes also denied the petition taking the same position the Georgia Supreme Court had taken on the matter. The question of Frank and his defense counsel not being present during the reading of the verdict, Holmes believed, was a question that should have been raised in the initial appeal.

Holmes would express an opinion which fueled the fury of newspapers throughout the country who believed Frank's case should be overturned. Justice Holmes expressed doubt Leo Frank had received proper due process of law citing "the presence of a hostile demonstration and seemingly dangerous crowd, thought by the presiding judge to be ready for violence unless a verdict of guilty was rendered."

Defense attorneys eventually appealed to the entire Supreme Court who agreed to hear the case. In just one week, the high court denied Frank's appeal with no accompanying written opinion. The Albany, New York, newspaper, Knickerbocker Press, printed an editorial which expressed the frustration of many. "Is it not an amazing commentary upon our judicial system that an associate Justice of the United States Supreme Court 'seriously doubts if Frank has had due process of law,' and yet there is no means at hand by which 'due process' may be had?"

In February of 1915, Frank's attorneys were given one more chance to be heard by the U.S. Supreme Court, this time petitioning for a writ of habeas corpus. The high court considered the petition for two months, but again denied the petition. The only allowable appeal left for Leo Frank was an appeal to the state for clemency. This could have come from either the Georgia Prison Commission or the governor.

The denial of the federal courts to grant a new trial was especially frustrating for Frank and his attorneys in light of a significant revelation which came in the fall of 1914. It would be a revelation which attorneys were sure would lead to Frank's acquittal if they could secure a second trial.

On October 2, 1914, William M. Smith, who had been sweeper Jim Conley's attorney, made an incredible announcement. Smith declared that he believed his own client, Conley, had murdered Mary Phagan. In answer to the apparent ethical conflict of such an announcement, Smith asserted that his statement was not in conflict with his obligations to his client because Conley's conviction for his complicity in the crime prevented him from ever being tried again in the matter. It was Smith's attempt at saving the life of what he believed was an innocent man.

Conley was seemingly unaffected by his lawyer's proclaiming of his guilt. Conley was serving his time at Bellwood convict camp, indifferent to the events unfolding in Atlanta. He had been assured by his attorney at the time of his conviction that he could never again be tried for his involvement in the death of Mary Phagan,

Tom Watson responded to Smith's statement the same way he responded to anyone who publicly defended Frank. He accused Smith of accepting a bribe. Watson did a convincing job of selling his readers on the theory that money from the North was trying to buy Frank's freedom. In one of Watson's articles, he either ominously threatened or accurately predicted what was about to happen. Watson asked his readers: "Are you going to provide encouragement and justification for future lynchings, by allowing Big Money to annul the well-weighed findings of unimpeachable jurors, whose verdict rests on unimpeachable testimony, and bears the approval of the highest court in the world?"

Rallies, encouraged by Watson, were held throughout the state. The mobs at these rallies would cheer Dorsey's and Watson's names and cheer for the hanging of Leo Frank. A fiddle player named "Fiddling John" Carson would attend and entertain the crowds with

"The Ballad of Mary Phagan."

Little Mary Phagan
She left her home one day;
She went to the pencil-factory
to see the big parade.

She left her home at eleven ,
She kissed her mother good-bye:
Not one time did the poor child think
That she was a-going to die.

Leo Frank he met her
With a brutish heart, we know;
He smiled, and said, "Little Mary,
You won't go home no more."

Sneaked along behind her
Till she reached the metalroom;
He laughed, and said, "Little Mary,
You have met your fatal doom."

Down upon her knees
To Leo Frank she plead;
He'd taken a stick from the trash-pile
And struck her across the head.

Tears flow down her rosy cheeks
While the blood flows down her back;
Remembered telling her mother
What time she would be back.

You killed little Mary Phagan,
It was on one holiday;
Called for old Jim Conley
To carry her body away.

He taken her to the basement,
She was bound both hand and feet;
Down in the basement
Little Mary she did sleep.

Newtley(sic) was the watchman
Who went to wind his key;
Down in the basement
Little Mary he did see.

Went in and called the officers
Whose names I do not know;
Come to the pencil-factory,
Said, "Newtley, you must go."

Taken him to the jail-house,
They locked him in a cell;
Poor old innocent negro
Knew nothing for to tell.

Have a notion in my head,
When Frank he comes to die,
Stand examination
In a court-house in the sky.

Come all you jolly people,
Wherever you may be,

Suppose little Mary Phagan
Belonged to you or me.

Now little Mary's mother
She weeps and mourns all day,
Praying to meet little Mary
In a better world some day.

Now little Mary's in Heaven,
Leo Frank's in jail,
Waiting for the day to come
When he can tell his tale.

Frank will be astonished
When the angels come to say,
"You killed little Mary Phagan;
It was on one holiday."

Judge he passed the sentence,
Then he reared back;
If he hang Leo Frank,
It won't bring little Mary back.

Frank he's got little children
And they will want for bread;
Look up at their papa's picture,
Say, "Now my papa's dead."

Judge he passed the sentence
He reared back in his chair;
He will hang Leo Frank,
And give the negro a year.

Next time he passed the sentence,
You bet he passed it well;
Well, Solicitor H.M. (Dorsey)
Sent Leo Frank to hell.

Within earshot of one such demonstration, the Georgia Prison Commission held a special session to consider Frank's appeal for commutation. At the March 31, 1915 hearing, Frank's attorneys presented as a part of their evidence a letter from Judge Roan. In the letter, Roan again expressed his doubt as to Frank's guilt. Roan had offered to appear in person to both the prison commission and the governor to express his doubts, but he died before the March hearing.

The prison commission also had before them a six-page letter written by Conley's attorney, William Smith. In his letter, Smith pleaded with the commission to not let Frank die. In part Smith wrote:

> There exists a large number of the strongest lines of evidence that reveals the error of charging Leo M. Frank with having any part in the murder of Mary Phagan. I believed it was my duty to speak. I had helped to destroy an innocent man before God. My sole purpose is to undo the wrong I have helped to do. With all the earnestness and seriousness of my life, I appeal to you not to let him die.

Solicitor Dorsey chose not to appear at the hearing, but instead opted to send a letter opposing commutation of the death penalty. The prison commission voted 2-1 to deny Frank's appeal for clemency, believing that no new evidence had been presented.

It was learned later that while Judge Roan was considering earlier appeals, attorney William Smith had visited him and relayed a story Conley had told him while Smith represented Conley.

Conley was assigned to work at the pencil factory on Confederate Memorial Day and wait for the night watchman Newt Lee to come on duty at six o'clock. At some point during the day, Conley had arranged to have some corn whiskey delivered to him at the basement door which led into the alley. Conley drank heavily that day, finishing off the entire bottle. Conley, drunkened by the whiskey, remembered seeing a girl in the factory that day. Conley followed her, and she screamed. A struggle ensued and Conley told his attorney he fought back. Conley claimed that from that point his mind went blank. He remembered that sometime later he found himself in the basement. He looked around and there was the girl, lying still, with a cord around her neck. He looked at her a long time and decided she was dead. He was scared. He didn't wait for Newt Lee. He hid the body the best he could, and left through the alley door in the basement.

Later writings revealed that both Smith and Judge Roan believed this to be the true story of how Mary Phagan was murdered. However Judge Roan, who was himself under death threats, believed public opinion was too hostile. He believed allowing the case to make its way through the appellate courts would give the public time to calm down. It was Judge Roan's belief that if the case was not overturned during the appeals process the governor would do the right thing when the case reached his desk. That day had come, and it was Leo Frank's last chance for justice.

Leo Frank's fate now rested in the hands of one man — Governor John Slaton. Governor Slaton was a popular governor who had been elected to office by an overwhelming margin with the support of Tom Watson. In 1914, he unsuccessfully vied for a U.S. Senate seat and consequently was in his final days in office as governor. The new governor, Nathaniel Harris, was scheduled to be inaugurated June 26,

1915. Since Frank's execution was scheduled for June 22, 1915, his plea for commutation would be heard by Governor Slaton. Since the incoming Governor Harris was considered to be a "Watson man," Frank's attorneys believed they would fare better with the current governor.

Slaton's goal was to one day hold one of Georgia's two U.S. Senate seats, but he lacked the political pull needed to achieve it. Tom Watson reportedly offered his substantial political weight to back Slaton in his next bid for the seat if he would let Frank die.

Slaton, a good man with a strong sense of justice, took the case very seriously. He set out to learn everything he could about the case in an attempt to come to the best informed decision. He heard arguments from both the state and defense. He visited the pencil factory and examined the crime scene. He had a letter from Judge Roan asking the governor to rectify his mistake of sentencing Frank to death.

Governor Slaton also learned of evidence that would not be made public for eight years. A federal prison doctor, treating a prisoner at the federal penitentiary in Atlanta who thought he was dying, relayed important information to the governor. The prisoner was identified only as Freeman. Freeman claimed he had been playing cards with Conley in the basement of the pencil factory the day of the murder. Around noon Freeman said Conley went up the ladder to the main floor. After a short while Freeman heard muffled screams and went up the ladder to see what was happening. He saw Conley in a struggle with someone. Freeman told his doctor the sight scared him and he fled into the alley through the basement.

Freeman went on to say that later that night Conley came to his door needing money. Freeman alleged that Conley told him he was trying to raise $3 and needed an additional $1.80. In exchange for the money, Conley gave Freeman a woman's mesh handbag. Freeman said that when he later read of the murder and the missing handbag, which had contained $1.20, he got rid of the purse and fled the city. He later was convicted of a federal crime and sent to the Atlanta penitentiary.

Governor Slaton considered the case for 12 days, poring over the information. He received scores of demands for both commutation of sentence and death for Leo Frank. In addition there were more than a thousand death threats against him and his wife should he let Leo Frank live.

In the early morning hours of June 21, 1915, Governor Slaton made his decision. At 2 a.m., he climbed the stairs and finding his wife still awake on the second floor, informed her of his decision. "It may mean my death or worse, but I have ordered the sentence commuted." Mrs. Slaton kissed her husband and responded, "I would rather be the widow of a brave and honorable man than the wife of a coward."

Before making his announcement, Governor Slaton instructed the sheriff of Fulton County to secret Frank out of the city and move him to a state prison away from Atlanta. The press was watching the Fulton County jail closely. The sheriff ordered a car to pull to the front of the jail and remain there idling. As the press watched the awaiting car, the sheriff and deputies escorted Frank through the basement and into another waiting car in the back alley. He was successfully and safely moved to the prison in Milledgeville.

The commutation of Frank's sentence was the headline story of almost every newspaper in the South and created a tremendous outpouring of emotion both for and against the decision. The day after Governor Slaton made his decision, he released a statement explaining his action. The statement covered an entire page of The Atlanta Constitution. The statement outlined the facts of the case, defended the actions of Judge Roan, and condemned some of the criticisms of Georgia's legal system. The governor wrote the following about the attack on Georgia:

Many newspapers and multitudes of people have attacked the state of Georgia because of the conviction of Leo M. Frank and have declared the conviction to have been through the domination of a mob and with no evidence to support the verdict. This opinion has been formed to a great extent by those who have not read the evidence and who are unacquainted with the judicial procedure in our state.

I have been unable to even open a large proportion of the letters sent me, because of their number and because I could not through them gain any assistance in determining my duty.

The murder committed was a most heinous one. A young girl was strangled to death by a cord tied around her throat and the offender deserves the punishment of death. The only question is as to the identity of the criminal.

The responsibility is upon the people of Georgia to protect the lives of her citizens and to maintain the dignity of her laws, and if the choice must be made between the approbation of citizens of other states and the enforcement of our laws against offenders, whether powerful or weak, we must choose the latter alternative.

In spite of the fact that Governor Slaton commuted Frank's sentence, he made it clear in his statement that although he could not be sure of Frank's guilt, neither could he be sure of his innocence. He also criticized those who second-guessed the jury's opinion, stating that the jurors were in the best position to know the truth. About the evidence Slaton wrote:

Many newspapers and non-residents have declared that Frank was convicted without any evidence to sustain the verdict. In large measure, those giving expression to this utterance have not read the evidence and are not acquainted with the facts. The same may be said regarding many of those who are demanding his execution.

In my judgement, no one has a right to an opinion who is not acquainted with the evidence in the case, and it must be conceded that the jury who saw the witnesses and beheld their demeanor upon the stand are in the best position as a general rule to reach the truth.

Governor Slaton's statement then began to outline the evidence presented at trial against Frank. When he came to the testimony presented by Jim Conley, Governor Slaton made it clear he believed Conley to be the weak link in the state's case. About Conley's story Slaton wrote:

The admission of Conley that he wrote the notes found at the body of the dead girl together with the part he admitted he played in the transaction, combined with his history and his explanation as to both the writing of the notes and the removal of the body to the basement, make the entire case revolve about him. Did Conley speak the truth?

Before going into the varying and conflicting affidavits made by Conley, it is advisable to refer to some incidents which cannot be reconciled to Conley's story. Wherever a physical fact is stated by Conley, which is admitted, this can be accepted, but under both the rules of law and of common sense, his statements cannot be received, excepting where clearly corroborated. He admits not only his participation as an accessory, but also glibly confesses his own infamy.

One fact in the case and that of most important force in arriving at the truth contradicts Conley's testimony. It is disagreeable to refer to it, but delicacy must yield to necessity when human life is at stake.

The mystery in the case is the question as to how Mary Phagan's body got into the basement. It was found 136 feet toward the end of the building where the body was found at a spot near the back door, which led out toward the street in the rear. Conley swears he did not return to the basement, but went back up in the elevator, while Frank went back on the ladder, constituting the only two methods of ingress and egress to the basement, excepting through the back door. This was between 1 and 2 o'clock on the afternoon of April 26.

Conley testified that on the morning of April 26 he went down into the basement to relieve his bowels and utilized the elevator shaft for the purpose.

On the morning of April 27 at 3 o'clock when the detectives came down into the basement by way of the ladder, they inspected the premises, including the shaft, and they found there human excrement in natural condition.

Subsequently, when they used the elevator, which everybody, including Conley, who had run the elevator for 1 ½ years admits only stops by hitting the ground in the basement, the elevator struck the excrement and mashed it, thus demonstrating that the elevator had not been used since Conley had been there.

Governor Slaton went on to outline many other facts which caused him doubt, such as the letters Conley had written to his girlfriend with similar phrases used in the murder notes, and the fact that the notes were written on pads normally kept in the basement and not in Leo Frank's office.

When Governor Slaton released his statement to the press he announced to them, "Feeling as I do about this case, I would be a murderer if I allowed that man to hang."

A few days later Governor Slaton was quoted in another publication stating:

> Two thousand years ago another governor washed his hands of a case and turned over a Jew to a mob. For two thousand years that governor's name has been accursed. If today another Jew were lying in his grave because I had failed to do my duty I would all through life find his blood on my hands and would consider myself an assassin through cowardice.

The larger daily papers, as well as some of the rural news editors, commended Governor Slaton's courage. In many towns, including Marietta, Columbus and Newnan, dummies with Governor Slaton's name on them were burned in effigy. In Marietta, the sign read, "John M. Slaton, King of the Jews and Georgia's Traitor Forever."

Some angry Georgians lashed out at all Jews. In Canton, Jews were given 24 hours to leave town or face the threat of "summary judgement."

In Marietta fliers were reportedly given to Jewish merchants purporting to be from the "Marietta Vigilance Committee" which read as follows:

> You are hereby notified to close up this business and quit Marietta by Saturday night, June 29, 1915, or else stand the consequences. We mean to rid Marietta of all Jews by the above date. You can heed this warning or stand the punishment the committee may see fit to deal out to you.

Predictably, Tom Watson used The Jeffersonian to lash out at Governor Slaton with fury over his decision. Watson wrote, **"Our grand old Empire State has been Raped!"** The words that followed seem to encourage Georgians to do what the law had not. Watson wrote, "...let no man reproach the South with Lynch law: let him remember the unendurable provocation: and let him say whether Lynch law is not better than no law at all."

In Atlanta, Solicitor Hugh Dorsey also denounced the governor for his action. As soon as the announcement of commutation was received, people began to gather in the streets of Atlanta. When the crowd swelled to a capacity that could overcome the squads of city policemen, the mob – reportedly armed – overran them and marched on the governor's home in Ansley Park. Governor Slaton had declared martial law within a half-mile radius of his home. An entire state militia battalion stood guard behind barbed-wire barriers.

The crowd threw stones and bottles towards the English-style mansion, but the militia effectively stopped the crowd. The following night another armed mob was detained when they attempted to approach the rear of the governor's home. They were released after Governor Slaton declined to prosecute them. Martial law remained in effect around the mansion until the governor and his family left the

70

state the following week after the inauguration of the new governor, Nathaniel Harris.

The Atlanta Constitution called for an end to the mob violence. Newspapers in other parts of the country looked on Georgia with disdain. In Wisconsin, The Madison Journal editorialized: "The public condemnation of Governor Slaton proves not so much that Georgia has besmirched her honor as that Georgia has no honor."

Life on the prison farm for Leo Frank consisted of four to five hours labor. That allowed Frank the remainder of the day to write letters to his wife and others who had rallied behind him. At night he slept on a cot in a room with several other prisoners until one night in late July when he was violently awakened.

Another prisoner named William Creen skulked up to a sleeping Leo Frank and plunged a butcher knife into his throat! The guard and two other prisoners rushed to Frank's aid as Creen proceeded to attempt to further slice open Frank's throat. By the time the two could be separated, Frank was bleeding profusely from a 7 1/2 inch gaping wound.

Fortunately for Frank, two of the prisoners were doctors who quickly applied pressure to Frank's jugular vein and successfully stopped the bleeding. Frank was moved to the prison hospital where the two inmate doctors, along with the prison doctor, stitched up the wound and placed his head in a brace in an attempt maintain the integrity of the stitches. Frank's life hung in peril for several days, but he eventually improved.

The assaulting prisoner Creen told Governor Harris, who came to the prison to investigate, that he had been called "from on high" to murder Frank. Creen also told the new governor that he tried to kill Frank to save other prisoners from possible harm from future invading lynch mobs.

When it became apparent that Frank would recover he wrote triumphantly to a friend about his survival: "Certainly my escape was providential, and the good Lord must sure have in store for me a brighter and happier day when that honor, justly mine now, will be restored to me." He was wrong.

On August 16, 1915, 25 men approached the prison farm by automobile. There were only two guards on duty at the time. One of the guards heard the approaching automobiles and asked for permission to move Frank to a safer place, but permission was denied. Five of the men went to the warden's house where the warden was handcuffed without incident. Some of the other men captured and also handcuffed the prison superintendent. Four of the men went to Frank's room. The door was opened, and one of the men said to Frank, "We want you to come with us." Frank got of bed and began to dress when another of them spoke. "Don't bother with the clothes; come just as you are." Frank then was handcuffed and led out of the room. His demeanor was reported to be calm, acting neither terrified nor surprised. The entire kidnaping was reported to have taken less than five minutes.

Later it was learned that the abduction had been carefully planned by some of the highest caliber people in Marietta. In fact, one publication reported that the "riffraff" were intentionally left out of the plan. The men had left Marietta in small groups throughout the day, traveling to Milledgeville in different intervals using different routes to avoid drawing unwanted attention. Two were dispatched to disable the telephone and telegraph wires leading to the prison.

The men met at a prearranged location near the prison and executed their plan, wearing goggles and hats to avoid being identified. After taking their prisoner, the men drove the 175 miles northwest to Marietta. Their original intention was to hang Frank near the grave of Mary Phagan. When time slipped away from them and dawn broke before they were ready, they chose an alternative site.

During the all-night drive, Frank rode in the back seat of the vehicle with two of his abductors. Unbeknownst to them all, the phone line saboteur had missed one of the phone lines going out of the prison, and the governor had been alerted about the kidnaping. The governor in turn alerted the sheriff of every county to be on the lookout for a caravan of cars passing through their jurisdictions. Not one sheriff reported sighting the caravan.

During the ride, the men in the car encouraged Frank to confess to the murder but he would not — not even when they offered to spare his life if he confessed. His words were so believable that when they reached their destination, two of the kidnappers had begun to believe Frank and told the others so. The men were shocked, but then Frank began to plead his case to the rest of the men. It was later reported that after Frank talked to the mob, all but four of the 25 men had indicated a willingness to abort the lynching. But then one of the remaining four reminded the rest that daybreak had come and there was likely a posse looking for them. It also was pointed out that safely returning Frank to the prison was not feasible. The crowd then resigned themselves to finish what they had started.

Frank was led to a large oak tree despite the objections of one or possibly more of the original conspirators, who protested and refused to take part any further. While being escorted to the tree, Frank said to his captors, "I care more about my wife and my mother than I do of my life."

Frank was asked again if he murdered Mary Phagan. Frank did not reply. Frank was asked if he wanted to make a statement. He said no. He removed his wedding ring from his finger, handed it to one of his abductors and asked that it be given to a newspaper man who would forward the ring to his wife. The request was granted, and the ring eventually was returned to Mrs. Frank.

Frank was placed on a table, and a manila rope placed around his neck. The table was then kicked out from under him, and Leo Frank was hanged. Within hours of the lynching, most of the town of Marietta had learned of the lynching, and a large crowd of sightseers had gathered around the body, some shouting at the lifeless figure as it hung from the branch of the oak tree, blindfolded, handcuffed with his feet bound and barefoot.

Photo taken as sightseers surrounded the body of Leo Frank before he was cut down from the tree. Courtesy, Georgia Department of Archives.

Photo taken as sightseers surrounded the body of Leo Frank before he was cut down from the tree. Courtesy, Georgia Department of Archives.

Governor Nathaniel Harris denounced the lynching and called for an investigation. Most of the newspapers throughout the nation also denounced the actions of the mob. The local Marietta paper, however, praised the action writing, "We regard the hanging of Leo M. Frank in Cobb County as an act of law abiding citizens." Mayor Woodward of Atlanta told a conference group in California that Frank suffered a "just penalty for an unspeakable crime."

Although everyone in Marietta was said to have known the identities of the lynch mob, no one was arrested. The coroner's jury ruled that Leo Frank's death was committed "at the hands of person or persons unknown."

Frank's body was turned over to his family. He was buried in Mount Carmel Cemetery in Brooklyn, New York. After the funeral, his wife Lucile returned to Atlanta where she lived the remainder of her life. Whenever her signature was required, she proudly penned the name "Mrs. Leo Frank." She protested his innocence until her death.

During World War II, Governor John M. Slaton's long-time friend, Judge Arthur Powell, a prominent Atlanta attorney, wrote a book entitled *I Can Go Home Again.* In that book Judge Powell wrote, "I am one of the few people who know that Leo Frank was innocent of the crime for which he was lynched." Judge Powell continued, "I know who killed Mary Phagan, but I know it in such a way that I can never honorably make the information public as long as certain persons are still living."

He said he would write the information out, seal it and leave it in his office to be opened upon his death. At the time the book was published, Atlanta Constitution crime reporter Celestine Sibley tracked down Lucile Frank to seek her reaction to Judge Powell's book.

"I found her rolling bandages for the Red Cross at the Temple — a plump gray-haired woman in her late 50s," Celestine later remembered. "She just broke down crying and said, 'If Judge Powell knows anything that will clear my husband's name he should speak now!'"

Judge Powell did not speak. After he died, his family said they found nothing among his effects that would throw any additional light on the case.

In the 1950s, Alonzo Mann came forward for the first time. Mann had been the 13-year-old boy who saw Mary Phagan's seemingly lifeless body being carried down the stairwell which led to the basement of the pencil factory by her probable lone killer. Mann told his story to a reporter with The Atlanta Journal - Constitution. Mann supposedly was told that the editors of the paper would not run the story because of fear the Atlanta Jewish community would not want the case brought back up. Lucile Frank was never told the new information had surfaced. She died April 23, 1957, at the age of 69, never knowing if her husband's name would ever officially be cleared.

Alonzo Mann's story did not surface again until March of 1982 when a reporter named Jerry Thompson from the Nashville Tennessean went to a trailer home in Bristol, Virginia, and listened to the 82-year-old man known to him as Lonnie. Lonnie explained that he wanted to tell his story and clear Leo Frank's name before he went to his maker. He told the Tennessee paper that it was the sweeper Jim Conley whom he saw that Confederate Memorial Day carrying Mary Phagan's body towards the basement — alone with Leo Frank nowhere in site. Mann remembered Conley's growling words to a frightened teenager: "If you tell anyone about this, I'll kill you!"

On March 7, 1982, the Tennessean broke the Alonzo Mann story, and the nation sat up and took notice. Thompson's article was picked up by the wire services and the resulting efforts sparked by Mann's story led to a posthumous pardon by Georgia Board of Pardons and Parole. Although the board initially rejected the request, the official pardon was granted in 1985. None of the main players involved with the case lived to see the pardon.

The commutation of Leo Frank's sentence virtually ended Governor Slaton's political career. Although he eventually was able to return to Atlanta and was embraced by his fellow jurists, he was never again elected to public office. He lived on his 75-acre farm in the heart of Buckhead until his death in 1955. He was 88 years old. His mansion at the corner of Peachtree Road and West Paces Ferry Road, where Georgia troops fought back angry lynch mobs in 1915, sold for $1,356,000 after his death.

In 1916, Hugh Dorsey was elected Governor of Georgia riding the coattails of his popularity over the prosecution of Leo Frank and with the substantial endorsement of Tom Watson. With the help of Watson, Dorsey beat the incumbent governor Nat Harris, who ran on a campaign based on his belief in prohibition. During the campaign, Watson described Dorsey as "the fearless, incorruptible solicitor general who won the great fight for LAW AND ORDER, and the PROTECTION OF WOMANHOOD in the Leo Frank Case."

Dorsey was elected again in 1918 with no opposition. In 1920, Dorsey ran for the U.S. Senate seat that Governor Slaton had coveted for so long. During Dorsey's second term as governor, he published a pamphlet attacking the state's treatment of blacks. This enraged Watson, who in turn handily defeated Dorsey in his race and claimed the U.S. Senate seat for himself. Watson quickly earned the reputation in the senate as a belligerent. He died in September of 1922 from an asthma attack while in Washington D.C. Of his funeral, historian C. Vann Woodward wrote, "Most conspicuous among the floral tributes was a cross of roses 8 feet high, sent by the Ku Klux Klan."

The home in which Dorsey lived still stands today just off the square in Fayettteville and is named the Dorsey-Fife-Holliday house. Dorsey, because Hugh Dorsey had lived there; Fife, after the last prominent family to live in the home; and Holliday, after Doc Holliday whose grandparents also once lived in the home.

The National Pencil Company was sold to M.A. Ferst, who later founded The Scripto Company.

On the 80th anniversary of the lynching of Leo Frank, Rabbi

Steven Lebow had a plaque placed on an office building near the intersection of Roswell and Frey's Gin roads at the site where Frank was hanged. It reads, "Wrongly accused. Falsely convicted. Wantonly murdered."

Eighty-seven years after the murder of Mary Phagan, in the year 2000, Mary Phagan's great-niece, Mary Phagan Kean lives in Cobb County, Ga., working as a special education administrator. For years she had been keeping a list of people who came to her and bragged that their family members had been part of the lynch mob that killed Frank. Kean intended that the list "be opened at my demise." But her list slipped out and is now being published on an Internet web site that claims to expose the killers of Leo Frank.

Tom Watson died in 1922. After his death a 12-foot statue was placed on the grounds of Georgia's state capitol. The inscription hailed Watson as a champion of right. The August 13, 2000, edition of The Atlanta Journal-Constitution contained an editorial which strongly disagreed. The editorial called for the removal of Watson's statue from the lawn of the state capitol. The editorial said in part:

> As the 85th anniversary of one of Watson's most notorious causes, the lynching of Leo Frank, approaches, it's time to address the terrible symbolism of this statue and the need for its removal.
>
> To paraphrase Shakespeare, it has come time not to praise Tom Watson but to bury him.
>
> Watson's life was a disturbing testament to the power of hate.

Jim Conley, the factory sweeper who claimed Leo Frank was the murderer, died in 1962. He had lived most of the remainder of his life in and out of prison. After being released for his admitted part in disposing of Mary Phagan's body, he soon was arrested again and

79

sentenced to 20 years after being shot during an attempted burglary of a drug store in Atlanta. After being released for that, he was arrested various times for drunkenness and gambling. He never publicly confessed to killing Mary Phagan.

A careful review of the evidence known in 2000 reveals that it is doubtful that Leo Frank could be convicted today by a non-biased jury based on the evidence presented at his trial in 1914. Based on the evidence now known against Jim Conley — he most probably could be.

2

THE DEATH FARM
Jasper County
1921

He laid across the gasoline barrel — held there by others who, until then, he thought were his friends. Clyde Freeman had one arm and Charlie Chisolm the other. They held him there, wincing at what was being done to him. Another supposed friend held a buggy whip and struck him repeatedly as he lay over the barrel. He cried and begged them for mercy, but mercy was not theirs to give. The beating continued. It had to continue because they were all slaves, and the white son of the owner of the plantation had ordered it. The plantation owner's son stood there supervising the torture, reminding the slave cracking the whip that if he didn't do an adequate job he would be next.

The victim of the beating was known only as "Iron John" or some times "Iron Jaw." He took the whipping as long as he could stand it. He said in anger, "Don't hit me no more. I'd rather be dead than treated this way." The supervisor of the torture stepped forward without another word and shot him in the shoulder blade. Iron John again screamed out in pain. The son of the man who ruled the plantation asked him, "Do you want more?" In spite of the resilience that earned him the name Iron John, he could take no more. "Yes," he said. "Shoot me." The plantation owner's son did as his father had taught him — he placed a hand gun to the back of the slave's head and pulled the trigger. The man known as Iron John died with his true name never being recorded. The reason for his torture; he had laid a hog fence crooked.

It wasn't the 1800s. It wasn't pre-Civil War. In fact, it was 1921, 58 years after the Emancipation Proclamation. But slavery was still alive in parts of Jasper County, Georgia, particularly on the Williams' plantations.

The plantation where Iron John had worked was owned by John S. Williams. Williams was born in Meriwether County in 1866, one year after the Thirteenth Amendment to the Constitution forbade slavery. Unlike plantation owners of a century before, Williams had found a more economical way to procure slave labor. Rather than buying them off the auction block, Williams bought his slaves out of jail.

Iron John, and most of the other workers on the two Williams plantations were "bought out," a term describing the practice of John S. Williams and three of his sons, Huland, Leroy and Marvin. John and Huland Williams traveled to the Atlanta and Macon stockades in search of their farm labor. They were looking for black prisoners, imprisoned for various petty crimes, who were unable to pay their fines. The plantation owners would pay the fine and tell the prisoner he could come back to the farm and work off the debt. It was a scam.

On the plantation of John S. Williams there was no record of a single laborer ever leaving the plantation of his own free will after satisfying his debt. Except for a few who escaped, those who left the Williams plantation left this world.

The reason the Williams traveled to Atlanta and Macon for their labor was because Negroes from far away didn't know their way around Jasper County. They had no allies in the area to aid in escape and didn't know the area well enough to get away before being tracked down. The plantations had tracking dogs for the specific purpose of catching escaping slaves. In 1921, they were not referred to as slaves, but no other word in the English language better describes their plight.

There were two plantations in the Williams family. John S. Williams' sprawling 2000-acre farm was the home place. Huland Williams had moved to other land and was successfully running his own plantation with "bought out" labor as his main work force.

There were three exceptions to this work force — Clyde Manning and Clyde and Claude Freeman. Clyde Manning was the overseer, or as the press dubbed him, the "Negro boss" of the slaves on John's farm. Claude, with the help of his brother Clyde, oversaw the slaves on Huland's farm. Huland was usually the one who traveled to the Atlanta and Macon stockades bringing back the slaves.

Both of the Williams' farms had what the press called "stockades." They were redwood buildings divided into two rooms which did not connect internally. It was a crude sort of duplex with cracks in the walls. You could carry on a conversation with the person in the adjoining room.

The overseer stayed on one side and the farm labor on the other. The overseer was free to come and go as he pleased. The slaves were locked in their room at night, forced in their first days of arrival to sleep on a bare wooden floor.

On John Williams' plantation, Clyde Manning would lock the slaves up with a lock and chain he ran through a hole in the door. He lived on the other side with his wife and children. Claude Freeman would lock up his labor with a wooden bar across the door.

Two of John Williams' other sons, Leroy and Marvin, lived on John's farm in separate houses and helped run the plantations. A fourth son of John's, Gus, was a World War I veteran and successful doctor in McDonough, Georgia.

The nation had a new president, Warren G. Harding. Hugh Dorsey was serving his second term as Governor of Georgia. After the lynching of Leo Frank, Governor Dorsey was spending his final term as governor trying to change his image with his condemnation of lynching and the treatment of blacks.

There were laws in the United States which prohibited the Williams' conduct in Jasper County. Peonage was outlawed by the U.S. Congress in 1867 in response to problems in New Mexico. Peonage was wide-spread throughout Mexico and other parts of Spanish America.

Clyde Manning, the Negro boss on the main plantation, was 27 years old and had lived on the plantation since his father was shot and killed about 1907 when Clyde was young. John S. Williams took in Clyde and his family. As Clyde grew older, Williams began grooming Clyde to be foreman to his labor. According to his eventual testimony, Clyde's loyalty to the elder Williams was based more on fear than appreciation. However, his loyalty ran deep no matter what that loyalty was based on.

Clyde was to Williams what would have been referred to in that time as a trusty Negro. Williams even allowed Clyde to carry a pistol — unheard of for a Negro farmhand on a white-owned plantation but necessary for Clyde to maintain control over the slaves. Claude Freeman also was allowed to carry a pistol on the Huland Williams farm.

There were successful escapes. First Frank Dozier, then James Strickland and then Gus Chapman, but Chapman did not get away on his first attempt. After somehow convincing Clyde Manning to unlock the chain in the middle of the night and set him free, Chapman ran south. He was heading for Macon, one of the larger cities in middle Georgia, where he hoped to find work that was less back-breaking. He trusted no one on his journey and tried to travel mostly at night, battling Georgia's summer heat and mosquitos. He was looking for railroad tracks he could follow to Macon. Just as he found those tracks, the dogs from Williams plantation found him. A group from the plantation, which included Clyde Manning, captured Chapman near the town of Shady Dale, Georgia and took him back to the waiting fury of John S. Williams.

Chapman knew his life was in danger. When Will Napier was captured after an escape attempt, Huland Williams beat him so severely that he finally asked to be killed. When Will said to Huland, "Kill me," Huland handed a .38 caliber pistol to another slave, Charlie Chisolm. Without having to be told, Charlie put the pistol to the back of Will's head and pulled the trigger killing Will Napier.

When Chapman was brought back to John Williams, he was beaten by John himself. The beating was severe, but Chapman was allowed to live. Chapman later told investigators he though he was allowed to live because he was old. The beating did not break his determination to be free.

Five months afterward, in November, Gus Chapman escaped again. This time he traveled north and made it all the way to Atlanta. After discussing his situation with other blacks, he decided that someone needed to be told what was going on in Jasper County. He made his way to the offices of the United States Bureau of Investigation (named the FBI in 1935).

A.J. Wismer and George W. Brown were assigned by the bureau to investigate peonage in Georgia. They had no shortage of complaints to deal with. Peonage, to various degrees, was going on all over Georgia. Vincent Hughes, the head of the Bureau of Investigation, described the situation in Georgia to The Atlanta Constitution in the following statement:

> This office receives and investigates every complaint of peonage arising in the territory comprising almost the whole state of Georgia. The bulk of our work now is on peonage complaints. There are more of these than all other cases combined. We find ourselves handicapped in handling most of the complaints because the law is not broad enough.
>
> The technical crime of peonage is only committed when involuntary servitude exists on a basis of debt and many Negroes are held in servitude through fear and other coercion, perhaps more so than for debt. On a basis of geographical original complaints we receive, I should say that peonage in Georgia is widespread in the sense of being state-wide. Judging from the complaints we receive a far greater part of Georgia is free from the practice which seems to centered in two or three sore spots where social conditions are less advanced.

Hughes pointed to a map and told the Constitution that Jasper County, 50 miles from Atlanta, was the worst peonage county in the state. He then pointed to Pike County as another and indicated an area in south central Georgia as the third worst region in the state.

Gus Chapman had no idea the problem was so widespread. He had no reason to believe that his complaint would not be one of hundreds with little chance of stirring definitive action. In spite of the odds against it, Gus' story would get the attention of Agents Wismer and Brown. Gus's complaint had been well timed, coming on the heels of one filed by James Strickland, another black worker who had escaped earlier that same year.

Gus Chapman went to the federal agents with the best of intentions. He wanted to end the suffering of the friends he left behind on the Williams plantation. That he would do, but it would come at the expense of most of their lives.

On February 19, 1921, Agents Brown and Wismer made a surprise visit to both Williams' plantations. When they first arrived, John Williams was not home, and they were able to speak with several of the field hands without Williams being present.

It was a red flag to Agent Brown that something was going on when he found Clyde Manning wearing a sidearm. It was very unusual for a white farmer to allow a black field hand to be armed. Agent Brown questioned Manning about the first escape of Gus Chapman and asked Manning if he and others had tracked down Chapman and brought him back. Manning denied this to Agent Brown. It was an important question because in order to charge someone with peonage, the agents had to prove the service was involuntary. Manning knew that tracking someone down with dogs and forcing them to return to the farm would be strong evidence of peonage.

When John Williams returned to the plantation, he saw the federal agents before they saw him. He hurried to the other workers on the

2,000-acre farm and told them to watch what they said to the agents. Then he went to Huland's farm and told those slaves to say nothing disparaging to the agents when they came.

When Williams finally approached the agents he presented himself as a humble gentleman willing to cooperate in any way possible. When the agents told Williams they were investigating peonage, he asked the agents to define peonage. Agent Brown told him peonage was when you worked "bonded Negroes." In response to that Williams said, "Well then I might technically be guilty of that, but so would most Georgia farmers if that definition is correct."

The agents told Williams that the conditions on the farm were not as bad as they had expected. The agents considered the more severe cases of peonage to be the ones where the laborers were not well-fed or cared for. The Williams' field hands were well fed and fairly well-dressed. They had observed one worker making shoes for all the others out of old automobile tires. The workers acted as if they were content.

When the two agents left, they told Williams he probably was guilty of peonage but that they were not overly concerned with what they had seen. The last words Williams heard from them was that he probably would not be taken before a federal grand jury.

None of the field hands interviewed had said anything incriminating against John Williams, but Williams could not be sure of this. In spite of the assurances of federal agents that they would not return, Williams made a crucial decision that drastic action was in order.

On the following day, he pulled Clyde Manning aside and said, "It won't do for these boys to go up yonder and swear against me. It would ruin me. They got to be done away with." When Clyde showed reluctance Williams said to him, "If you don't want to do it, it just means your neck or theirs."

Before the killing started, John Williams ordered his sons to leave the state so they would not be involved in what was about to come. Two days later the killing started.

Johnnie Williams was a black slave with the same name as his plantation owner. He had been sent into the field that morning by John S. Williams to move some cows. Williams then went to Clyde Manning and told Clyde it was time to kill Johnnie. Clyde accompanied the plantation owner down to the pasture where Johnnie was moving cows. "Hit him and be sure you get him!" was the order that prosecutors would later claim became John S. Williams' standing order. Johnnie heard the wealthy land owner order his death and begged for his life to no avail. Clyde killed him with only one swing of the axe, striking Johnnie in the head. Together John S. Williams and Clyde Manning buried him near the site where he was killed.

The following day Clyde learned the identity of the next victim — John Will Gaither. Gaither was a large slave whose size had earned him the nick-name "Big John." Because of Big John's size, John Williams knew Clyde would need help with him. Williams turned to another of his "trusty Negroes" who had killed for the Williams before, Charlie Chisolm. Williams told Clyde to go get Charlie and then take Big John to the Campbell house and pretend to be digging a well there. When Clyde told Charlie what they had been instructed to do, Charlie asked no questions. If John Williams said it was to be done Charlie knew he had to do it.

The Campbell house was an unoccupied home John Williams had recently purchased. It had never been lived in and did not yet have a well. Clyde, Charlie and Big John went there and began digging what Big John thought would be a well but instead would be his grave. When John Williams came by and found they had dug the hole almost as deep as Big John was tall, he picked up an axe, handed it to Charlie and motioned for him to do the job he had been sent to do. Charlie killed John Will Gaither without Big John ever knowing what hit him. One swing crumpled him to the bottom of the hole.

Not knowing if the blow was fatal or not, Clyde and Charlie quickly filled the hole with dirt.

———————————

Jackson Lake was a man-made lake created in 1910 with the Lloyd Shoals Dam. The lake was fed by three rivers, Yellow, South and Alcovy, which all pooled together in Newton County. The new lake had changed the face of the rural counties it engulfed. Jasper, Newton and Butts county residents all were affected by the lake and the people drawn there. There was now fishing, boating and the other recreation associated with a large lake. There was also deep water.

———————————

Several days went by without any more killing, but on Friday, February 25, the killing would resume. It was well after dark when John Williams knocked on the door of the slave stockade where Clyde and several of the slave hands were socializing around a table. Williams made the amazing announcement to the slaves that he intended to allow any of them to go home if they wanted to go. He offered to give whoever wanted to go, a ride to the train station. After a few moments of silence, one by one the men spoke up and told the plantation owner that they did want to go home. Clyde Manning sat among his friends listening, knowing it was a lie. He knew there was no way John Williams would let them leave.

Although many of the slaves asked to leave, Williams told the group he could only take a couple at a time, but that he would take more the following day. He chose John Brown, whom he called "Red", and one of the younger slaves, Johnny Benson. Everybody called Benson "Little Bit." Williams told Clyde to summon Charlie Chisolm to ride with them to the train station.

They traveled towards the railroad station in Williams' car. Clyde rode in the front seat; Charlie rode in the back with Red and Little Bit. After driving a while, Williams stopped the car and told everyone to get out. When Williams opened the trunk and began to remove chains from the trunk, Little Bit panicked.

"What we doing, Mr. Johnny? What we gonna do Clyde?" He asked in terror, "Ain't we going to the train station?" Little Bit knew the answer when he saw Williams begin to wrap the chains around Red's legs. Little Bit went into such a panic that Williams had to take hold of him and assure him that nothing was going to happen to him. Williams told Little Bit they were only there to scare Red.

Little Bit watched in horror as Williams tied Red's hands with wire, wrapped him in chains and placed a large iron wheel around his neck. While he worked, Red begged for his life and tried to assure Williams that he would not talk to authorities, but Williams ignored him.

Williams then began to wrap Little Bit in chains. Little Bit tried to resist, but Clyde and Charlie grabbed him and held him. He was crying so hard that his words could not be understood as he tried to beg and plead for his life. After Williams had wrapped Little Bit in chains, he tied his hands with wire. Then he took a chain and connected the two men together. Now bound to each other at the hands, the two men were placed back into the car for the ride to their final destiny.

Williams drove to Water's Bridge on the Alcovy River and

stopped in the middle of the bridge. Clyde and Charlie dragged Red and Little Bit from the car and dragged them to the side of the bridge while both men begged for their lives. Red began pleading directly to Clyde, "Oh god, Clyde, please don't throw me over in that water!" "Clyde, please, I don't want to drown in no river like that. Please, Clyde, please don't throw me in that water," he cried.

Then he surprised Clyde with a request. "Can't you just knock me in the head before you throw me over Clyde?" Red begged him, "I don't want to drown Clyde. Can't you knock me in the head first?" Clyde looked at Williams who appeared impatient, then turned back and, along with Charlie, shoved both men hard sending them over the railing. Manning would later say that he heard their final screams of terror, and would probably hear them forever, but he never heard the splash.

On the following night, almost the same scenario occurred. John Williams went to the stockade late in the evening and made the offer to take more slaves to the train station and set them free. This time Williams chose Lindsey Peterson, Willie Preston, and Harry Price, whom everyone called "Foots." Johnny Green, one of the slaves from Huland's farm had also wanted badly to go. Williams told him, "You come back first thing in the morning Johnny, and I'll take you."

Again they loaded into the car with Williams, Clyde and Charlie. Again they stopped before they got to the train station and before they knew what was happening Peterson, Preston and Price were in chains, riding down the dirt roads that led to Jackson Lake. Williams stopped his car on Allen's Bridge over the Yellow River.

Once again Clyde and Charlie drug the men from the back seat, except for Harry Price. Williams told them to leave Price in the car. Price sat, watched and probably contemplated his own fate. Peterson and Preston tried to run but couldn't. This time Williams had fitted bags around each of their necks with a hundred pounds of rocks in each bag. The bags were so heavy that Williams himself had to help lift the bags from the car.

They desperately struggled for their lives. Manning would later say the horror in their eyes was so unbearable that he tried not to look them in the face. The chains around them prevented their successful escape. The two begged for their lives, again to no avail. They were thrown over the railing and into the Yellow River, their feet momentarily bobbing from the water as the rocks yanked them head-first towards the bottom. It was a terrible way to die. Harry Price had to sit and watch the horror and anticipate what was next for him.

Without much conversation Williams, Clyde and Charlie got back into the car and drove away. Williams stopped the car again when he got to Mann's Bridge overlooking the South River. Harry Price now knew what his fate was to be. The other men helped him from the car, and Charlie and Clyde led him to the rail of the bridge. Harry had no plans to resist. He had seen the futility of it with Peterson and Preston. "Don't throw me over," he told the men. "I'll get over." He sat there quietly for a moment and then said, "Lord have mercy," and quietly went over the railing on his own. Seven men were dead, and the killing wasn't over.

The following morning, John Williams found Johnny Green on his front door step waiting to go to the train station. Beside him was a small cloth bundle which contained his only possessions. Williams told him he needed him to go with Clyde to fix a fence in the pasture and that they would catch the train later in the day. Greene gathered the tools needed and went down to the fence, never to return. Clyde killed him with a blow to the head with an axe while Charlie Chisolm watched. They left him lying in the field and went back to their homes for their Sunday lunch.

Later that evening John Williams approached the stockade where several of the workers had gathered. One of the workers, Willie Givens, was leaning against a tree. Williams told him he was going to walk to Homer's store and asked Willie if he wanted to walk with him. Willie jumped at the chance to get off the farm. Then Williams turned to Clyde and told him to come along. He told Clyde to bring an axe to cut a log for crossing the creek. Clyde knew what that meant, but dutifully did what he was told.

They walked a trail towards the store. Clyde was trailing behind the other two as Williams had instructed. When they reached the wood-line, Clyde swung the axe striking Willie in the neck almost decapitating him. Acting under Williams instructions, Clyde covered up the body with pine straw. Later that night, Clyde and Williams would return and bury both Willie and Johnny Green. Williams and Clyde returned to their homes without another word. Manning later would say that when he got back to the stockade, Williams threatened to shoot him if he heard anything about that day.

Several days went by with no more killing. Clyde Manning and Charlie Chisolm talked about the killings having stopped. They speculated on whether or not that would be the end of it. They talked about how they hated what they had done but reveled in the fact that they had survived. Their jubilation was premature. One of them would die.

The following Saturday evening, Williams approached Charlie Chisolm and told him he was taking him to the train station to set him free. Williams told Chisolm, "No use in having you around to talk to them if they bring a case. You might as well go on wherever you want."

Chisolm got into the car with Williams. When Clyde got into the backseat, Chisolm must have known his fate. He knew what had happened to the others on their ride to the train station. He also had to know that he knew too much. His worst fears were realized when just before they reached the Alcovy River, Williams pulled the car to the shoulder of the roadway.

All three men got out of the car. Williams reportedly said to Charlie, "I heard some of your damn talk boy. I'm going to teach you a lesson." Charlie replied, "I ain't said nothing to nobody, Mr. Johnny." "I ain't said nothing and I ain't going to, neither." Williams told him to hush and then began to gather the tools Chisolm had to know would be used to sink him into one of the rivers of Jackson Lake.

This time Williams had not brought the rocks with him needed to weigh his victim down. Williams had Clyde gather rocks from the area while Charlie stood there in a strange state of submission, knowing by then, what was about to occur.

Williams and Clyde tied Charlie's feet together, and then they tied the bags of rocks to his neck and feet. For some unknown reason they did not tie his hands, but Charlie continued his capitulation. They put him in the front seat, Clyde got in the back seat, and Williams drove the remaining mile to the Alcovy River. It was probably the longest ride of Charlie's life, riding down that dirt road towards the same fate he had helped send others to.

Williams stopped the car in the middle of Water's Bridge, and they all got out. Williams and Clyde dragged Charlie to the railing. No words were spoken between any of them. Charlie stood there trembling as tears streamed down his cheek. Williams reached down to grab Charlie's feet and Clyde shoved Charlie in the chest, sending him over the railing, into the dark water of the Alcovy River, to his death. On the ride back to the plantation, Williams once again reminded Clyde if he told anyone what he knew he too would wind up in that river.

A few days later Manning was working several of the slaves in Huland's fields when John Williams walked up carrying a double-barreled shotgun. Williams sent Claude and Clyde Freeman up to Huland's house, leaving just Clyde Manning and Fletcher Smith. Once the Freeman brothers were gone, Williams shot Fletcher and Williams and Clyde buried him where he was killed. Williams then instructed Clyde to plow over the grave so that it would be consistent with the rest of the field. It was to be the end of the killing.

It was early March when Carl Wheeler and Randall Parker were walking across Allen's Bridge and made their startling discovery. Their attention was drawn to something floating just beneath the surface of the water. When they looked closer, they realized it was two bodies tied together. They had found Willie Preston and Lindsey Peterson. Newton County Sheriff B.L. Johnson was summoned to the scene, fished the bodies from the river and began his investigation.

The following day, Harry Price's body was discovered under Mann's Bridge in the South River. The discovery of the bodies were the headline stories of the Covington newspapers. The local papers, which frequently reported conjecture in the early 1920s, immediately tied the three discovered Negro bodies to "recent peonage problems in Jasper County." The story eventually also made it to The Atlanta Constitution, and then came to the attention of Agents Brown and Wismer, as did Eberhardt Crawford.

Eberhardt Crawford was a black man who lived in Covington and even though he didn't work on the Williams plantation, he was almost the next victim.

Crawford sat down with the agents and told them his story. Crawford had the unfortunate luck of being in attendance at the riverside inquest of Willie Preston and Lindsey. Peterson. When others were unable to identify the bodies, Dr. C.T. Hardeman, who was examining the bodies, turned to Crawford and asked if he recognized the men. Crawford told him he did not, but he also said,

"I bet some of the hands on the Williams place would know them."

On the evening of that inquest, Crawford heard a loud knock on his door. He opened the door and was undoubtedly shocked to be face-to-face with John S. Williams. "I hear you been talking about me and my boys!" Williams said to Crawford, "You been telling folks we had something to do with those dead niggers in the river?"

"No sir Mr. Williams, I ain't said nothing like that." Crawford replied. "All I said was some of your hands might know who them boys are. That's all I said."

"Don't you lie to me, nigger!" Williams screamed at Crawford as he walked toward him and warned him. "I know what you been saying and I won't have it. If you know what's good for you, you'll keep your damn mouth shut." Crawford simply responded, "Yes sir, boss." Williams left angry and left Crawford scared.

Although Crawford's nephew was asleep in the home, Crawford left him there and went to a neighbor's home seeking refuge from Williams. He later told investigators he was afraid to take the boy with him for fear of coming across Williams on the roadway. Desperate to get out of the house, Crawford left the boy alone.

He hadn't been at his neighbors long when he heard gunshots. His worst fears were realized when he looked towards his house and realized the gunshots were coming from there. When the shooting stopped, a vehicle sped by. It was Williams and several other white men with guns. After they left, Crawford ran to his house and found it shot to pieces with the front door knocked off of its hinges.

To Crawford's horror, his nephew was not in his bed. He searched frantically and found his nephew hiding in the outhouse, frightened but unharmed.

When Agents Brown and Wismer heard the story, they realized they would need to take action. When Crawford told them his story, he added a piece of information they believed was just the evidence they needed. While describing the bodies of Preston and Peterson (who police had not yet identified), Crawford mentioned that the dead men were wearing shoes made of old automobile tires.

The investigators remembered seeing one of the hands at the Williams plantation making shoes from old tires and had noticed that all of the field hands wore those type of shoes. It was the clue they needed to connect the dead men to the Williams farm. They took their evidence — and their witness — to the governor of Georgia.

It is unclear whether or not the Bureau of Investigation had the federal authority to intervene. Wismer and Brown decided to take their case to the state. The sheriff of Jasper County had a peonage case pending against him and the federal agents doubted they would get the cooperation they would need.

Governor Hugh Dorsey had been openly condemning lynching, and his criticism over the poor treatment of blacks made agents believe he would be receptive to their visit. After two visits to the governor's office, the agents got results.

Upon their second visit, Governor Dorsey decided to take action. He persuaded the judge and solicitor general of the Stone Mountain Circuit Court, which included Newton County, to issue grand jury subpoenas on the matter.

Based on the subpoenas, and accompanied by the federal agents, Newton County Sheriff B.L. Johnson went to the Williams plantation and arrested John S. Williams. Arresting citizens based upon subpoenas for the purpose of bringing them before a grand jury was not uncommon in those days. They had intended to arrest his sons Huland, Leroy and Marvin as well, but none of them could be found on either farm. The lawmen also arrested Clyde Manning, Clyde

Freeman and several other field hands who the agents had interviewed on the day of their visit.

Sheriff Johnson also found a man named Frank Dozier who previously worked on the Williams plantation but had escaped. They were all taken to the Covington Police Department (Covington is the county seat of Newton) where Covington Police Chief B.B. Bohannan assisted with the interrogations.

Initially, none of the field hands would talk except for Frank Dozier. Dozier had escaped and was no longer under the spell of fear that John Williams held over his other slaves. Dozier told the agents everything about the conditions on the farm, the stockade and the beatings – everything.

Once the agents learned of the conditions on the plantation, they leaned hard on the two Negro bosses, Clyde Freeman and Clyde Manning. It took several hours to get to the truth. Freeman broke first. Before he told the truth, he warned the agents about his speaking out. "If I do and you send me back, Mr. Johnny'll kill me right away."

After the agents assured Freeman that he would not be sent back, he told the agents what had been happening over the last couple of weeks. Field hands were disappearing, Freeman told the agents. "They told us them boys done gone home but I knew that wasn't right," he said.

The agents pressed Freeman to tell them what happened to the field hands, but Freeman insisted he didn't know. When they asked him who would know, Freeman replied, "I believe Clyde can tell you all about it."

After hearing that, the agents interrogated Clyde Manning vigorously for hours. When he refused to talk, the sheriff and agents decided to take both Manning and Freeman to Allen's bridge to have them view the two bodies that were in the jurisdiction of Newton County.

When a body or bodies are found in a river which separates two counties the jurisdiction lies with the agency the body is floating closest to. Law enforcement agencies have historically bickered over which agency would be burdened with such cases. The law enforcement agency that arrived on the scene last would sometimes claim the agency on the other side had pushed the body away from their own jurisdiction. That had not happened at Allen's bridge. Sheriff Johnson had pulled the bodies to the Newton County side and accepted jurisdiction on the case.

When the sheriff and federal agents arrived at Allen's Bridge, they had the bodies dug up for the purpose of having them identified. Manning said nothing as Freeman identified the bodies of Lindsey Peterson and Willie Preston. Freeman pointed to the rubber soles on the two men's feet and told the lawmen that he remembered that Rufus Manning, Clyde Manning's uncle, had recently resoled the shoes of both of the victims.

Freeman and Manning were taken back to the Covington Police Department and the lawmen questioned Manning until late in the night. At around 3 a.m., he finally talked. Before he talked, he also warned the agents. "I can tell it, but I can't go back to Jasper County if I tell it. I'll be dead just like them other boys."

Once Sheriff Johnson assured Manning he would be protected, he told everything. He didn't just tell of the 11 men he had killed or helped to kill in the last two weeks. He systematically told the sheriff and agents of every black man he remembered having been killed on the Williams plantation. His memory was excellent.

Manning, Freeman and eight other field hands from the Williams plantation were taken before the Newton County Grand Jury by Solicitor A.M. Brand to tell their stories. Many of them were asked to remove their shirts revealing horrible scars from the many beatings they had taken on the Williams' farms.

Much of Clyde Manning's chilling grand jury testimony was reported in the April 5, 1921, edition of The Atlanta Constitution. The Constitution spelled Charlie Chisolm's name with an "h" but later writings would not. The following is a partial excerpt of that testimony:

> I knocked four Negroes in the head with an ax in one week and buried them in a pasture back of Mr. Johnny's (Williams) house.
>
> Why did I do it? Because the boss said he wanted to get rid of them Negroes and that if I didn't make 'em disappear, he'd kill me. And I knew he meant what he said.
>
> Mr. Charlie Chisholm, another of Mr. Johnny's trusty Negroes put in a little work — he killed one suspicious Negro by braining him with an ax. Then a little later Mr. Williams got uneasy about Charlie and made me get him. Me and Mr. Johnny took him to the river one night and pitched him off the bridge after we weighted him down. Charlie begged hard but Mr. Johnny said: 'Let's throw him over and have it over with.'
>
> I don't know how many Negroes there are in the river, but I helped Mr. Williams to drown six, including Charlie Chisholm. We took the other five at night, after getting them out of their houses, and

chained 'em down with rocks and threw 'em in.

Yes sir, they all cried and begged — and some of 'em asked to be knocked in the head before being thrown in, but Mr. Johnny wouldn't do it and wouldn't let me do it — we just threw them off the bridge and rode on back to the plantation.

Most of the drowned Negroes came off the farm of Mr. Huland Williams — my boss' son. But a few of the ones Mr. Johnny called 'bad' and wanted done away with came off of his own farm.

Most of these dead negroes was originally from Atlanta, Macon or somewhere else — they didn't come from Jasper County. Mr. Huland Williams, the son of my boss, would go to Atlanta and Macon and get the Negroes out of the stockade by paying their fines. I used to hear him and his father talking about all that.

Well, they brought the Negroes to the farm and put 'em to work, and kept guards over 'em all the time so as not to let 'em get away or talk too much. I don't know whether they got any pay or not — I know Mr. Johnny paid me $20 a month and board.

Of course mister, I'm sorry I knocked all them boys in the head and helped Mr. Johnny do away with them others, but there wasn't nothing else I could do — the boss told me if I didn't do as he said I would be the next dead Negro around there. I admits I have always been mighty afraid of Mr. Williams.

When he got ready to kill a Negro, he would come to me and say, 'Clyde, I'm scared of that Negro.' Then he would tell me what he wanted done, and being as I was working for him and couldn't get away myself, I had to go ahead and do it.

After Manning's testimony, authorities told the grand jury that a total of 15 bodies had been found in the rivers and buried on the Williams plantations.

In a move which would later be forbidden by state law, John S. Williams was also allowed to testify before the grand jury and plead his case. In front of the grand jury Williams admitted that one "Negro" had been killed by his son Huland, but the elder Williams told the grand jury that killing was in self-defense. Williams acknowledged to the grand jury that the killing was never reported to the authorities.

Williams pleaded with the grand jury not to press the case against him, and he promised to release any "Negro desiring to leave" his farm.

The grand jury did not honor his request. Clyde Manning had, by that time, taken investigators back to the plantation and shown them where all of the bodies were buried. The mass murder had shocked the entire nation and was being reported all across America. The press had dubbed the Williams plantation the "death farm." Williams had given Jasper and Newton counties, as well as the entire South, a black eye of incivility. The good people of Newton County were out to show the nation that John S. Williams was simply a bad seed, and not representative of the rest of that region.

The sports world of the nation had their eyes on Georgia because baseball legend Babe Ruth was in Atlanta. The same front pages of the Atlanta papers that reported on the "death farm" murders were also reporting that Ruth's 1920 pennant-winning Brooklyn team was coming to Atlanta on April 5, 1921, to play an exhibition game with the New York Yankees.

One New York newspaper was sending a reporter to travel

Georgia and try and learn if the entire state was as primitive as Jasper County. The reporter wrote that most of Georgia had good decent people, including the people of Jasper and Newton Counties, and that most of the South deplored what had occurred on the Williams plantation.

John S. Williams, reprinted with the permission of The Atlanta Journal.

Williams was housed in the Fulton County Jail Tower and transported to and from the trial by train. Scores of blacks would gather as the train passed and watch the white plantation owner travel to justice. The Atlanta Constitution reported that on one trip, as Williams observed a small town where "a large crowd of Negroes had gathered," Williams said to his guards: "Just throw me out among them, and you'll see them scatter."

At the Newton County courthouse, Williams told the press, "I'll come clear. Don't you worry." Williams' war hero son, Dr. Gus Williams, was also on hand assuring the press that his father was innocent and defending his three brothers, who had also been indicted and were fugitives at large.

On the first day of the trial, April 6, 1921, the courtroom was so crowded most of those present did not even notice when the elder Williams was escorted into the courtroom and seated next to his lead defense attorney, Green F. Johnson.

The prosecution would be led by Solicitor A.M. Brand who was being assisted by former Congressman W.M. Howard and Assistant Attorney General Graham Wright. Both Howard and Wright had been sent to Covington by Governor Dorsey to help in the prosecution of Williams. In the early proceeding of the trial, defense attorney Johnson called Howard and Wright to the stand and insinuated they had been hired by outside influences like the NAACP. Both denied the charges. Solicitor Brand brought laughter to the courtroom when he stood up and asked, "Your Honor, does he wish to question me too?"

Clyde Manning, reprinted with the permission of The Atlanta Constitution.

Solicitor Brand decided to keep the first trial simple by only trying Williams for the death of Lindsey Peterson. Defense attorney Johnson would argue during the trial that trying Williams for only one murder should preclude the prosecution from introducing evidence on the other murders, but presiding Judge John B. Hutcheson allowed all of the evidence on all the killings to be introduced.

One of the more dramatic points of the trial was when Clyde Manning was given what the press called the "roll call of the dead."

The questioning by prosecuting former Congressman Howard went as follows:

> Howard: "Do you know Lindsey Peterson?"
> Manning: "I do."
> Howard: "Where is Lindsey Peterson?"
> Manning: "He's dead."
> Howard: "Now Clyde, where is Harry Price?"
> Manning: "He's dead."
> Howard: "And Charlie Chisolm?"
> Manning: "He's dead too."
> Howard: "And Willie Givens?"
> Manning: "He's dead."
> Howard: "Fletcher Smith?"
> Manning: "He's dead."
> Howard: "The Negro named Johnnie Williams?"
> Manning: "Him too."
> Howard: "Johnny Green?"
> Manning: "He's dead."
> Howard: "How about John Brown?"
> Manning: "He's dead too."
> Howard: "Little Bit?"
> Manning: "He's dead."

> Howard: "Big John?"
> Manning: "He's dead."
> Howard: "And Willie Preston?"
> Manning: "He's dead."

Manning would go on to testify as to the details of each murder and about his eventual identification of all of the bodies.

Another remarkable witness for the state was Lessie May Benton. Lessie gave the sad testimony of how excited Lindsey Peterson was the day he came to her and told her he was going home. She patched his overalls, got him a clean shirt and a pair of shoes and then he left, never to be seen by her again.

The only witness for the defense was John S. Williams himself. Williams' statement was unsworn, which meant that Williams could not be cross-examined. But it also meant his testimony was to be given less credibility. In Williams' statement, he denied killing any of the men.

Williams told the jury he had released several of the men to go home and gave them five dollars for the trip. He claimed he thought the men had gone home and inferred that Manning may have killed them for the money they had. Williams tried to make the jury believe that Manning had done all of the killings alone, calling Manning a "bad, hard-headed nigger." Williams was the only witness the defense offered and the only evidence they presented.

Williams was cocky and confident at the end of his trial slapping his lawyer on the back and telling him, "I believe we whipped 'em."

The jury was given the case on Friday, April 8, 1921, at 4 p.m. The jury deliberated until 1 a.m., when they all retired to bed. The following morning, the jury had reconvened before being called into the courtroom. During that time, they deliberated some and then took another vote. At 9 a.m, Judge Hutcheson called the jury into the room to see if they had any questions before they once again began their deliberations. He was shocked when the jury foreman informed him that the jury had a verdict. The judge instructed the foreman not to publish the verdict until all of the proper persons were present.

At 10:30 a.m. that Saturday, April 9, 1921, the courtroom was once again packed with observers as the jury filed back into the jury box to announce their verdict. Williams had been present in the courtroom at 9 a.m., but had appeared ruffled, unkept and was without a tie. For his 10:30 a.m. appearance, he was neat with a tie and a carnation in his lapel. His wife and younger children sat behind him.

The verdict was guilty with a recommendation of mercy. The following Sunday edition of The Atlanta Constitution described Williams' demeanor as the Judge told Williams his sentence:

> Will you stand up Mr. Williams, the court asked in a voice that shook with emotion despite its modulated tones. John Williams arose, his great shoulders squared, his head thrown back, his eyes fixed on the judge with a gleam that bespoke defiance to the words he knew would make him a striped felon for the rest of his days. There was a twitching in the muscles of his brawny throat, but otherwise his whole being seemed to shout the unspoken thought, 'There is no punishment that law can mete out to me that I cannot bear.'

Judge Hutcheson asked Williams, "Do you have anything to say to this court before I sentence you?" Williams answered, "I am innocent of the charge." Judge Hutcheson said "Mr. Williams, having been found guilty of the murder of Lindsey Peterson by this court, it is my duty to sentence you to life imprisonment."

It was later reported that there was never any argument as to the guilt or innocence of Williams, only the question of whether they would allow him to hang based on the testimony of a black man. The vote was reportedly 8 - 4 in favor of hanging, but the four that wanted life in prison to be the sentence held out and won. The press reported, "The only conclusion to be drawn is that the evidence was so overwhelming as to justify no other verdict than that returned."

Clyde Manning's trial began on May 30, 1921. The eight surviving slaves from the Williams plantation were held in the Fulton Tower jail as witnesses for the nearly two months between the trials. As unjust as that was, their lifestyle — although boring — was much less stressful sitting in jail and being fed by the government. In fact, one Atlanta Constitution front page article complained they were "NEGROS LIVING ON FAT OF LAND AND GETTING PAID." The article complained the survivors were sitting back in their jail cells collecting a dollar a day and eating "goodly portions of side meat and corn" at the expense of the taxpayers. The survivors were: Emma Freeman, Clyde Freeman, Claude Freeman, Gus Chapman, John Freeman, Gladdis Manning and Julius Manning.

Clyde Manning had good legal representation. E. Marvin Underwood and A.D. Meadows, a local Covington judge were his attorneys. Both had been recruited by Governor Dorsey and paid by wealthy Atlanta citizens the governor had organized.

Manning's defense was that he had to kill everyone he killed to survive himself. He was supported by all of the survivors of the "death farm." The jury did not accept his defense. After a two-day trial, a jury found Manning guilty after 40 minutes of deliberation, the jurors recommended a life sentence.

Judge Hutcheson treated Clyde Manning with much less respect than he had John Williams. "Stand up Clyde," the judge ordered. After Manning stood up, the judge continued, "Clyde, the jury has found you guilty with a recommendation for mercy, and the sentence of the court is that you spend the rest of your life in the penitentiary. Have a seat."

John Williams' three sons remained fugitives for several years, reportedly hiding out in Florida. After four years, Leroy Williams turned himself into Jasper County authorities, as both of his brothers did two years later. They all posted bonds and were released from jail. The state could not collect enough witnesses from the farm to present a successful case, and none of them were ever prosecuted.

The Williams farm stands abandoned today off of Cook Road, north of Monticello. The crumbling brick chimney that once was the only surviving sign of life on the land is now gone, too.

Clyde Manning spent the next six years working on a chain gang, continuing his life as a slave until his death from tuberculosis.

John Williams served 10 years in prison in Milledgeville where he had earned the status of trusty. He was crushed to death in 1931 when he was pinned against a wall by a stolen truck full of escaping prisoners. In his 10 years of prison time, he never confessed to murder or remorse.

3

MURDER IN DRUID HILLS
The Murder of Henry C. Heinz

Druid Hills, an exclusive community of prestigious northeast Atlanta homes, was established in 1908. One of the main people responsible for the development of Druid Hills was Coca-Cola founder Asa Griggs Candler. Thirty-five years later his daughter, Lucy Candler Heinz still lived in Druid Hills at 1610 Ponce de Leon Ave. with her husband, Atlanta banker Henry C. Heinz.

It was the fall of 1943. The governor of Georgia was Ellis Arnall, the president of the nation was Franklin D. Roosevelt. World War II continued in Europe, Russia and the Pacific as America fought

Germany and Japan at the same time. Every country in Europe faced the threat of Hitler's Nazis and in the Pacific, Japan was the aggressor. Few families in the world felt secure. The Heinz family was no exception, but for reasons seemingly less sinister.

Druid Hills was being prowled by a burglar. Marion Blackwell and Bill Miller were Atlanta police officers who patrolled the exclusive subdivision of sprawling lawns and expensive housing. Officers Blackwell and Miller knew the Heinz home on Ponce de Leon because of problems there in recent years. The officers had responded to several burglaries at that address as well as others in the Druid Hills area. On one occasion, Henry Heinz had awakened to find an intruder in his home and actually got a glimpse of the thief, a man he described as a large Negro man. It was the second time a Druid Hills resident had seen the prowler and identified him in that way. The rash of burglaries had spanned more than two years.

It was a matter of considerable concern for the Atlanta Police Department. Many of Atlanta's elite lived in the area, and the problem had lingered too long. Blackwell and Miller had been specifically assigned by Atlanta Police Chief M.A. Hornsby to patrol nightly, checking the homes that had been hit. They knew the Heinz grounds well because they checked them frequently at night— shining their spotlight to let Mr. Heinz know it was them. Henry Heinz had told them he had armed himself but assured them there would be no danger of him shooting at them as long as he saw their spotlight. They did not, however, have the same assurances from his neighbors, a fact that would place them in peril.

On the night of September 29, 1943, Blackwell and Miller were on patrol. It was nearing 10 p.m. A call was dispatched to the Heinz residence at 1610 Ponce de Leon — a signal 4. A signal 4 meant a burglar in the house. Although the call was dispatched to another car Blackwell and Miller, who were traveling nearby on Moreland Avenue, maneuvered a U-turn and sped towards the location given. They recognized the address and knew exactly where to go. Their patrol car was a 1941 Ford with the traditional black and white police markings of the time. Blackwell was driving. Traffic was light due to war-time gas rationing.

When they arrived at the Heinz home they found the grounds in total darkness. "It was pitch-black, you couldn't see two feet in front of yourself," Blackwell would later say to the press. Officer Miller bailed and headed for the front door which was lighted at the entryway. He found the front door locked and then heard a woman scream. He found a side door unlocked and entered a screened porch. He discovered Lucy Candler Heinz, the daughter of the founder of Coca-Cola, in the library screaming. When she recognized Miller as a policeman she said, "Thank God you've come. He's still in the house." Miller also discovered Henry C. Heinz with several gunshot wounds, which he examined beneath the blood soaked clothing. Miller would later say he knew immediately that Heinz was dead.

Outside Blackwell had maneuvered his patrol car so the headlights shined on the back of the house. Then he got out of the car, unsuspecting of the gun battle in which he was about to be engaged. Others would later corroborate it was an extremely dark night. When Blackwell stepped into the glow of his headlights the first shot was fired. The muzzle blast was all that Blackwell saw as he heard the percussion of a .45 caliber gunshot. Blackwell yelled to Miller, "Here he is out here. He's shooting at me."

Blackwell returned fire in the direction of the muzzle blast. Miller

113

heard the gunfire and his partner yelling. He ran out of the house, exiting through a door of the library onto a lighted porch. Blackwell yelled for him to get down and at that point the gunman turned his attention to Miller and began firing. Blackwell saw Miller go down. He charged at the gunman, exchanging gunfire with him while on the run.

When Blackwell reached the gunman he pointed directly at the gunman's head and fired. The gun made a fizzling sound and the lead bullet simply rolled out of the end of the barrel. Blackwell's gun had misfired, and he later would be very thankful for that. Miller limped his way to the bushes where the gunman was located. At the same time Officers I.A. Thomas and Ralph Hulsey ran up, and all four officers jumped the gunman. When the man realized it was policemen he was fighting with, he yelled. "I'm not the burglar, I've been shot."

To the officer's horror they stood and listened to the man explain that he was a neighbor who Mrs. Heinz had called in a panic while the burglary was in progress. He had responded on foot in his pajamas with his army .45, and upon observing Officer Blackwell and mistaking him for the burglar, he opened fire. He was Dr. Bryant K. Vann, a prominent dentist and former son-in-law of Mrs. Heinz. They took him to the house where they discovered they had shot him in his chest and arm. Blackwell learned that his partner, Miller, had not been shot but had fallen and broken his ankle.

Blackwell and Miller quickly realized the magnitude of their situation and immediately called for more help. One prominent Druid Hills citizen lay dead and now another was seriously wounded at the hands of police. Mrs. Heinz fainted upon being told that Dr. Vann had also been shot.

Blackwell later told the press that the initial hour after arriving on the scene was mass confusion. He described officers stumbling to find light switches and bandages while Mrs. Heinz chased them all

114

around trying to tell them what had happened.

In response to Blackwell's radio call, what seemed like a brigade of Atlanta police arrived at the Heinz home. In addition DeKalb County police officers and sheriff deputies responded, including DeKalb County Police Chief J.T. Daily and Sheriff Jake Hall. Although most of the city of Atlanta is inside Fulton County, this small portion of Druid Hills lies in western DeKalb.

In addition to swarms of police, dozens of family members and friends rushed to the Mediterranean-style Heinz mansion. A streetcar had been passing by during the excitement and when the motorman stopped to see what happened, all of the passengers followed him onto the grounds to investigate the commotion.

In spite of the crowd of people on the property, police were able to preserve evidence in the library and dining room areas; evidence which would eventually help bring resolution to the case.

Mrs. Heinz had been nervous about the frequent prowlers and break-ins in the neighborhood. She told police she and her husband sat in the library awaiting a 10 p.m. radio news broadcast when her husband heard a barking dog and a commotion outside the left wing of the house. She would not let her husband go out to investigate.

She grew sleepy, went upstairs and was just stepping out of the shower when she first heard her husband cry out; "Mama, mama, that devil is in here. Get the gun quick." She knew immediately what "devil" her husband was referring to. He had many times referred to the person responsible for the thefts around the house as the devil.

She was putting on her robe when she heard gunshots. She ran

115

into the library and saw her husband wrestling with a large Negro man. Mrs. Heinz told police the man was wearing a skull cap and had a handkerchief tied around his face, masking his identity. He was dressed in a blue shirt and brown trousers.

On most days in the fall of 1943, the daily editions of the Atlanta Journal and the Constitution led with news about the war, but the lead story on Sept. 29 was the murder of Henry C. Heinz. The Atlanta Journal read, **"Greatest Atlanta Manhunt Launched For Heinz Killer."** The stories ran alongside photos of Henry Heinz, Dr. Vann, the Heinz mansion and the window thought to be the murderer's entry point. War news had been moved to less prominent areas of the papers. The reporting included a biography of Henry Heinz.

Henry Heinz in his younger years.
Courtesy of the Special Collections Department, Atlanta Fulton Library

Heinz had begun his career with the Central Bank and Trust Company, founded by the man who would later become his father-in-law, Asa G. Candler. When that bank merged with the Citizens and Southern in 1922, Henry Heinz was named vice-president and director of the C&S bank, a position he held until his death. Heinz had spent the next 21 years building a name for himself as a civic leader in Atlanta. He was a founder of the Atlanta Boys' Club and was still president of that organization at the time of his death. He was city chairman of the banking division of the third War Loan Drive. In a sad touch of irony, it could be argued that his participation in that drive may have contributed to his death. Heinz had stayed up later than his usual bedtime waiting in the library for a news report to learn if the War Loan Drive he had chaired had reached its goal.

There was controversy in the press about the shooting among Blackwell, Miller and Vann. Dr. Vann told the press that Blackwell fired on him first. Blackwell countered that he couldn't have fired upon Dr. Vann first because it was too dark to know Dr. Vann was there until he saw the muzzle blast from Dr. Vann's pistol shots. There was also the question of why Dr. Vann had fired upon Officer Miller, who had been standing on a lighted porch in full uniform. Dr. Vann explained that when he received the call from Mrs. Heinz she had said to him, "Come over here this instant! *They* are killing Mr. Heinz!" He had grabbed his Army .45 and set out believing that he might encounter more than one intruder, the reason he traversed the roadways and approached the mansion from the road instead of using a more direct route to the Heinz home from the rear.

Dr. Vann's first wife, then deceased, had been the Heinz's daughter. A sunken garden and private pathway led from the Heinz mansion to Dr. Vann's backyard. Dr. Vann told the press he had feared that if he had taken the garden route he might have encountered one of the murderer's accomplices in the darkness. In

117

fact, had he taken that route he would have encountered the murderer himself.

While in the hospital recovering from his wounds Dr. Vann gave the following version of events on the night of the murder:

> I had been to a State Guard meeting and was upstairs in the shower when I heard the telephone ringing. At first I decided not to answer it, but it seemed to ring so insistently, as if the call was urgent, that I finally ran downstairs naked to answer it.
>
> Even before I placed the receiver to my ear I heard Mrs. Heinz, half screaming, half sobbing: "By, come over here this instant. They are killing Mr. Heinz."
>
> I started to go through the gardens but then I decided that whoever was over there might be outside or have accomplices so I went down Lullwater Road to Ponce de Leon and up Ponce de Leon to the gates.
>
> My first inclination was to run up the driveway directly to the house, but I couldn't hear a sound in the house and I decided I had better approach the house cautiously. I then moved as quickly and quietly as I could along the coping at the left side of the estate, keeping in the shadows and straining to hear some sound.
>
> Suddenly I heard a shot and thought: 'My God are they trying to kill Mrs. Heinz now, or are they shooting at me?'

Dr. Vann said he felt something warm flowing down his arm but did not realize that he had been shot. He crouched behind a tree and saw someone approaching him with a flashlight which sent "a bright beam of light across the pitch-dark yard." Dr. Vann continued:

>
> I thought the man holding the flashlight was the burglar and I shot at him. I don't know how many shots were fired but it wasn't long until I saw the silhouette of a man standing on the screened porch and I shot at him. The two men then moved in opposite directions about 60 degrees each way and with me in the apex of the triangle. I was still on the ground. It was about this time that I was shot again.
>
> The police came on toward me and when I recognized them I said: 'Boys, I'm not the burglar. I am a friend of Mr. Heinz. I came here to help Mrs. Heinz. Please let me up.' I do not recall struggling with the police I really thought at first that they were burglars and I believe they thought the same of me. There is no doubt in my mind that the shooting was accidental.

The Heinz murder caused the citizens of Druid Hills as well as the rest of Atlanta to lock their doors as panic spread through the city. The murder had occurred on a Tuesday night. On the following night — so late in the night that it was actually Thursday morning around 2 a.m. — terror would again strike DeKalb County residents. A lodger on the poultry farm of Mrs. Gene Harrell on Valley View

119

Road was awakened by the sound of a match striking. As others in the home woke up, it was discovered that the home had been ransacked.

A neighbor, Mrs. Hicks, was then awakened by a Negro knocking on her door asking if she wanted to buy some eggs. Knowing she was only a few miles from where the Heinz murder had occurred and doubting the validity of an egg salesman at 2:30 in the morning, Mrs. Hicks refused to open her door. She instead called the DeKalb County police. DeKalb County officers Hill and Austin responded and found that the Harrell chicken barn had been set on fire.

Nitty Jones was a Negro woman who lived further down the road. At 2:40 a.m. she was awakened by a knock on her door. A Negro male voice demanded to be let in. She, too, refused to let him enter. The man asked Nitty to give him some matches. Nitty slid them under her back door. The man left and told her he was leaving her a present. Nitty opened the door after he was gone and found three dozen eggs marked with the brand of the Harrell poultry farm.

By then police were swarming the area and some neighbors had been alerted. Neighbors noticed a fire in the garage of D.T. Oliver. They found that a total of three fires had been set in the home including one on the living room sofa. The house also had been burglarized.

The suspect succeeded in eluding police all night. It was 7:45 in the morning when trouble escalated to violence at the residence of Mrs. Carl Roberts of Valley Brook Road. She was home alone when she walked into her dining room and was grabbed by the throat by a large Negro man. He was armed with an ice pick but she fought him anyway. She struggled and made it to the back porch where they both fell to the ground. Her resistance startled her assailant. He got up and fled into a patch of woods behind the residence. Mrs. Roberts escaped with only cuts and bruises.

By 9 a.m., a posse with bloodhounds captured the suspect in

Clarkston. He was identified by DeKalb County authorities as Randall McHenry, a 32-year-old escapee from the Stonewall Prison Camp in Fulton County. McHenry had an extensive criminal record dating back to 1936. He was wearing a tight-fitting hat that could be mistaken for a skull cap. In spite of early optimism that police had captured their man, the case against McHenry in the Heinz murder quickly fell apart. His fingerprints failed to match those found on the Venetian blinds in the Heinz dining room and Mrs. Heinz could not identify him as the man she saw struggling with her husband.

Although many suspects were taken into custody and questioned, the investigation continued for more than a year. As with any high profile murder not quickly solved, lack of resolution led to conspiracy theories, even among some police detectives. Some detectives turned their suspicions towards Dr. Vann and Mrs. Heinz.

In 1943, memories of the Great Depression persisted. Many still harbored animosity towards rich capitalists, believing their money could buy them out of anything — even murder. Most of the theories were ridiculous and caused additional stress and hardship on both Dr. Vann and Mrs. Heinz.

Even though Mrs. Heinz tried to assure police that the intruder she saw was a Negro man, some investigators insisted on a theory that the mask was worn by a white man who had somehow darkened his skin to masquerade as a Negro.

Mrs. Heinz had told police that the last words she heard her husband speak to the intruder were, "Don't shoot me... you will get more if you don't shoot me!" Some presented these words as evidence that Dr. Vann and Mrs. Heinz had murdered Henry Heinz for money so that they could marry. The longer the case went unresolved the more strenuously conspiracy theorists argued there had been a deeper motive than burglary. They were wrong. Even when the strongest of evidence came forward proving the truth some chose never to believe it, clinging to the ridiculous and refusing to believe the obvious.

It was Sunday, January 14, 1945. The war had continued for more than three years. Traffic on Atlanta's roadways continued to be light, and not just because of gas rationing. Spare parts for cars were hard to find, and people were having trouble keeping their automobiles roadworthy.

It had been almost a year and a half since the murder of Henry Heinz. It was a little past 7:30 p.m., but already dark. Two Fulton County police officers were patrolling the north end of the county when they observed a blue car traveling without headlights.

The vehicle was stopped and Officer Thompson approached to find a single black male driving the vehicle. When questioned about his headlights the driver responded, "I just a railroad nigger trying to get home. My lights went out." Thompson observed the driver to be sober and believed his story. He sent him on his way but, not before writing down the tag number of the car.

Hughes Spalding, a prominent Atlanta attorney, lived on Peachtree Road only a couple of miles west of the Druid Hills area. At 8:30 p.m., his wife walked into her well lit bedroom and came face-to-face with a large black male wearing a blue bandana and holding a pistol in his hand. He calmly walked around her bedroom as she demanded to know what he wanted and what he was doing there. He ignored her. He walked to a bedroom closet and removed a pocketbook from the shelf, and then left.

Mrs. Spalding called the police who issued a radio lookout for the man she saw leave her home in a blue car. Responding police found the blue bandana in the Spalding's front yard.

When Officer Thompson heard the lookout for the burglar in the blue car, he was immediately convinced that the man he had stopped with no headlights was the same man. Thankful he had made note of the tag number, he broadcast it over the radio.

At 9:40 p.m., Atlanta policemen who heard that broadcast spotted the vehicle on Simpson Road in Atlanta. Officers stopped the vehicle and transported the occupant to Atlanta police headquarters and then to the Fulton Tower jail. The driver was identified as Horace Blalock, a large black male who lived at 1986 Simpson Road.

He initially denied having been at or near the Spalding residence. When police went to his home and interviewed his wife she identified the blue bandana found at the Spalding home as belonging to Horace Blalock. Mrs. Blalock said the bandana was one of four given to her husband by one of her children.

When Blalock learned that his wife had identified the blue bandana he confessed to the Spalding burglary as well as 14 others in north Atlanta. Blalock, who gave his occupation as a porter, was an eighth grade dropout weighing more than 230 pounds and standing 6'3" tall. He had no criminal record other than traffic citations. Up to this point, he had never been fingerprinted by police. If he had, the Heinz murder would have been solved much sooner.

It had become policy to compare all residential burglars' prints to the prints found at the Heinz murder. After a year and four months of rumors and wild speculation in the press about the Heinz murder, high-ranking officials within the Atlanta Police Department proceeded cautiously whenever they were provided with clues on the case.

Fulton County police notified Atlanta police that the fingerprints of Horace Blalock were very similar to the latent (unknown) fingerprints found on the Venetian blinds at the Heinz home on the night of the murder. Captain Ben Seabrook of the Atlanta Police

Identification Bureau examined the prints. He also believed the prints were similar. The Georgia Bureau of Investigation was asked to examine the prints and concurred with the previous police agencies' opinions that the known index and small fingerprints of Horace Blalock matched two of the unknown prints lifted from the Heinz's Venetian blinds. In a final attempt at being reassured of their accuracy, Atlanta Police Chief Hornsby ordered the latent prints and known prints sent to the Federal Bureau of Investigation in Washington D.C. for comparison. He received his answer in 24 hours. It came by way of a one-line telegraph from the head of the FBI.

Latent print identical with print of suspect Blalock.
Hoover

It was the assurance Chief Hornsby had hoped for. Horace Blalock was not aware of the existing fingerprints from the Heinz home being compared to his own. On January 18, 1945, four days after his arrest, Blalock was confronted with the fact that his fingerprints could now positively be placed in the Heinz home. His first reaction was to confess that he had burglarized the home several weeks before the murder.

Blalock went with police to the Heinz home and told them he entered during the burglary through a library window and took $80 from a purse on a dressing table. Blalock attempted to explain this earlier burglary as the reason his fingerprints were found on the Venetian blind. However, later in the day Mrs. Heinz picked him out of a lineup as the man she had seen struggling with her husband on the night he was murdered. After 15 more hours of questioning Horace Blalock confessed to the murder of Henry Heinz.

Herbert Jenkins was the evening shift captain and senior man on duty for the Atlanta Police Department on the night Henry Heinz was killed. He would, in later years, succeed Chief Hornsby as Atlanta's Chief of Police. In 1981, his son James S. Jenkins wrote a book entitled *Murder in Atlanta!* (Cherokee Publishing Company).

Murder in Atlanta! is a book which chronicled the infamous murders of the author's father's tenure. In this book, Jenkins published a statement written by someone who was present in the room during the interrogation and eventual confession of Horace Blalock. Jenkins never identified the author of the following description of events other than stating he was one of the policeman in the room at the time Blalock wrote his statement.

Everybody was seated about the office very casual like. We would talk among ourselves about the case. Officers would come in and out on other business, there would be discussion of other cases, of routine police business and then we would begin talking about the Heinz case again. We would ask Blalock questions, mainly about his activities the night of the murder. Blalock was seated at a desk — an ordinary desk there in the office. There were no bright lights or the suspect being subjected to any discomfort, except the questions. Blalock was friendly and agreeable and showed no anger toward any of us. His replies were always well thought out and intelligent. He was a very likeable person and in the questioning there was none of the seething hostility that often develops in this type of situation. Food and soft drinks were brought in from time to time, and we would not talk about Heinz during these breaks. Blalock gave the appearance of being very fond of his family. I don't know how to say it exactly except that he was not carefree. In many ways he was different from your ordinary suspect: his manner, his very conservative way of behaving, his politeness, and his intelligence. All this made him different. Talking about his family and children seemed to get to him. We went over again and again all we knew about the case — which was a good deal — and tried to get Blalock to fill in the answers. Bit by bit he began to tell us things we hadn't known before. When he realized this, and this was quickly, he sat quietly for a long time and would not talk to us. We were on the verge of sending him back to his cell and giving it up for the night when he suddenly asked for a paper and pencil. It was handed to him and he began writing vigorously. While he was writing no one in the room said anything, and no one came in to interrupt while he was writing. He took a long time. It was kind of eerie ... the long silence.

The following is Blalock's statement, as it was written, in its entirety:

On the day of September 14, 1943 I had to go to the hospital for a serious operation on the brest left side and I stay in the hospital until September 18 cause I had a cold. They operated on me on the 18th day of September 1943. I left the hospital on the 23 to go home. I was very weak until the 15 day of October 1943. I began to gain my strain, I need some money. I was get $7.00 a week out of my policy that was not anof and I try to figer out some way to get some more money. I was at home that nite. My wife and myself. So somebody came by my house going to Dallas, Ga. to see my sister-in-law. They ask my wife and myself to go with them so I say I am to weak to ride up there so I demand my wife to go ahead so she did but she say will you be allwright. I say sure I will be so when she left I come out of my house and got in my car and left. I went down on out in Druid Hill and look around. I stop and Mr. Heinzy home on ponde de leon Ave. I went up there and I look around it was about 7:30 at night so I spoted them sitting in the side room. They were reading so I waited until Mrs. Heinzy went into the bedroom then I went to the winder and walk slower to the side room I thought both of them was goind to the bed room and I thought I spotted a red pocketbook on the sofa but it was a sewing bag and I hat a gun in my pocket when I got there there he was I was sorprised I turned to run and fell over the tables and he grab me and we tussle for a few minute he was so strong I could hardly hold him so he got my gun before I did and point it at me and shoot my thum half in two, and I got the best of him but I did never get the gun he had the gun but I twisted the gun point at him and it was fire every once in awhile. I don't know how may times it fire I got it in a little while in my hand and I ran out. Then I saw my finger was bleeding so and I all ready weak I could hard make it. I went strait home got me some little stick and did it up. I went to bed it bled all night. I went to the doctor the next morning and he fix it up. But I have not rested a nite since it have been worried me so much I could not sleep I say awake al night if it had not been for my wife and

127

children I would have done give up. I go to church I could feel right it was sometime on my mind all the time I am sorrow I don't no what to do. I bought the gun from a boy on the west side of town. I dont no who he was. I throw the gun in the river at Marietta Bridge I was brought up in the church and made to do wright. My mother and father are dead they made me do wright but when I got up I staid away from her and his raised. They was very nice to me I have worked for some very good white people in Atlanta I work for Mr. Clay for a year or more. I do wont Mr. Clay to speak for me at my trial gentleman I need mercy of you all for my family I have a wife and 3 little children. One 3-8-9 for the sake of my little children I ask mercy of Mrs. Heinzy please mirm just in order to see my children grow up and not let the make the same mistake I have made in life I am ask that you gentlemen please sir, I am so sorrow have mercy on me for wife and my children. Crime dont pay everybody that is doing wrong quit it now dont pay. The trial will come off in Decatur, Ga. High Cort some time in March. I hope you gentlemen will please sir, I am so sorrow I turned out to be what I did I married a fine girl for a wife she is a chrisen woman and not a better one she beleave in wright and wright a long I hope she will be happier again someday. She is a mitre sweet girl I will have to give her critic for my little children that so much of me and there mother it is hard for me to part from them but the lord says the best of friend must part from one another I wont you all to pray for me and I will pray for me. My time is all mose up but I hope not cose I am so sorrow

I don't know what to do please pray for me and my family and children I hope no more of my people dont no crime. So sorrow.

Horace Blalock

Press had gotten wind of what was going on and were outside waiting for the 15 hour interrogation to end. After Blalock had written his confession, police allowed the press into the room. Blalock was flooded with questions about the crime by a room full of reporters. It was then the press learned what really killed Henry Heinz. It was the "bug."

The bug was a numbers racket popular among the poor in the 1940s. It was a type of lottery long before the days when the lottery became legal in Georgia. People, mostly those who could least afford it, would pay their money at "bug" drop-off points, betting on the last four digits of the stock market's closing price.

When the press learned that Blalock earned $200 a month with the railroad, a good salary for 1945, they wondered why a self-proclaimed family man with no prior criminal history would become a thief. Blalock explained that shortly after he moved to Atlanta he began to play the bug. He soon became addicted, playing $15 a day. He told the press he had tried to quit but the bug had become a part of his everyday life. He turned to thievery to feed his family and his habit. Blalock told the press he took $45 from Heinz after killing him.

The trial began in March, 1945, before DeKalb County Superior Court Judge James C. Davis. Lawyers for Blalock recanted his confession and unsuccessfully tried to have it thrown out. They also attempted to have the fingerprint evidence thrown out, again to no avail.

The trial lasted three days. One of the key witnesses was Mrs. Heinz, whose reputation had been dragged through the mud by the rumor-monger press. She appeared visibly shaken by the attacks on her in the press. There were accusations that police were railroading a black man to protect "the widow of a rich capitalist." The all-white, male jury deliberated for 50 hours over a three-day period, sleeping on cots in the courthouse at night. The eventual verdict was guilty with a recommendation of mercy, meaning Blalock would not be sent to the electric chair.

Even the conviction of Blalock did not stop the ridiculous rumors surrounding the Heinz murder. In James S. Jenkin's book *Murder in Atlanta!,* Jenkins wrote about the gossip in the city and within the Atlanta Police Department. Presumably drawing from the knowledge of his high-ranking father:

> It was the opinion of many that Blalock took the blame for higher-ups. No manner of evidence or reasoning could convince some people otherwise. The police were severely stung by the rumors and

accusations in the Heinz case. They felt that a super-human effort had been made to solve it. However, many of the rumors developing around the case could be traced directly to certain police investigators who were influenced by and believed in the conspiracy theory — and became captives of it, themselves prisoners of the prejudice against people of wealth. Certainly the possibility of a conspiracy was thoroughly gone into, for the investigators wanted to find a basis for their beliefs. But no evidence of a conspiracy was ever uncovered. The officers closest to the case and the best informed from all the police departments involved felt then, and later, that any implication linking Mrs. Heinz with the murder of her husband was absurd.

Years later Mrs. Heinz married Atlanta Symphony Conductor Enrico Leide. She enjoyed social prominence in spite of the vicious rumors that followed her until her death in September, 1962.

Horace Blalock served 10 years of his life sentence and was paroled on May 18,1955. He moved to Vidalia, Ga., and became a porter for a car dealer.

After the murder of Henry Heinz, the Heinz mansion was rumored to be haunted. Occupants reported hearing gunshots in the night and believed the mansion was being haunted by Henry Heinz. The mansion fell into disrepair and became an overgrown monument to the tragedy.

4

THE MOORE'S FORD LYNCHING
1946

Roger Malcom was a 27-year-old black man who lived in Walton County, Ga. He lived in an area called Hestertown, six miles southeast of the town of Monroe, in a tenant shack with his wife, Dorothy. The shack was owned by Barnette Hester Sr. but Roger no longer worked for Hester.

Roger enjoyed a good reputation in Walton County among both blacks and whites, and was known around town as "a good boy." But trouble was brewing in Hestertown between Roger and the Hesters.

It was 1946. Ellis Arnall was in his final year as governor of Georgia. The sheriff of Walton County was E.S. Gordon. The president of the nation was Harry Truman. World War II had ended the previous year and America was thankful to all its veterans, black and white.

Two years earlier in <u>Smith v. Allwright,</u> the Supreme Court ruled that white primary elections were unconstitutional. In 1946, the U.S. District Court in Atlanta ruled that the Supreme Court decision applied to Georgia. Georgia could no longer hold "white only" primaries.

In spite of the high court's ruling, blacks were in danger in certain areas if they attempted to vote.

In south Georgia's Taylor County, Macie Snipes was the only black to vote in his district. The following day he was called into his front yard and gunned down by four white men.

Eugene Talmadge, who had previously served two other terms as governor, was seeking a third. In one of his speeches that summer, Talmadge told the crowd how he thought blacks should be treated:

> I was raised among niggers and I understand them.
> I want to see them treated fairly and I want them to
> have justice in the courts. But I want to deal with the
> nigger this way; he must come to my back door, take
> off his hat, and say, 'Yes sir.'

Talmadge promised voters he would restore the "white only" primaries and keep blacks from voting as long as he held office. He asked "good" blacks to stay away from the polls.

Talmadge's request went unheeded, and hundreds of blacks did turn up at the polls in Walton County. Some would say this later led to the trouble that would besiege Walton County.

The results of that summer's primaries is an indication of the division between the citizens of the county seat of Monroe and the outlying areas of Walton County. Monroe residents voted against Talmadge by a 2-1 margin, opting instead for business progressive James V. Carmichael. In spite of the voters of Monroe, Talmadge still carried Walton County by 78 votes because of the support he had out in the country. There was a big difference in attitudes between city and country in 1946 in Walton County.

There is no official record of how the trouble began between Roger Malcom and the Hesters — only the rumors told to the press after it occurred.

It was said that Weldon Hester, Barnette Hester Sr.'s son, had tried to run down Dorothy Malcom in a car. There was also a rumor that the senior Hester's other son, Barnette Hester Jr., known as Barney, had been making advances on Dorothy. It was said those rumors likely led to the trouble that came on Sunday, July 14, 1946.

Roger spent the afternoon drinking and then went home and angrily confronted Dorothy. When Dorothy thought Roger was becoming abusive, Dorothy fled to Barney for protection. Roger followed her there. A serious fight broke out between Barney and Roger. During the fight, Malcom stabbed and seriously wounded Barney. Malcom ran home as others rushed Barney to the hospital.

There was serious racial tension in the county over the voting situation. Whites feared that blacks were overstepping what whites thought should be their boundaries. Later that night, approximately 10 white men went to Roger's tenant shack, pulled him into the yard, and beat him. A white woman who had known Malcom since he was a child notified Sheriff Gordon of the trouble.

134

Sheriff Gordon arrived in time to save Malcom's life. He found him in the front yard, surrounded by his attackers, beaten and bound by ropes.

The sheriff dispersed the crowd and arrested Malcom for having stabbed Barney Hester. The sheriff likely knew that jail was the safest place Malcom could be. Sheriff Gordon had saved blacks from lynching before. In 1939, he called for the aid of 50 state troopers to hold back an angry mob of 1,500 who were after a black man named J.D. Vaughn. Vaughn was accused of attacking a white woman. Sheriff Gordon successfully saved Vaughn from the mob. He would not be so successful with Malcom.

The second attempt on Malcom's life came on Monday night, July 15, 1946. An angry mob, reportedly from Hestertown, came to the Walton County jail and demanded Malcom's release. Sheriff Gordon refused to release him to the crowd and eventually convinced the mob to disperse.

On Friday July 19, 1946, a local paper, the Walton Tribune, reported the fight between Barney Hester and Roger Malcom. The Tribune reported that Malcom was drunk and beating his wife when Hester "remonstrated with him, whereupon the Negro pulled out his knife and stabbed him." The Tribune described Barney Hester as a "splendid citizen of the Blasingame district."

Malcom's wife, Dorothy, fled to Oconee County to live with her brother, George Dorsey, and his wife, Mae Murray Dorsey. George Dorsey was a World War II hero. He served five years in the Army Air Corps in the Pacific and was the recipient the Good Conduct Medal, the Bronze Star, the Army Defense Award, and several campaign stars.

Dorsey had fought for five years to keep America free. When he returned to Walton County, he did not return the humble Negro many of his white neighbors thought he should be, but Dorsey didn't care. He had used his Army discharge money to stay out of debt while he raised a bumper crop of cotton, sharecropping on the land of J. Loy Harrrison.

Forty-two-year-old Loy Harrison was a landowner and reputed bootlegger. He was a large man, weighing 275 pounds, and was described by the press as "red-jowled, broad shouldered and big-bellied." Dorsey, his wife Mae, and Malcom's wife, Dorothy had all been pleading with Harrison to drive them to Monroe and bond Malcom out of jail. On Thursday, July 25, 1946, Harrison agreed to drive them all to Walton County and do just that.

Harrison drove them to Monroe in his Pontiac early that afternoon. Harrison posted, or at least he claimed to have posted, the $600 bail needed to release Roger Malcom from jail. It was later deemed suspicious that although the paperwork necessary to release Malcom would take only 10 minutes, it took sheriff's deputies three hours to do so.

After the release, Harrison drove Roger and Dorothy Malcom and George and Mae Dorsey back towards the Harrison Farm in Oconee County. Instead of returning by way of the Atlanta-Athens Highway, Harrison detoured to an isolated lane called Moore's Ford Road. Moore's Ford Road was a dirt road that led to Moore's Ford Bridge, a wooden structure which crossed the Apalachee River. After the incident Harrison told *Time* magazine he had been taking a short cut.

Harrison told *Time* that thirty minutes later he telephoned the Walton County Sheriff's Office and claimed he spoke with Deputy Sheriff Louis Howard. Harrison said, "Mr. Howard, they just hijacked me and killed my niggers."

The Aug. 5, 1946, edition of *Time* magazine described the incident in the following way:

> Loy Harrison, his 275 pounds sweating uncomfortably behind the wheel of an old Pontiac, started on the road toward home while Roger Malcom

136

chattered happily. Six miles out from Monroe, Harrison turned off on a rough, sun-drenched, red-clay shortcut between the cotton fields.

When he reached the wooden bridge over muddy Apalachee creek, Harrison jammed on the brakes. A car blocked the bridge. A band of 20 white men, unmasked, armed with pistols and shotguns, moved silently out of the roadblock.

Said Loy Harrison: "A big man who was dressed mighty proud in a double-breasted brown suit was giving the orders. He pointed to Malcom and said, 'We want that nigger.' Then he pointed to George Dorsey, my nigger, and said, 'We want you too, Charlie.' I said, 'His name ain't Charlie, he's George.' Someone said "Keep your damned big mouth shut. This ain't your party."

Harrison watched part of the mob lead quivering Roger Malcom and George Dorsey down a sandy track toward an oak tree. The Negro wives left behind in the car began to shriek. Harrison heard one of them call out the name of one of the mob, but swore he couldn't remember what it was.

Then "the big man said 'Git them bitches, too.' A little fellow wearing Army shoes, clothes and an Army cap held a shotgun on me. One man said, 'Let's shoot him too.' The big man thought it over. He asked me twice, 'Do you recognize anybody?' I said, 'No, you shouldn't shoot me."

Loy Harrison silently looked on as the men dragged the struggling women over to the oak tree and shoved them beside the bound figures of their husbands. Then the mob fired three pointblank volleys into their prisoners.

Harrison told authorities that after the shooting, he drove to a store two miles away and called the sheriff's office.

The lynching touched off nationwide criticism of the South. The *Time* magazine article said of the lynching:

> Gene Talmadge's campaign to be governor of Georgia had ripped the thin gauze of decency from the body of his state. Last week the nation saw the running sores beneath it....
>
> The hate of white men for their Negro neighbors burst forth in a lynching seldom equaled for viciousness in the state.

Sheriff Gordon announced early on that he was at a dead end with his investigation. County Coroner Tom Brown held an inquest. The only witness was Loy Harrision. The six-man jury returned the verdict, "death at the hands of unknown parties," a verdict frequently used in cases of lynching. Sheriff Gordon asked the Georgia Bureau of Investigation to take over the investigation.

Loy Harrison, reprinted with the permission of *Time*.

The nation was in an uproar over the killing. It was assumed early in the investigation the lynching came as a result of Roger Malcom stabbing a white man. If that were the reason, then George Dorsey was an innocent party, and Dorsey was a war hero.

It was reported initially that President Truman would have no direct involvement in the case, but political pressure would change his mind. On July 30, 1946, President Truman ordered the U.S. Justice Department to throw all of its resources into the case. The Federal Bureau of Investigation was sent to Georgia.

They soon discovered that there was no record in the sheriff's office of Harrison ever actually paying the $600 that should have been required before Malcom's release, casting a cloud of suspicion over deputies in the sheriff's office. Deputy Sheriff Louis Howard came under more suspicion when a black man named Johnnie Burdette placed Howard at the scene of the lynching.

Burdette told NAACP officials sent to investigate that he (Burdette) was at Moore's Ford, parking with a girlfriend, shortly before the lynching. Burdette said that Deputy Howard and another armed man approached him, told him to leave and to not allow ,"any other niggers to come down the road." Burdette was too afraid to testify, and NAACP officials helped him leave the area for his own safety.

Observers around the courthouse linked the lynching to the black voter turnout on election day. One such observer, unnamed by the media said, "The sight of that long line of niggers waiting to vote put the finishing touches to it." Another rationalized the killing as necessary saying, "This thing's got to be done to keep Mister Nigger in his place. Since the state said he could vote, there ain't been any holding him."

Investigators did not believe that Loy Harrison, who had lived in the area all of his life, failed to recognize anyone in the mob of 20 men. They eventually arrested Lester Little, a beer tavern employee who police believed to be the mob leader, but Harrison refused to identify him. Investigators became angry at Harrison, and Harrison defended himself to the press saying, "They think I had something to do with it. Why, I'm mad as anybody, the way they killed my niggers. I need all the nigger hands I can get."

U.S. Attorney General John Cowert eventually convened a federal grand jury to hear the matter. More than one hundred witnesses were called to testify, but no indictments were returned. It would be the end of the matter.

A thorough probe by both the FBI and the GBI led nowhere. Major William Spence, who headed the GBI's investigation, told *Time* magazine in frustration, "The best people in town won't talk." And the best people in town didn't talk for 46 years.

In 1992, Clinton Adams, a white man living in Florida at the time, came forward and said he had witnessed the murders at Moore's Ford when he was 10-years-old. According to Adams, Loy Harrison took part in the shooting along with three other farmers who lived in the area, all of whom were dead by the time Adams came forward. None of the accused were from Hestertown.

The final motive might have been greed more than prejudice. During the investigation, rumors had surfaced that Loy Harrison had been trying to pick fights with George Dorsey, hoping he would take off and leave his crop of cotton for Harrison. Whether Harrison took part in the shooting or not, when the killing was done, Harrison was left with Dorsey's crop.

No one was ever convicted for the murders of Roger and Dorothy Malcom or George and Mae Dorsey.

In July, 1999, the Georgia Historical Society and Moore's Ford Memorial Committee erected a historical marker on U.S. 78 near its intersection with Locklin Road. Committee member Richard Rusk told the Atlanta Journal-Constitution "For a half century anonymous killers have had the last word on Moore's Ford but we the good citizens of Athens/Clark County, Morgan, Oconee and Walton Counties will write the final chapter."

5

THE BLACK WIDOW OF MACON
The Story of Anjette Lyles
1958

It was early spring when Mrs. W.K. Bagley strolled up the driveway of her Cochran, Ga. home to retrieve the morning's mail. She paused to open and read an odd letter with no return address that had caught her attention. The brief anonymous letter spoke volumes. It would bring justice but not salvation.

Please come at once. She is getting the same dose as the others.

The letter was postmarked from Macon, Georgia. Mrs. Bagley

had two grand-nieces in Macon. They were the daughters of her sister, Julia Lyles' son Ben F. Lyles Jr. Both Julia and her son Ben Jr. had died mysteriously. Ben in 1952 and Julia in 1957. Mrs. Bagley recognized the letter to be the first clue in solving those mysterious deaths. She traveled to Macon and learned that her oldest grand-niece, nine-year-old Marcia, had suddenly taken ill and had been hospitalized.

Mrs. Bagley took her letter to a city police detective, the solicitor general, a postal inspector, and eventually the F.B.I. All of the authorities considered the letter to be from a "crack pot" and took no action. Three weeks later on April 4, nine-year-old Marcia Elaine Lyles, Mrs. Bagley's grand-niece, was pronounced dead at a Macon hospital.

It was 1958. The sheriff of Bibb County was James L. Wood. The governor of Georgia was Marvin Griffin. The president of the nation was Dwight D. Eisenhower

Macon was the county seat of Bibb County, incorporated in 1823 in the "heart of Georgia" as they like to call it.

Its downtown streets are named for trees — Walnut, Cherry, Poplar, Plum, Pine, Hemlock, and Mulberry.

Mrs. Bagley's sister Julia had married into a well-known family in Macon. For nearly three decades Julia and her husband, Ben F. Lyles Sr. ran a popular restaurant on Mulberry Street, across the street from the Bibb County Courthouse. The "meat and two vegetables" restaurant was convenient to employees of the U.S. Post Office, nearby law offices and shoppers patronizing thriving downtown stores. Upon Ben Sr.'s death, Ben Jr. continued to run the family restaurant with the help of his new wife, Anjette Donovan Lyles.

Anjette Lyles was an attractive, prematurely gray, 27-year-old woman with dark eyebrows and striking features. She wore tight-fitting clothes to display what the press described as a "buxom" figure. She quickly became a popular figure in the busy restaurant

143

that catered to the courthouse crowd and to what Anjette called the "brass hats" of Macon.

Tragedy began only three years into Ben and Anjette's marriage, when Ben was struck with a strange illness that took his life at the young age of 29.

Anjette rebounded quickly and remarried a young, strapping, 200-pound airline pilot from Texas named Joe Neal "Buddy" Gabbert, a man she met in the restaurant. When they married, Buddy was the picture of health. Five months after his marriage to Anjette, Buddy died a mysterious, torturous death that stunned his family back in Texas. At the time of his death he was 26 years old.

Anjette collected $20,000 in life insurance, went to court to legally assume her former name of Lyles, purchased and remodeled her first husband's family restaurant and changed its name to Anjette's. Her former mother-in-law, Mrs. Bagley's sister Julia Lyles, moved in with Anjette to help run her former husband's family business.

Two years later Julia Lyles became mysteriously ill and within weeks she, too, succumbed to her illness and died on Sept. 29, 1957. Anjette produced what purported to be the Last Will and Testament of Julia Lyles, dated one month before Julia's death, making Anjette sole executrix. The will provided for Anjette and her children to inherit two-thirds of Julia's estate. The remaining third was left to Julia's other son, Joseph Hamilton Lyles Sr.

It was about this time that Anjette began to act very strangely. She began to practice voodoo. Root doctors, spiritual advisers and fortune tellers guided her daily life. She lit candles throughout the restaurant — green ones for good luck and red ones for romance. She also began to set her sights on a new beau, another young airline pilot named Bob Frank. She lit red candles and told patrons of the restaurant that when the candle flickered brighter her new love was coming nearer to her. She also was acting very hostile towards her oldest daughter, Marcia — snatching her up in front of restaurant employees and snapping at her, "You little Lyles-looking thing, I'll kill you if it's the last thing I do."

In March of 1958 Marcia became ill. Shortly after she was hospitalized Anjette told her employees that the child was going to die. Two weeks before Marcia actually died, Anjette purchased her coffin, arranged for her funeral, packed her suitcase in her hospital room and sent the flowers away. Marcia passed away on April 4, 1958.

After receiving the anonymous letter Mrs. Bagley was sure all of the deaths surrounding Anjette were related and that someone close to Anjette knew more. After the death of Marcia, police took the letter sent to Mrs. Bagley much more seriously.

Coroner L.H. Chapman sent Marcia's organs to the State Crime Lab's deputy director, Larry Howard, a poison expert. Dr. Howard confirmed what Mrs. Bagley had long suspected. Marcia had been poisoned with arsenic.

Sheriff's investigators began questioning relatives and restaurant employees about Marcia's death. Anjette quickly realized that Marcia's death might not be the only one to be questioned. Just days into the investigation, Anjette came home one day frantically speaking of a letter she must find. She encouraged her maid, Carmen Howard, to help her look for the alleged letter. Carmen was unable to find any letter and went home that day having found nothing. The following morning when Carmen arrived at Anjette's split-level home, Anjette immediately called her upstairs and showed her a letter Anjette claimed she found in the lining of one of Julia Lyles' old purses. The letter appeared to be from Julia and stated that Anjette was not responsible for "little Ben's" death nor her own. The letter implied that Julia herself was responsible for both.

Anjette told her maid, Carmen, that if anyone were to ask she was to say that she found the letter. With letter in hand Anjette began telling friends that she had a "hot piece of evidence" that would clear her of any wrongdoing.

Reprinted with the permission of The Atlanta Journal-Constitution

146

During the first week of May, almost four weeks after Marcia's death, charges were filed against Anjette charging her with the murder of her daughter.

Anjette was in the hospital at the time being treated for phlebitis. Guards were posted with her and on May 9, 1958, she was transferred to the Bibb County Jail.

On that same day Sheriff James L. Wood and his deputies searched Anjette's home. In her bedroom the sheriff found what he described to the press as a "witch's lair, complete with voodoo charms of various types." The sheriff and his investigators found love potions, root oil, socks and stockings pinned in various places, including under her mattress. The socks and stockings contained photographs of Bob Franks, Anjette's latest love pursuit. They also found four bottles of rat poison.

The trial of then 33-year-old Anjette Lyles began in October, 1958. The voodoo angle, the popularity of the restaurant, the horrific allegation that Anjette had poisoned her own daughter and Anjette's unique appearance were all circumstances which caused the matter to be the "story of the decade" in the press for months leading up to the trial. The case was reported nationwide, and every article gave detailed descriptions of Anjette's style and appearance each day at court. Initially the press referred to her as a "pretty widow" or "attractive and buxom." But things changed as the trial grew near. When it came time for her trial, either the months in jail took away from her appearance or the press lost some of their attraction. On Oct. 9, 1958, Atlanta Constitution columnist Celestine Sibley wrote

147

the following about Anjette's appearance:

> The press worries over adjectives to describe her. "We stopped calling her 'attractive' last summer," a wire service reporter remarked. "But what else are you going to call her? I've worn out 'plump' and I hate 'comely.'"
>
> You try to be precise but it's difficult. She changes. One moment she looks middle-aged and frankly fat. And then you catch her looking over her shoulder, searching the face of a prospective juror and you are astonished by her beauty — the clear cut, finely molded features, the startling combination of dark eyes, black eyebrows and white hair, the bright red lips, the phenomenal baby-like skin. You catch —or imagine you catch—a momentary look of wistful vulnerability.
>
> And then her back is turned and you see the thick shoulders, the short plump neck, the hands ostentatiously fingering the little Testament.

By the time the trial began, Anjette was charged with the deaths of both of her husbands, her mother-in-law and Marcia. The first trial, however, would only be for the murder of Marcia. The main prosecutor was H.T. O'Neal; the main defense attorney, William E. Buffington. Presiding over the trial was Judge Oscar Long. Because of the similarities in the four deaths Judge Long allowed the prosecution to enter evidence involving all four victims.

The trial began with testimony about the bodies being exhumed, and the gruesome autopsies that followed. Things quickly became

148

sensational when Dr. Larry Howard testified that all four of the bodies contained fatal doses of arsenic poison consistent with the rat poison found in Anjette's bedroom.

Another interesting witness was Carrie Jackson. Carrie Jackson was a 43-year-old the press described as a "Negro cook" who had worked in the Lyles' restaurant for nearly three decades. Carrie had worked for both Ben Lyles Sr., Julia, Ben Jr. and then Anjette. Carrie admitted during her testimony that she wrote the mysterious anonymous letter to Mrs. Bagley telling her to "Come at once, she's getting the same dose as the others."

Carrie testified that she wrote the note because of her observations of Anjette whenever one of her loved ones was in the hospital. Carrie testified that Anjette would always take whomever was ill something to eat or drink and that the patient's condition would always worsen. On each occasion the illnesses ended in death. With Julia Lyles it had been buttermilk, but with Marcia it was lemonade.

Carrie testified that she watched Anjette squeeze lemons into a glass of water, preparing lemonade for Marcia who by then was already in the hospital. Carrie then watched Anjette take the lemonade, pick up her purse and carry both into the lavatory of the restaurant. Carrie testified that she later observed rat poison in that same purse. "Thank God for Carrie!" prosecutor O'Neal said in his closing argument.

Anjette's maid, Carmen Howard, testified about the letter Anjette asked her to claim she found. Carmen told the jury that she did not find the letter, and had later told Anjette she would not lie for her.

Prosecutors then put up one of their most damaging witnesses: State Represenative-elect Taylor Phillips, an attorney Anjette had visited for legal advice. Phillips testified that she always approached him as a friend — that he never accepted any of the legal work she was requesting and was therefore not bound by the attorney-client privilege.

Phillips testified that he was in the hospital at the same time as Buddy Gabbert, Anjette's second husband. Phillips said Anjette came to him in his hospital room and asked him to come and prepare a will for her husband of less than one year. Phillips testified that when he put on a robe and went down to Gabbert's room, he found Gabbert in such a state of distress, feverishly scratching rashes around his eyes and ears, that Phillips was unable to talk to him.

Phillips also testified that Anjette had asked him to try to persuade Julia Lyles into preparing a will. Phillips testified that Anjette told him that Julia "didn't want one and was against having one."

Phillips testified that he went to the hospital when Anjette was being treated for phlebitis to tell her she was probably going to be arrested on multiple counts of murder and that he would not be available to represent her. Phillips told Anjette she needed to go out and get herself "a couple of good lawyers." During that visit Anjette showed him the letter she claimed was written by Julia Lyles in which Julia allegedly cleared Anjette in her and her son's death. Phillips testified he believed the letter was a forgery.

The prosecution went on to establish through a series of witnesses that Anjette had become quite proficient at forgery. A Veterans Administration employee testified that four days before Anjette and Buddy Gabbart were married the VA received a letter purporting to be from Buddy inquiring whether or not a $10,000 life insurance policy on him was still current. Four months after Buddy and Anjette were married that policy was changed to reflect Anjette as the beneficiary. Within one month of the change Buddy died of what the state had established was arsenic poisoning. The state's next witness, Mary Beacon of the state crime lab, testified that the letter of inquiry to the insurance company was a forgery and did not contain Buddy's known signature.

Later in the trial it was also established that the will purporting to be the Last Will and Testament of Julia Lyles, leaving two-thirds of her estate to Anjette, also had been a forgery. (After the trial a former employee of Anjette's and her real estate agent would be indicted for signing false witness on the will).

A representative from The Metropolitan Life Insurance Company testified that his company also issued a $10,000 check to Anjette after the death of her second husband, Buddy Gabbart. William N. George testified that the payoff was based on a policy sold by Anjette's brother, William Donovan.

John Henry West Jr., a car dealer from Warner Robins, testified that a few months before Julia Lyles' death he drove a flashy white Oldsmobile convertible to Macon for Anjette to test drive. West testified that Anjette told him she could not afford the automobile yet, but that Mrs. Lyles was sick at the time and Anjette told him the illness was serious and she was not expected to pull through. Anjette told the car dealer that she and her children stood to inherit two-thirds of Mrs. Lyles estate.

The prosecution's case, although totally circumstantial, did a convincing job of painting the picture of a greedy, conniving, ruthless woman who would even kill her first-born child because as one prosecutor put it to the jury, "she was a little in the way" of Anjette's pursuit of her new perspective beau.

The only evidence the defense put up was Anjette herself. The law allowed for Anjette to make an unsworn statement and not be cross examined. The judge would be required to instruct the jury that the statement would hold less credibility because it was not sworn and could not be questioned by the state.

151

The Oct. 14, 1958 edition of The Atlanta Journal described Anjette's statement to the jury as follows:

Anjette's story of her life, as related to the jury in her unsworn statement, was that of a widow who had only a dime to her name on the day that her whiskey-drinking first husband died. She said she had to borrow money for milk for her two little girls.

Speaking in a conversational voice, Anjette pictured herself as a woman struggling to make a living for her children while beset by one tragedy after another in her personal life. She was a loyal wife, daughter-in-law and mother under trying circumstances, according to the way she told it.

Anjette denied giving poison to any of her four alleged victims. She insisted that, instead, she tried to help them all "get well" during their final illnesses, ruining her business and endangering her health in the process.

The jury was given the case on Oct. 14, 1958, at 8:35 p.m. Observers in the courtroom patiently watched a light above the courtroom clock which, when illuminated, indicated that the jury had reached a verdict. The light came on at 10 p.m. The jury had debated the case for one hour and 35 minutes. The verdict was guilty. There was no recommendation for mercy. In 1958 this meant the death penalty was automatic.

In a soft-spoken voice Judge Long told Anjette she could remain seated while he pronounced sentence. The sentence was death by electrocution to be carried out on Dec. 5 of that same year. The Atlanta Journal reported that Anjette was "cold, or stoic, or stunned — who knows?"

The sentence date of Dec. 5 was unrealistic as the defense made a motion for a hearing, and Judge Long set a date for the hearing which was beyond her scheduled execution date. The date basically had the effect of immediately postponing the execution.

The press reported that Anjette left the courtroom "with the brisk, heel-clicking stride that had marked her previous exits during the seven days of her trial. She characteristically carried her chin rather high, and it was high as she went out — a condemned woman."

The press was reporting that if Anjette were electrocuted she would be the first white woman executed in Georgia's history. Columnist Celestine Sibley later learned through research that there was a white woman executed in Georgia before it became a state. While Georgia was a colony a white Irish girl named Alice Riley was executed in Feb. 1745 on Hutchinson Island, which was directly across from Savannah. Riley was hanged after being accused of killing an Englishman for whom she worked as a servant.

Riley was pregnant at the time and was allowed to live several months until the baby was born. After the birth of her baby she was taken to the gallows where her sentence was carried out.

Anjette's attorneys spent the following year fighting to save her from the electric chair. Doctors who reviewed her mental state, which appeared to deteriorate during her confinement, described her as "psychotic and schizophrenic." Defense attorneys now were arguing that she was insane. Her sanity had never been questioned during the trial. It apparently became the opinion of her attorneys and doctors that her sanity had slipped away during her incarceration.

In her final desperate attempt to prove to her doctors she was innocent she turned against her biggest supporter, the one woman who sat behind her during the entire trial, her mother, Jetta Donovan. Anjette told the doctors that her mother was mean and had probably killed the child.

After the hearing, when this was first revealed to Anjette's mother, the press surrounded a crying Jetta Donovan, who continued to support her daughter. She told the reporters, "I don't care if she's killed everybody in Macon. That's my daughter in there. What do you expect me to do?"

State parole officials and a sanity commission eventually labeled her insane. Georgia law prohibits the execution of an insane person. Anjette was transferred to the Central State Hospital in Milledgeville. If it ever had been determined that she had regained her sanity the death penalty could have been reinstated. It never happened.

Celestine Sibley visited Anjette when she was first sent to Milledgeville. In 1998 Celestine recalled that visit. "She was cheerful the day I visited. They had her working in the kitchen then. Can you believe they would put her in the kitchen?"

Anjette Donovan Lyles died of natural causes in 1976 at the age of 52, at the Central State Hospital. People who knew her told the press she had worked daily in the hospital laundry until the time of her death. Not because she had to but because she wanted to "just to pass the time in here." She often told her friends there, "God is going to let me out of here one of these days."

6

THE OLD MAN AND HIS MONEY
1967

It was early August, 1967, in the seemingly sleepy town of Jefferson, Georgia. Shortly after midnight he crept through the yards of the town's good people while they slept. He slithered towards the home of his unsuspecting victim. In spite of his recent escape from the Pickens County Jail he was not the hunted but the hunter. He thought he had arrived, but the vehicle they told him to look for was not there. He walked back down the dirt road with ten sticks of dynamite in his hand to the car where they waited. He reported there was not a 1965 Ford Galaxy in the yard with a radio pole, the car he found was a newer model. With no apparent concern of striking at the wrong victim, they told him to go back and do it anyway. And he did.

High on pills chased with beer, undaunted by the sounds of dogs barking in the distance, he made his way through the dark, back to the modest home. He raised the hood of the green 1967 Ford Galaxy and began placing the dynamite on the engine. Fumbling in the dark, he ran a wire from the dynamite to the point of ignition. Connecting the dynamite to the wrong wire would have been instant death for him and quick justice for the good people of the town. His name was John Blackwell. He did not know who the intended victim was. He would be paid $1,500, and his actions would shake the neighborhood and scar the town for decades. His participation would prove to be the weak link in their conspiracy.

It was just before dawn when the prosecutor for the Piedmont Judicial Circuit, Floyd "Fuzzy" Hoard, attempted to crank his car. The explosion was horrific. The force of it propelled him into the backseat where he was quickly found by his panic-stricken wife and teenage daughter, who ran to the car after hearing the explosion. Also hearing the explosion, which shook him from a drifting sleep in his bunk bed, was Hoard's 15-year-old son, G. Richard Hoard. His mother called him "Dickey." Years later he wrote about that night and how it would affect the rest of his life. In *Alone Among the Living* (Brown Thrasher Books), Hoard wrote the following about the morning his father was killed:

> Reverberations of whatever it was shook the house. What in the world, I thought? Half falling from the bunk, I stumbled through the door leading to the back porch, rubbed sleep from my eyes as I walked barefoot and bewildered toward the front yard.
>
> "Dickey!" My mother screamed, coming into sight around the corner of the house. "Hurry! Come

156

quick!"

Suddenly she bolted toward me, weeping, turning to look at the front yard, as if running in a circle, tuning completely around again to face me, grabbing at her hair. "I think your daddy's just been killed."

It was just like my mother to imagine the worst, I thought. More than likely Daddy was in town somewhere. But what was the explosion? "Get some water. Quick!" she screamed, lurching toward me. "We've got to put out this fire."

She was uttering nonsense, I thought, and disregarding her command, I walked to the corner of the front yard to see that the Galaxy had been demolished, flames were leaping from the engine and Daddy was inside the car. "God," I said aloud and sprinted to the faucet in the back yard where Mama was already filling up a pail. I grabbed another of the plastic buckets and waited while the meager stream fell, Mama halfway filling one pail before carrying it toward the front yard, water sloshing with her every step. With my bucket only half full, I ran with it to the front yard, reeling at the sight of my father sprawled where the back seat should have been. I poured the water on the flames which hissed in reply but continued to leap from the engine. I ran for more water, stopping this time at a nearer faucet, then returning to the car to extinguish the fire. Peggy now stood where the door to the car should have been stooping over Daddy, patting his cheek. "Daddy, listen, Daddy. You're gonna be alright now. We're getting some help. Horace is coming. Everything is gonna be alright."

157

One hand at my heart, the other to my throat, I assessed the destruction; my father's face splintered by fragments of windshield, pants to his scorched suit shredded at one shin, flesh sliced to bone, torso impaled to car seat by blackened steering wheel, white shirt charred and bloodied beneath the buttons of suit ripped open to reveal intestinal wall. "Oh, God'l mighty, he's going to die." Somehow Horace must hurry. Get him to the hospital. Daddy might be there a long time, but he'd get over this. He couldn't die. God, he couldn't die. Not here. Not now.

"Peggy Jean!" Mama cried. "We've got to call the ambulance." She ran toward the house.

"Mama, I've already called. Horace is coming. He's on his way. And I've called Albert."

My mother stopped in mid-step and returned to the car. "Listen Daddy," Peggy Jean said. "Listen, I'm right here. Help is coming. You're gonna be alright. You'll be alright."

Suddenly he breathed — or groaned — a long guttural escaping of air. Quickly Peggy Jean was upon him parting his lips to give mouth-to-mouth resuscitation, but finding his throat blocked by a mass of broken teeth and gums she tried to force air through his nose. "Daddy," she said. "Daddy?" She raised his eyelids, saw nothing but white, and closed them. She felt for a pulse. "Oh, Mama, he's dead."

"No," Mama wailed, "No, Peggy Jean, no don't say that. Horace is coming. Albert is coming." She turned to dash toward the house. "Hurry, Horace. Hurry."

"Look, Dickey," Peggy Jean said. "I'd better go

see about Mama. She's crazy. She's liable to kill herself. See if you can get him breathing. I can't get any air into his mouth. All his teeth are gone. You're gonna have to breathe into his nose."

"In his nose?"

"Yes, you know how to do mouth-to-nose," she said, glowering at me.

I looked down at my father. His face was the color of dead ashes. Yes, I knew how to do mouth-to-nose, and I knew I had to do what I could to revive him. Lowering my face toward him, fighting nausea at the taste of burned flesh, I exhaled into his nose, one hand on his chest to feel the air fill his lungs, raising my head to let the air escape, breathing into him again, his lungs rejecting the air, breathing into him again, watching the air escape, breathing in...

Minutes later my sister was back. "Peggy Jean, it ain't doing any good." I said.

"Keep doing it," she said and returned to the house.

A neighbor strolled into the yard, a 12-year-old boy whose face wrinkled with curiosity and revulsion at the sight of the corpse. "Dickey," he asked as if apologizing for interrupting a surgery. "What happened?"

What I wanted to scream was, "What in the hell does it look like happened you stupid son of a bitch?" But instead I gritted my teeth and said grimly, "My father's just been killed."

"Why," he said, shaking his head backing away from the yard before turning to walk back across the field. I watched his progress after each rejection of

159

air, time slowing to a crawl until finally the white police car sped up the driveway and skidded to a halt. As if in a dream I walked toward Albert, who leapt from his car and froze in his tracks. "Goddamn!" He pounded his fist into the palm of him hand, tears steaming down his face. "Who would have done this? Goddamn! Who would have done this?"

He glared at me as if expecting me to answer. I shook my head, my mouth hanging open in disbelief as I realized for the first time that someone had meant for this to happen.

"Oh, God damn," he sobbed again. "Who would've done this?" I shook my head as if to say that I didn't know.

Floyd, Peggy Jean and G. Richard "Dickey" Hoard. Reprinted with permission of the Jackson Herald.

160

In communities the size of Jefferson, murders were always shocking. The murder of the solicitor general, the title district attorneys held during that time, was devastating. The man elected by the community to ensure enforcement of the law was lawlessly eliminated; the good people of the community seemingly stripped of the wall of protection the law was meant to represent.

It was 1967. The president of the nation was Lyndon B. Johnson. The U.S. was at war in Vietnam as additional U.S. troops sent there the year before by President Johnson began to invade what had been the Demilitarized Zones. The times were filled with turmoil and more would follow in the coming year when Martin Luther King, Jr. was to visit Memphis, Tenn. Although Prohibition had ended decades earlier, many of the smaller communities in the heart of the Bible Belt forbade the sale of alcohol. The governor of Georgia was Lester Maddox. The sheriff of Jackson County was R. "Snuffy" Perry.

The shock waves from the murder of "Fuzzy" Hoard rippled throughout the state. Governor Maddox ordered a contingent of agents from the Georgia Bureau of Investigation to Jefferson to launch an investigation. G.B.I. Capt. James Carnes was to head the investigation. Assisting him were Lt. R.J. Cleghorn, Sgt. Robert Hightower and Agents Bonnie Pike and Ron Angel.

Special Agent Angel was no stranger to Jackson County, and he had been no stranger to Fuzzy Hoard. Hoard was in his first term of office having been elected on the "reform ticket." The Piedmont Judicial Circuit had become a notorious territory. Auto theft rings were rampant, and bootlegged beer and liquor flowed freely in the dry communities which made up the circuit. The Piedmont Circuit covered Barrow, Jackson and Banks counties.

Voters in the circuit had totally revamped their legal system by electing a new sheriff, solicitor general, and Superior Court judge on

161

the reform ticket. All three candidates had pledged to take a stand against the blatant lawlessness in the circuit.

There had been raids and arrests in the past — arrests significant enough to clearly reflect the magnitude of the problems. In 1962, massive raids were conducted at 12 locations in Jackson County. Fourteen people were arrested; 2,400 cases of beer and 31 cases of liquor were seized. The raids were conducted by agents from the G.B.I. and state and federal revenue agents. Charges were filed in Federal Court. Federal Court Judge Richard B. Russell, III complained that the bootleggers were refusing to come to court. The sheriff at the time, John Brooks, was less than cooperative, claiming he could never find any of the bootleggers when it was time for their appearance. Judge Russell threatened to seek aid from then Gov. Carl Sanders if the defendants were not brought to court.

The people in Jackson County apparently had enough of the corruption, or at least those within the voting majority had had enough. During the 1964 elections, the entire reform ticket was elected. Mark Dunahoo was elected Superior Court judge, Hoard as solicitor general, and Snuffy Perry as sheriff. Hoard had taken office early upon the resignation of his predecessor. The former solicitor general had given up his office shortly after learning of his defeat.

Voters in the circuit were optimistic. In spite of the fact they had elected a sheriff and prosecutor with the nicknames "Snuffy" and "Fuzzy,"citizens of the Piedmont Circuit had been promised a tough crackdown on those living outside of the law in northeast Georgia. But after only a short time in office, Hoard became concerned about the effectiveness of the reform ticket. Hoard did not believe Sheriff Perry was dealing with the bootleggers as decisively as promised. Raids were not taking place despite his pleas to the sheriff for action.

Hoard contacted the Georgia Bureau of Investigation for help. Special Agent Ron Angel was assigned the task of dealing with illegal beer and liquor sales in the Piedmont Circuit. One of the agencies responsible for enforcing liquor laws in Georgia was the State Revenue Department, whose agents operated throughout the state making undercover buys and conducting raids. The participation of the local sheriffs was imperative to the agents' safety and effectiveness but Prosecutor Hoard was ordering buys and raids of which Sheriff Perry was unaware. The revenue agent for that area, John Perdue, was concerned about insulting the new Jackson County sheriff. "He (Perdue) helped us, but he did it in a way so that the sheriff wouldn't know he had," Special Agent Angel later recalled. "He was trying to not get crossed up with the sheriff. He would point out the bootleggers to me, and then I'd let him out up the road and come back to make the undercover buys." Angel recalled.

In all, Angel made 54 buys of beer and liquor sold illegally in the circuit. "Some of them were long-time bootleggers and some were just scratching out a dollar to get by," Angel remembered. Like †Nay Johnson, who was selling beer and liquor off of her front porch to raise an invalid daughter. But Angel's most memorable purchases were from an old man who was doing much better than just scratching out a dollar.

It was in the town of Pendergrass. When Angel pulled off U.S. Highway 129 and made his way up the 200-foot driveway, the structure that came into view was not your typical bootlegger's shanty. It was a sprawling white-columned, Southern plantation. The driveway led him to a detached, two-car garage behind the house. It was there Angel saw him for the first time. He was a polite, older man with a pleasing gentleman's Southern accent. His name was Cliff Park. He was the one they called "the old man". His seemingly pleasant demeanor was deceptive.

The garage was neatly adorned with well-stocked beer coolers and neon clocks on the wall advertising the beers he sold. The counters were filled with large jars of pickled eggs and hot sausages. The old man rose from his chair and made illegal sales of beer and whiskey to Angel on that day and on three other occasions.

On the day the raids went down, Cliff Park was one of dozens on the list to be arrested. Fifty-four hundred cases of beer and 19 cases of liquor were seized as Prosecutor Fuzzy Hoard carried out his promise to the people to clean up the Piedmont Circuit.

When Ron Angel drove out of his home-town in August of 1967, he did not realize he would not return or see his family again until Thanksgiving. His thoughts were elsewhere. He had just gotten a phone call from Lt. Cleghorn advising him of the death of Fuzzy Hoard and of his assignment to join the investigation in Jefferson.

In addition to the bootlegging problems in Jackson County, the area also had been plagued with abandoned, stripped, stolen cars from Atlanta. One of the most notorious leaders of the auto theft rings was A.D. Allen, owner of Allen's Auto Parts. In 1963 during a raid of his business in Commerce, agents from the G.B.I. reportedly discovered garages full of late model motors, seats, dashboards, windshields, hubcaps, taillights, and other various parts from cars. Directly across the street behind Allen's home, police found the hull remains of more than 100 late model cars along with transmissions, bumpers, and doors neatly aligned for customers to peruse and choose the parts they needed. Upon his arrest, which took place before Hoard took office, Allen pleaded guilty to 25 counts of auto theft. He received a minimal sentence for the crimes and openly stated during his sentencing that he was aided by corrupt lawmen in the operation of his stolen car "chop shop." In a short period of time, Allen was back on the streets of Jackson County and continuing in his criminal enterprises.

He was typical of the chop shop operators in northeast Georgia who felt threatened by the aggressive new prosecutor. In the first days after Hoard's death, the press was reporting the murder was linked to the northeast Georgia car theft rings.

The Macon News headline on August 7, 1967, read **AUTO BOMB KILLS GEORGIA SOLICITOR: Act Believed Linked to Car-Theft Racket.** The Aug. 9 edition of The Atlanta Journal featured a cartoon of auto thieves stripping a car in the woods along with an editorial speculating that Georgia had become the auto theft capital of the world. Athens State Senator Paul Broun told the press: "Mr. Hoard had done a fine job of gathering evidence they knew he was going to present to the grand jury and the big auto theft people eliminated him from the picture."

Most of the speculation that the murder was linked to the auto theft rings was due to the fact that Hoard had planned several auto theft-related indictments on the day of his murder.

The tragedy quickly became a national event, being reported in papers throughout the nation as well as *Time* magazine. It was one of Georgia's darkest hours.

A total of seven G.B.I. Agents were sent to Jackson County. The Aug. 9, 1967, edition of The Griffin Daily News announced that Sheriff Perry was "heading up an all out search for the killer." But tension grew quickly between the sheriff and agents from the G.B.I.

On Aug. 17, 1967, both The Atlanta Journal and The Atlanta Constitution reported that G.B.I. Director Barney Ragsdale had ordered his agents to remove Sheriff Perry from their investigation.

Some of the suspicion about Perry was based on the discovery that he had been ordered to padlock the doors of two bootleggers arrested in the May raids. In July, three of the accused bootleggers pleaded guilty and were fined and placed on probation. The heaviest fines were placed on Cliff Park. Sheriff Perry was alleged to have been ordered to padlock the doors at Park's bootlegging operation and had failed to do so. Additionally, it was being reported that much of the alcohol turned over to the sheriff after the May raids was now missing.

The press began reporting that Gov. Maddox was exploring the possibility of removing the Jackson County sheriff from office. Sheriff Perry denied all allegations and vowed to continue his own probe of the murder.

In spite of the black cloud hanging over the town of Jefferson there were still good people in the town who believed Jefferson could be a decent place to live.

The following is part of an Aug. 21, 1967, editorial about the town written by The Athens Banner-Herald News Editor Bill Carpenter:

JEFFERSON — Flakes of mica sparkle like diamonds on the red clay hillsides of Jackson County. Soils are good here and things grow green and healthy.

Jackson County has a population of approximately 18,500 men, women and children. It covers about 377 square miles. Jefferson is the county seat.

According to the menu in Marlowe's Cafe, Jefferson is "a great town. We are proud of it" and

"We are progressive and growing but we take pride in our old-fashioned hospitality."

The same slogan could easily be applied to Commerce, Braselton, Hoschton, Pendergrass, Arcade of any of the other small towns in the county.

All have their churches of various denominations and all have their own stores, shops and civic clubs. Commerce and Jefferson have their own schools while the county provides for the rest.

Industry has come into Jackson County, bringing a welcome boost to the area's economy. Jefferson has two modern textile plants and Commerce hosts the clothing industry.

Poultry production — Northeast Georgia's booming industry — has taken root in Jackson County. Farming long has been an economic mainstay.

Physically speaking, the county is a beautiful place with rolling hills and lush green vegetation. Its rivers and streams provide good fishing for the afternoon angler.

Much of the county's land is in timber. Tall, heavy pines cover the forest floor in a mat of brown pinestraw and litter it with dark cones. Game flourishes in the forests.

But what is not in timber or under cultivation or inhabited by people is covered in the almost indestructible kudzu vine. It grows rapidly and can completely cover abandoned houses.

Vines make good cover for hiding and stripping an automobile stolen from Atlanta or from nearby Gainesville or Athens. The vines quickly cover rusting hulks.

Auto theft is one of the county's lesser known but nevertheless booming industries. It's usually carried out under cover of dark and it issues no annual financial report.

The buying and selling of liquor, however, is performed fairly openly and the shopkeepers have acquired the kind of reputations that accompany years of business.

Of course, the thirsty buyer has to know where to go because the bootleggers don't buy commercials or use outdoor advertising but they aren't hard to find. All you do is ask.

After you've been in the same business under the same name for at least 10 years, people tend to know where you are.

The column reflects common knowledge throughout the town of the darker industries in the community. There were editorials calling for the county's decent people to stop ignoring the corruption and take action to improve the reputation of the community.

G.B.I. agents investigating the case knew the people in Jackson County could never reform their community without a resolution to the murder of Floyd Hoard. Their big break came in the fall of 1967.

Special Agents Bob Hightower and Ron Angel were interviewing † Tillie Mathews, Lloyd Seay's girlfriend. Lloyd Seay and John Blackwell's names had surfaced because of their activities in the bootlegging business in Jackson County.

Lloyd Seay had been raised in the moonshine business. His grandfather of the same name was a premier stock car driver in the early days of racing. But his grandfather was also a moonshiner, killed in 1941 during an argument over a load of sugar intended for making moonshine.

Tillie Mathews had been a large part of Seay and Blackwell's alibi when they were questioned by the G.B.I. But someone forgot to tell that to Tillie Mathews. She failed to corroborate their stories, and the G.B.I. began to take a serious look at Seay and Blackwell. The G.B.I. agents got their first chance to confront the two shortly after the Mathews interview, when Seay and Blackwell were arrested in Wrightsville. A house in which they were accused of operating a moonshine still had blown up and burned to the ground.

Blackwell broke down first and relayed to the agents the events which led up to his planting the sticks of dynamite under the hood of Floyd Hoard's car. Blackwell had been hiding out at Lloyd Seay's house after having escaped from the Pickens County jail. During the stay, Seay asked Blackwell if he "had the nerve to kill a man." Blackwell told the agents he agreed to assist Seay in the conspiracy.

Cliff Park, reprinted with the permission of the Jackson Herald

169

After being confronted with Blackwell's statements, Seay also confessed and filled in the rest of the story of the man behind the murder. Seay told agents that he had been approached by Doug Pinion on June 11, 1967, and offered $5,000 to kill Solicitor Hoard. Pinion told Seay "the old man" was putting up the money and wanted Hoard dead. Seay eventually would testify that everybody knew "the old man" was Cliff Park.

Seay told the agents that he agreed to find someone who would do the job. After asking several people, Seay came upon Iris Worley. Worley had agreed to do the job but said he thought the job was worth $7,500. Seay had gone back to Pinion with Worley's offer. According to Seay, Pinion agree to pitch in an additional $500 of his own money to get the job done, Worley eventually agreed on the new terms.

Investigators learned through Seay's and Blackwell's statements that although Worley and Seay drove Blackwell to Hoard's home on the night of the murder, it was Blackwell who actually planted the dynamite. But it was Cliff Park, the old man, who had arranged everything.

Cliff Park and Doug Pinion were arrested on Dec. 4, 1967, and indicted only four days after their arrest. Iris Worley was not so easy for lawmen to find and was not arrested until after Park's trial which began on Jan. 2, 1968. The prosecuting attorney was Luther Hames. Park was represented by Horace Wood and Atlanta attorney Wesley Asinof.

The most dramatic moments of the trial were during the testimony of 16-year-old Peggy Jean Hoard when she described the morning her father was killed. One of the key witnesses against Park was John Blackwell, the man who admitted planting the bomb. Blackwell testified the money he was paid for the job came from "the old man", the man also known to him as Cliff Park.

On Jan. 10, 1968, a jury convicted Cliff Park of financing the murder of Floyd Hoard — his sentence was death. This was later commuted to life in prison. He died there serving his sentence. Doug Pinion, Iris Worley, Lloyd Seay and John Blackwell all received life sentences. Doug Pinion served almost 20 years before being paroled. The rest were paroled after 14 years.

Lloyd Seay, like his grandfather, was gunned down in a violent shootout in 1991.

In the year following the death of Floyd Hoard, Jackson County voters were given the choice on the ballot of allowing the sale of beer and wine in the county. The attempt failed by a narrow margin of just over 300 votes.

Floyd Hoard eventually was recognized as a hero by the people of Jackson County. In 1997, a monument was erected on his behalf on the grounds of the Jackson County Courthouse. He paid the ultimate price for his conviction to clean up his community because of an old man's love of money.

7

THE COLUMBUS STOCKING STRANGLER
1977-1986

It was springtime in New York. A retired school teacher, she lived alone in a small, cramped, retirement hotel. She never knew he was there — until it was too late. He climbed a patio wall and then into her bed. He raped her, then strangled her to death with a scarf. It would not be realized for 16 years, but in that small apartment in Albany, New York, Nellie Farmer had become the first victim of the man who would come to be known in Georgia as the Columbus Stocking Strangler.

One thousand eighteen miles and two distinctively different

cultures separated the cities of Albany, New York, and Columbus, Georgia, but one fatal link between the two was in the early stages of development.

The year was 1970. After having pulled 90,000 troops from Vietnam in his first year as president, Richard Nixon was sending troops into Cambodia and reinitiating bombing raids over North Vietnam. His attempts at Vietnamization of the war — making the Vietnamese fight their own war— were not working, and Americans at home had begun to believe it was not winnable.

A 26-year-old catcher led the National League in home runs for the first time in his career. In his third year in the majors, the Cincinnati Reds' Johnny Bench was building a name and a reputation he eventually would carry to baseball's Hall of Fame.

In New York, Ferdinand Lewis Alcindor Jr., a New York native, led the Milwaukee Bucs to the first of two straight National Basketball Association championships. The following year, after becoming a member of the Muslim faith, he would change his name to Kareem Abdul-Jabbar.

There were gubernatorial races in New York and in Georgia. Nelson A. Rockefeller, who was later named the nation's 41st vice-president, was elected governor of New York for the fourth time.

In Georgia, a controversial gubernatorial campaign was under way. A peanut farmer named James Earl "Jimmy" Carter was running his first race for governor. He was accusing his opponent, Carl Sanders, of being a "Humphrey Democrat" — a reference to former Vice-President Hubert Humphrey's liberal policies such as civil rights for blacks.

Carter organized his campaign appealing to the white conservative rural voters and refused to condemn Alabama Governor George Wallace's segregationist policies. Carter campaign workers were accused of passing around pictures of Sanders joking with a black athlete. Carter was elected to his first and only term as governor that year, receiving only 10 percent of Georgia's black vote. The world would later come to know a very different Jimmy Carter.

Albany, New York, is one of the oldest chartered cities in America, with its history dating back to the founding of America. The city became the capital of the state of New York in 1777 and remains so today, despite the fact that its population of just over 100,000 pales in comparison to New York City's staggering population of more than seven million.

Although strikingly different from New York City, Albany was no stranger to crime. Even so, the grim circumstances surrounding the murder of Nellie Farmer shocked the city. There had been an attack two months earlier at the nearby Hampton Hotel, but that victim survived. Police were afraid a pattern was emerging.

Nellie Farmer was found molested, murdered, and left by her assailant face down on the floor of her apartment, her body and face covered with her own bed clothes.

The apartment had been ransacked. The city wanted answers. Albany police detective Anthony Sedotti thought he had found those answers.

On July 10, 1970, around 10 p.m., Josephine Deitz was attacked at her residence on North Main Avenue. She told police her assailant grabbed her by the throat, threw her to the ground, grabbed her purse and ran. Four days later, Albany police arrested a man and charged him with second degree robbery in connection with the Deitz assault. Police compared his fingerprints with unknown fingerprints found in Nellie Farmer's apartment. Detective Sedotti learned that this man's fingerprint had been found on a steamer trunk that had been opened and ransacked on Farmer's bed.

The man identified himself to police as Carl Michaels. He told Detective Sedotti that if he were allowed to talk to his wife, Sheila, he would waive his right to his lawyer and tell Sedotti who had killed Nellie Farmer. Detective Sedotti contacted Sheila, who was not even aware that her husband was in jail. She came to the jail and spoke privately with her husband. After their conversation, Michaels agreed to talk to Detective Sedotti. With his wife Sheila sitting on his knee in the interrogation room (and expecting their third child) Carl Michaels gave detectives what the press would later call a "rambling statement" of his involvement in the robbery and death of Nellie Farmer.

Michaels said he acted as a lookout while a man named John Lee Mitchell raped and murdered Ms. Farmer. Michaels claimed he had entered the apartment and barely caught a glimpse of her body as he ransacked the apartment of Nellie Farmer looking for items he could take and sell. Michaels said that Mitchell told him, "Man I did a job on that bitch."

Michaels explained that Mitchell wore latex gloves during the incident and his fingerprints would not be found in the apartment. He later provided police with a letter, purportedly written by Mitchell, admitting involvement in the crime. Albany police arrested John "Pop" Mitchell and charged him with the murder of Nellie Farmer. Mitchell denied any involvement in the crime.

The case went to trial December 10, 1970. The state's case against John Mitchell crumbled when the defense proved through an expert witness that the letter Carl Michaels had presented to police, and had sworn was written by Mitchell, was actually written by Carl Michaels. Mitchell was acquitted on all charges. On March 16, 1971, Carl Michaels pled guilty to first degree robbery in the case of Nellie Farmer and received a sentence of 10 years.

Even if they had bothered to check, it would have meant nothing to the police at the time to know that one of their two suspects was born in Columbus, Georgia.

No one was ever successfully tried for the murder of Nellie Farmer.

It was the city of Syracuse, New York, named for the ancient

Greek city of Syracuse in Sicily, that had become the temporary home of the man who would become known as the Columbus Stocking Strangler.

Jean Frost had just celebrated her 55th birthday. She lived alone in apartment 4H at 126 Jamesville Ave. in Syracuse. It was a cold January night. She was awakened by a noise. She struggled to open her eyes from a deep sleep. When she did, she saw a dark figure standing in the doorway of her bedroom. Before she could react, he was on top of her. She tried to shove him aside and run. He grabbed her and said, "You shouldn't have struggled."

He tore her nightgown off and stuffed it down her throat so that she couldn't scream. He began to beat her severely in the face. She then felt something around her neck — he was strangling her with a scarf. She passed out. Later she was again awakened —Jean Frost had survived.

She was bleeding severely from the vaginal area —so severely, a doctor would later note, that it would be impossible to test for the presence of sperm. She told police that night that her assailant was a black man who had a mustache.

It was the second rape and robbery in four days in Syracuse. On December 31, 1976, 59-year-old Janet Karnes† was raped and strangled with a pillow case while in her apartment on West Castle Street. She also survived.

On January 4, the day after Jean Frost's attack, police arrested two individuals at a bank in Syracuse. They were attempting to cash in $191 in coins allegedly stolen from William Holland. Holland lived in an apartment at 126 Jamesville Ave. the same apartment building as Jean Frost. One of the men arrested fought with police when confronted. He was reportedly found to be in possession of marijuana and a gold pendant watch—Jean Frost's watch that had been taken from her dresser during her assault.

When police searched this man's apartment, they found linens

176

which had been taken from Janet Karnes' apartment. The suspect identified himself to police as Carlton Michaels. He was later found to be the same Carl Michaels whose fingerprint was found in Nellie Farmer's apartment. He had been paroled in March of 1975.

Michaels had been arrested with David Parker†. Michaels told the Syracuse police that he had gone to the home of Jean Frost with Parker, but had waited in a nearby cemetery while Parker entered the apartments then returned to the car with the coins.

Michaels again was claiming to have been nothing more than a lookout. He also told police that the linens found in the apartment where he stayed, which had been taken from Janet Karnes' apartment, had been brought there by Parker. Parker told police he knew nothing of the linens found at Michaels' apartment. He also told them that the only thing he knew about the coins was that Michaels had asked him to help cash them in.

Jean Frost could not identify her attacker. Syracuse police could find no evidence to prove which, if either, had attacked Frost. Again, it would have meant nothing to police at that point to have learned that one of the two suspects was born in Columbus, Ga.

Neither Michaels nor Parker were ever charged in the attack of Jean Frost. Michaels' parole was revoked, and he received a one-year concurrent sentence on charges related to the coins and watch. He was sent to New York's Onondaga Correctional Institute to serve his time. On August 22 of that same year, he escaped.

Columbus, Georgia is located in southwestern Georgia. The city is situated on land acquired from the Creek Indians. It was founded in 1828 in the last of the original 13 colonies and strategically placed on the banks of the Chattahoochee River to take advantage of riverboat traffic. It later became home to Dr. John S. Pemberton. From his colonial-style residence, he began to create a formula which would later become known as Coca-Cola.

In 1918, Fort Benning was established nearby, introducing ethnic diversity to the third-largest city in the state of Georgia. It was a city that, by 1977, had found racial harmony in a once-torn South. In 1971, Columbus became the first consolidated government in the state and one of only 30 in the nation by combining the city of Columbus with Muscogee County, bringing further conformity to the city and her people. The promoter of the consolidation, J.R. Allen, became the first mayor of the consolidated government. He later died in a plane crash while returning from a speaking engagement in Rome, Georgia, where he had discussed the consolidation.

It was 1977. While President Nixon had been struggling to pull American troops out of Vietnam, his staff had been conspiring to send burglars into the Democratic National Headquarters in the Watergate Hotel. The subsequent scandal and the president's involvement in the attempted cover-up had cost him the presidency.

It also severely shook the faith of the American people in their government, and most particularly, in the Republican Party. Although Gerald Ford served as president for the remainder of Nixon's term, the first time voters had a say in the matter a Democrat from Georgia was elected President of the United States.

His name was James Earl Carter, but he became universally known as "Jimmy." He was in his first year as the nation's 39th president. It was when the rest of the nation learned of Plains, Georgia, and a gas station owner there named Billy whose brother was now the President. Billy was an outspoken, big-bellied beer

178

drinker the press loved exposing to the world.

It was also the year a young actress made her way into the master bathroom of Graceland in Memphis and learned that the "King" was dead. The nation, and a good portion of the world, was mourning the loss of a music legend, Elvis Aaron Presley.

The governor of Georgia was George Busbee. The mayor of Columbus was Jack Mickle; the sheriff was Jack Rutledge; and the chief of police was Curtis McClung.

Ferne Jackson was the director of the Columbus Health Department's education division. Her name was Mary Willis Jackson, but everyone knew her as Ferne. A dedicated public servant, she had spent years tackling the problems of smoking, premature marriages, and venereal disease among the youth of Columbus.

She became interested in health education in 1950, after helping the health department with a tuberculosis survey. She took graduate training in the field of health education and in 1951, after receiving a master's degree in her field, returned to Muscogee County to serve as health education director.

On September 16 employees at the Health Department became concerned when she did not arrive for work. Ferne never failed to show up for work. She was last seen the evening before when a friend had dropped her off at home after attending an education meeting at the Lutheran Church. Police were sent to Ferne's home by her fellow employees.

It was a modest but elegant brick home located at 2505 17th Street. The front of the home was locked and secure. Police approached the rear of the residence and followed the terra cotta tiles from the patio through a door they found to be unsecured into the living room of the immaculate, well-furnished home. They continued through the kitchen and down a hallway to the last bedroom on the left. There they found Ferne Jackson.

She was lying on her bed in her night clothes. The clothes she had worn the night before were neatly draped across the back of a chair near the dresser. The first sign of foul play was the nylon stocking wrapped around her neck. A pillow covered her face. An open window on the other side of the house was believed to be the entry point for the assailant. Her car was missing, but it was found later in the day about a mile from the crime scene.

Although the Columbus press reported that the bedroom had been ransacked, Columbus police detective Ronald Lynn later recalled it differently. "I wouldn't say that the room was ransacked," he said. "The only real sign that anything had been gone through was an open dresser drawer. We found it peculiar because there was a bank envelope containing money in the drawer that he would had to have seen." If the motive for the murder was burglary, as Lynn and the other detectives suspected, they could not understand why the money was not taken.

The city was furious over what appeared to be a senseless attack of a defenseless woman. Rage was expressed by friends and family over the loss of a such a devoted asset to the community. The Columbus press praised the public service of the slain health educator who had been scheduled to be named the National Health Educator of the Year by the American Public Health Association.

Dr. A. J. Kravtin, a friend and professional associate, wrote a letter in the editorial section in the following Sunday's Columbus Ledger-Enquirer expressing his frustration towards whomever committed the murder. The Columbus doctor wrote:

> *Ferne Jackson fought for the under-privileged, the minority groups and against poverty and for better mental health...We do not at this point know who perpetrated such a dastardly act of violence against Ferne, but if it turns out to be one of the above, they killed the wrong person. They killed a friend.*

The letter was just the beginning of a controversy over the race of the strangler. While in the home of Ferne Jackson, Detective Lynn found coarse black hairs. The hairs were not consistent with those of the victim, and Detective Lynn believed they had been left there by the strangler. He also believed they were the hairs of a black male. Leaders in the black community wanted stronger proof of the race of the strangler before his race was declared. No one wanted to believe that one of their own could commit such horrible crimes. City officials and those in command of the police department gave strict orders regarding racial sensitivity. Detectives were told not to discuss their beliefs about the race of the strangler.

Ronald Lynn became a policeman in 1965 at the age of 21. It was the first real job he ever had. His mother, Grace Johnson, had always been around policemen. She owned and operated *The Depot Coffee Shop* at the corner of 6th Avenue and 12th Street for all of Ronald's life.

In the days before the city consolidated, both county and city police would come in for coffee, food and conversation. The conversations she overheard through the years left her leery when her own son donned the grey and blue uniform of the Columbus police department. He worked in uniform patrol for the first year and a half, then did a stint on motor patrol working traffic on the streets of Columbus on a city-issued Harley Davidson. In the early 1970s, during the race riots, he was assigned to the detective division.

The race riots of the early 70s in Columbus were sort of a backlash to the civil rights movements of a decade earlier. There were those in the city who were not satisfied with the progress of attempts at non-violent social change. The resulting tensions, which often became violent, divided the city. By 1977, the bruises of a city once divided were still in the process of healing, even within the police department itself.

The strangling had occurred in the Wynnton Road area of the city, a racially mixed, upper-middle class neighborhood of fine homes and long-time Columbus families. Quiet streets wind through rolling hills of brick and stone homes of varying and unique A-frame designs with well-manicured, landscaped yards. The attack on Ferne Jackson had been an isolated incident, or so police first thought, in what was believed to be a stable neighborhood.

Police had taken a report of an attack on Hood Street in the same Wynnton area. Geraldine Moore† was in the hospital in critical condition, still recovering, and had not yet been able to describe her ordeal to police. It had occurred five days before the attack on Ms. Jackson.

———————————

182

Margaret Stevens and her husband lived on 21st Street, less than a mile from Ferne Jackson. Like everyone else in the neighborhood, she knew of the Jackson murder. On the Friday following the attack on Ms. Jackson, an intruder had broken into the Steven's screened porch and attempted entry into their home. A locked sliding glass door thwarted the attempt. Their neighbor, 71-year-old Jean Dimenstien, lived alone next door. Ms. Dimenstien visited the Stevens and asked about their near break-in. The Stevens told her about footprints in the sand behind their house, presumably left by the prowler. They had circled the prints for police.

On the morning of September 26, 1977, the magnitude of the problem became painfully clear. Margaret Stevens walked out her door that Sunday morning and saw her neighbor's door removed from the hinges and leaning against the brick carport wall. She knew what it meant the instant she saw it. The interior of her neighbor's home had been exposed to the cool fall morning air ... and to the strangler. "We guessed the inevitable when we saw the door leaned up like that," she told The Columbus Enquirer later in the day.

Responding police found the Stevens' neighbor, Jean Dimenstien, murdered, lying on a twin bed, dressed in her night clothes, with a nylon stocking wrapped around her neck. Her purse was on a kitchen table — untouched. If there had been any doubt before, it had now been decisively erased: There was a serious problem in the Columbus neighborhood known as the Wynnton district.

In the 1830s, a land owner named Colonel William L. Wynn built a spacious Doric-columned mansion as his home. Although Wynn eventually moved on to Louisiana to run a sugar plantation, the Wynn House remained as the foundation of an upper class colony of the well-to-do in an area of Columbus which came to be known as Wynnton. One of the early pioneers responsible for the development of the Wynnton area was real estate developer John F. Flournoy. Flournoy was born in Wynnton and knew the beauty of its rolling hills. In 1887, with the help of Savannah investors, he developed it into the sprawling community which, after the turn of the century, would come to be known among some in Columbus as "A Colony of Millionaires."

Green Jefferson Jordan (pronounced Jerdan) operated "Jordan's Meat Market" in the area of Sixth Avenue and Eleventh Street. Jordan's was a grocery store which specialized in meats and delivered the finer cuts — hind quarters which supplied the richer beef steaks — to the wealthy people of Wynnton. Jordan's son Vernon delivered the meat by wagon. The business had flourished for a while due to these deliveries.

But Jordan's also had been selling meat on credit to railroad workers, attempting to carry them through the Great Depression. When the nation's economy plummeted, their inability to pay their bills put Jordan's out of business. He was one of many small business owners who were about to suffer as Columbus and America approached the hardest economic times ever known to the young nation. Although the residents of Wynnton had little or nothing to do with the plight of the smaller businessmen and workers suffering through those times, there was still evidence of resentment towards the people of the neighborhood who came to be known as "The Wynntonites."

A month after the stock market crash in October of 1929 a new publication went into print in Columbus. Saturday Evening announced in its first edition that it would not be a daily, and probably not even a weekly publication but would be "Issued on such Saturday Evenings as the Publisher and Public elect." The very first edition on November 30, 1929, was aimed entirely at the "Wynntonites". Publisher W.C. Woodall had intended for the first headline to be "The Millionaires' Colony — in which the Awful Truth Comes Out at Last on the Rich Wynntonites." The headline of the expected first issue was announced publicly and there was an immediately backlash from the distinguished men of Wynnton.

The headline was changed and the first page of the publication was almost entirely about the title and the reason for its change. The headline and first article read as follows:

The Millionaires' Colony
A Somewhat Intimate Study of the Rich Wynntonites

Change of Title --- and Why

The title first proposed for the initial issue of this publication was: "The Millionaires' Colony" — in which the Awful Truth Comes Out at Last on the Rich Wynntonites.

Scarcely had this been publicly announced before there came vague rumblings of apprehension and discontent. This uneasy feeling crystallized two or three days later in the receipt of a communication from various esteemed and highly respected citizens of Wynnton (and by that we mean the entire Eastern section of the city). Coming from such a representative collection of Rich Wynntonites, the

185

communication speaks for itself:

To the Publisher of SATURDAY EVENING —
Sir: You will, we are sure, receive this letter exactly
in the spirit in which it is written. We are peaceful
men, and don't want to start anything; also, we don't
want you to start anything.

The expression advertised in the public prints... 'In
Which the Awful Truth Comes Out at Last On the
Rich Wynntonites,' in connection with the subject
matter of the first issue of your new publication, is
possibly a little ambiguous and might be misconstrued
by the thoughtless or careless reader. (Note from the
Editor to the Committee: Our readers, dear sirs, are
neither thoughtless nor careless.)

Personally we are opposed to ambiguity, and think
that everything should be set forth in a clear-cut
manner that would leave no room for
misunderstanding or impressions that should be at
variance to any degree from the exact truth.

Frankly, we don't know just what you have in
mind. We know in our souls that we are innocent. No
truthful so-called expose' could affect us in the
slightest, we have no secrets, our lives are as an open
book. We are quite sure that the other citizens of
Wynnton are equally blameless but of course in
making detailed report can speak only for ourselves.

However, we do not believe that any promiscuous
rambling around in search of family skeletons or what
you might call just exuberances (sic) of human nature
as manifested (possibly indiscreetly at times) would be
a profitable undertaking. We are quite sure — we are
dead sure — that you would not dig up anything. So

why try? Understand, we are not speaking in behalf of ourselves, it is only a general goodwill movement we are sponsoring.

Why not tone down and modify your title? Or even get a new title? Personally, we are of course of the truth, even though the heavens fall. But who wants the heavens to fall? There has already been too much falling here of late, although of course we do not refer to stocks.   Respectfully,

J.E. Humes	Walter Byrd
Burrel C. Cole	W.C. Davidson
S.K. Dimon	H.R. McClatchey
Rev. G.N. Rainey	F.U. Garrard
A.J. Little	Dr. J.M. Baird
W.J. Rice	C.J. Swift
J.J. Pease	D.T. Sullenberger
T.O. Ott	J. Wodfin Woodruff
C.T. McDonald	L.G. Bowers

The letter did little to tone down the anti-rich rhetoric of the publication. The same front page had the following explanation box:

Abbreviations Used

Kindly keep in mind the following abbreviations used in this issue — it will save you time:

R.W.: "Rich Wynntonite"
V.W.W.: "Very Wealthy Wynntonite"
R.I.W.: "Rolling in Wealth"

C.E.C.I.: "Can't Even Count It"

Despite the obvious resentments expressed in some of the writings, others in the same publication accentuate the positive aspects of the neighborhood "on the hill." An article on page 10 titled "The Main Street Millionaires: A Cross-Section of the Rich Wynntonites" began with:

> Wynnton Drive, the Main Street of Wynnton, may be considered in its engaging personnel as a typical cross-section of The Millionaires' Colony. Wherefore, let us consider the high order of human beings who inhabit it. What is here put down in truth and soberness is written in that spirit of vast respect which a Rich Wynntonite naturally engenders. Here we have talent, bank books as big as dictionaries, human nature in sheer exuberance, nobility of character, and even a few instances of personal pulchritude.

On the previous page an article written by A.W. Cozart (who was himself from Wynnton) points out the prominent men of Georgia who lived in Wynnton. Four former Speakers of the Georgia House of Representatives had lived in Wynnton: William A. Little, Louis F. Garrard, John D. Little and W. Cecil Neill. Three of the four not only lived in Wynnton but were born there. Little also later served as a Georgia Supreme Court justice, and Neill was president of the State Senate.

The 1929 publication, which advertised bottles of Milk of Magnesia for 37 cents and 1930 Chevrolet Roadsters for $525, seemed to sometimes challenge, sometimes champion, the rich and elite of Wynnton.

Almost a half-a-century later, in 1977, most of the citizens of Columbus appreciated the contributions made by the people of Wynnton. But it was also painfully obvious that someone appeared to harbor deep animosity towards the women of Wynnton. A hatred so deep that the women were forced to suffer the ultimate degradations of humanity before their deaths.

Born in Philadelphia, Jean Dimenstien had lived alone in Columbus for 35 years, the last 23 spent in a modest brick home at 3027 21ˢᵗ St. She was retired and in declining health. In her prime she had co-owned and helped operate Fred and Jean's Department Store with her brother, Fred. She had spent the prior evening dining out with two of her friends at a steakhouse on Macon Road, just a mile from the Wynnton neighborhood.

She had made plans with one of them to have coffee and a snack the following day. They heard her latch the lock on the door as they left that night. It was to no avail. Whoever had installed that door had left the hinge pins exposed to the outside allowing anyone who would bother, the opportunity to remove the pins, then the door and make entry. Someone had done just that.

The following day, the citizens of Columbus read in their Monday paper shocking details and ominous preclusions by their county coroner, J. Donald Kilgore. Kilgore told the Columbus Ledger that autopsy reports revealed that both Ferne Jackson and Jean Dimenstien had been sexually assaulted before being killed. Kilgore said he believed the women were violated with "some sort of inflexible

189

object" and sexually tortured before their death while a pillow was held over their faces. Both women were reported to have been struck in the face. Both of the women's cars were stolen and abandoned less than a mile away.

"The motive is torture...and murder," Kilgore proclaimed to the Columbus newpaper. If the elderly women of Wynnton were not already in a panic before reading their afternoon paper, they were certain to have been after putting it down.

The Cross Country Plaza shopping mall was only a block away from the scene of the murder. The hardware section of the J.C. Penney store there quickly sold out of locks and deadbolts. The press reported that many of the residents of the neighborhood were arming themselves. It was reported that at one local gathering the women emptied their purses onto the floor, spilling the guns they all now owned.

Two other women reported that their doorbells had been rung at 2 a.m. on the same morning that Ferne Jackson was murdered. People throughout the neighborhood were telling the press they had recently been bothered by prowlers.

Columbus had become a city in distress, and the elderly citizens pleaded for a quick resolution. Even though the Jewish Orthodox tradition did not countenance autopsy or embalmment, Jean Dimenstien's rabbi, Theodore Feldman, consented for the body to be removed to the morgue for an autopsy after he performed a short ceremony at the scene of the crime — where Ms. Dimenstien's body still lay on her bed. Rabbi Feldman told police that "anything which could help authorities find her killer was allowed."

Geraldine Moore recovered enough to tell police that she too had been beaten, sexually assaulted, strangled and left for dead. Even though she was the first to have been attacked in the neighborhood, she had been the luckiest of the three: She had survived. She told police her attacker was a black male.

Columbus Police Chief Curtis McClung canceled all off days for the 45 men and women assigned to the police department's detective division. Stakeouts were arranged throughout the Wynnton area. Marked and unmarked patrol cars combed the neighborhood. Undercover police officers were hidden inside the homes of elderly residents who were thought to be the most likely targets.

On October 2, 1977, police got what they believed to be the break they had been looking for. Jerome Livas was arrested for the rape and beating death of Beatrice Brier, a 55-year-old woman who did not live in the Wynnton Road area. The press described Brier as Livas' girlfriend.

On October 14, 1977, authorities announced that Livas was officially a suspect in the Wynnton Road stranglings. The case was being turned over to the district attorney's office for presentment to the grand jury. The press got word that the suspect had confessed to the murders of both Ferne Jackson and Jean Dimenstien.

The stakeouts in the Wynnton Road area were called off. Residents in the neighborhood breathed a sigh of relief. Residents like Florence Sheible, who lived alone in an upstairs apartment at 1941 Dimon St.

She lived, basically, a lonely life, but this was her time of year. The season of her favorite pastime — baseball and the World Series. She knew all the players, their batting averages, and what positions each played. She would take time out each day to sit and listen to the games.

She was only 10 days away from her 90th birthday. It didn't matter that it was the middle of the day. He didn't have to sneak up on her because she was almost blind. He didn't have to chase her, because she was confined to a four-legged walker which the neighbors in the apartment below said she always scooted across the floor when she walked. He threw her down on her bed, struck her about the face, sexually assaulted her, then wrapped a stocking around her neck and strangled her.

On October 21 at 2:30 in the afternoon her son found her on her back in the bed, a pillow covering her face, and a stocking still wrapped around her neck. Neighbors had seen her earlier that morning. The time of death was estimated to be around 11 a.m.

The scores of police investigators working the case, and the entire City of Columbus, were devastated. The nightmare they had hoped was over was not. The strangling had occurred while law enforcement's main suspect, Jerome Livas — the man who had confessed to previous stranglings — was locked in jail.

The similarity of the strangling of Florence Scheible to the other stranglings severely diminished the viability of Livas as a suspect. It was diminished even further after a local reporter conducted a jailhouse interview with Livas in the presence of his attorney. During that interview, Livas signed a written confession to several murders — that of John F. Kennedy in 1963, William McKinley in 1901, and prior knowledge of the Lindbergh kidnaping and murder in 1932. One press report called Livas "a borderline idiot."

Three days later, on October 25, while Livas was still in jail accused now of only the death of his girlfriend, the Stocking Strangler struck again. There could be no remaining doubt about the strangler — he was still out there.

They stood trembling in the rain clinging to each other. Their street was filled with police, television cameras, the innocently curious and frightened, and those roving the crowd with a not-so-innocent curiosity.

Their eyes were filled with genuine tears. "Oh my God!" one exclaimed to another — "It's Martha, it's Martha." They talked among themselves — or so they thought. "Martha said we'd just have to wait and pray it wouldn't be us next." But Martha had been next.

Then they realized that one among them was not a neighbor but a reporter with the city newspaper. A member of the press who might expose their fears and vulnerability in print to the killer himself. "Oh God! Please don't use my name. I'm so frightened." She stared at the house as she trembled and cried. One of them turned to walk away but stopped and looked back at the house one more time. "I'm getting out of Columbus," she said. "I won't spend another night in this town."

The reporter in the crowd was Beverly Greer, the Living Today Editor for The Columbus Enquirer. She did what they asked of her — secured their names to the anonymity they requested — and wrote a gripping story for the October 26 edition of the Enquirer that captured the fear of the city and its people.

Their city had lost four women. The fourth victim was Martha Thurmond. The 69-year-old retired school teacher had been expected at her mother-in-law's house where she was to sit with her for the day. When she didn't arrive, a niece had gone to check on Martha. When she did not answer the door, police were summoned.

They found her strangled in a fashion similar to the other three women. She taught school, the second and fourth grade at Ridgon Road Elementary, for 19 years until her retirement. She lived alone after the death of her husband in their home at 2614 Marion St, within one mile of the other victims.

This time Coroner Kilgore realized the need to stop releasing so many clues to the press. On the morning Martha's body was found, he told the Columbus Enquirer, "She was strangled, but that's all I'm gonna say because we don't want to give away too many clues. People have been finding out too much about the details of the crime." But Kilgore's earlier statements about the women being tortured made imaginations run wild each time another victim was found.

The State of Georgia earlier had offered a $5,000 reward for the arrest of the strangler. The consolidated government of Columbus had matched that $5,000. After the fourth body was found, an anonymous donor came forward with another $5,000. There was now a $15,000 bounty on the head of the man no one could seem to find except those who desperately needed to elude him.

Gov. George Busbee told the press, "This reign of terror in Columbus must be stopped in its tracks and I'm offering these rewards as the maximum allowable under the law." He also offered the city the assistance of the Georgia Bureau of Investigation.

It was October 25, 1977. Columbus police were faced with the startling realization that the Wynnton area, and the rest of the city, would soon be filled with hundreds of masked people roaming the streets of Columbus. Halloween was just six days away.

Mayor Jack Mickle began making appearances on local television stations. He told the city, "On the recommendation of our responsible law enforcement authorities, I am asking that the traditional 'trick or treat' Halloween activities be terminated not later than 6 p.m. on Monday evening." Virtually every generation in Columbus was being affected by the fear of one man — somewhere in the city — who preyed on the weakest within the population.

The people of the Wynnton Road area who did not flee their homes locked themselves behind dead bolts and burglar bars. The balloon of confidence they should have enjoyed with this extra security had burst with the murder of Martha Thurmond. Martha Thurmond had done everything the police said to do: dead bolts;

194

windows nailed shut with burglar bars attached. But still he found a way inside. Police never were able to determine how.

Then came an uneasy period of peace. For the next two months no one else was killed. There was varying speculation about where he had gone. Had he been arrested? Had he gone away? Or was the answer simply that, for a short while, he had gotten a job? A night job that allowed no time for prowling the neighborhoods of Wynnton.

Golden's Foundries was a foundry and machine company in the Linwood area of Columbus. On November 14, 1977, they hired a 28-year-old black male who used the name Michael Anthony David. He was hired to work a night shift which ran from 8 p.m. to 4:30 a.m.

His attendance was good for most of the first month. Then, in early December an unexcused absence, then a few days later another. A few days later he failed to report for work two days in a row. On December 20, 1977, Michael Anthony David was dismissed from Golden's Foundries for excessive absenteeism. On that same day there was a burglary at the William Swift residence at 1710 Buena Vista Road — in the Wynnton area.

George C. Woodruff Sr. was an industrialist and former football coach at the University of Georgia. He lived with his wife Kathleen at 1811 Buena Vista Road until his death. The Woodruff family was a well-known and highly respected. Their only son, George Jr., served for a while as the president of the Columbus Chamber of Commerce. The Woodruff name had been synonymous with Wynnton since the turn of the century, even appearing on the infamous letter written by the men of Wynnton in 1929 responding to "The Millionaires'

195

Colony" article.

After George Sr.'s death, Kathleen lived alone in their home in the Wynnton area. She was 74 years old. She celebrated her last Christmas there in 1977. Three days later she was found raped and strangled her home. The strangler was back.

Kathleen's death was a shock to the community. It was now unmistakably clear — nothing and no one was sacred to the strangler, no matter how big the name. The Columbus press wrote of Mrs. Woodruff's death:

> Few events in the history of the neighborhood — or of the city, for that matter — have produced a reaction more profound than the murder of Mrs. Woodruff. Mrs. Thurmond had been known throughout the neighborhood, but Mrs. Woodruff — wealthy, socially prominent, known for her interest in education and charitable causes, gracious to all who knew her — was a symbol of everything the people of Wynnton cherished. It was as if the killer had stuck a knife into the heart of the neighborhood.

A year of terror had barely ended, and a new year was just beginning. Then police learned the problems in the Wynnton area were not over. Abraham and Virginia Illges were an affluent elderly couple who lived at 2021 Brookside Drive. On New Year's Day someone broke into their home and took, among other things, one of their cars. The car was later recovered at the Motel 6 on Victory Drive, a major road through Columbus.

Detective Ronald Lynn was now part of a task force working the strangler cases. The task force was comprised of officers of the Georgia State Patrol, the Georgia Bureau of Investigation and the Columbus Police Department. The task force was headed by Deputy Commander James B. Hicks and Director Ronald A. Jones. The task force was called "The Stocking Strangler Detail," but many of the investigators at that time were calling the suspect "The Chattahoochee Choker."

Ruth Schwob had always been a courageous woman. She was the wife of Simon Schwob, founder of Schwob Manufacturing Company, established in 1912. Schwob manufacturing made men's suits and distributed them to 40 stores in Georgia. When Simon passed away in 1954, Ruth was left as president of a company she had seldom participated in running. She had never even been in the shop. She ran it successfully, though, for 20 years after her husband's death. In 1966, she was named woman of the year in Columbus.

In 1976, she sold the company and retired a wealthy woman but continued an active life, involving herself in civic and cultural activities throughout the community. She raised, almost single handedly, more than a half-million dollars for the fine arts building at Columbus College. She had never met Lynn, but soon she would. On February 11, 1978, she would experience the most desperate struggle of her life.

It would be another night of Wynnton surveillance for Detective Lynn and the partner with whom he rode, Robert Matthews. Lining the winding neighborhood streets were a series of seemingly never-ending, expensive homes positioned on rolling hills behind lush thick shrubberies and surrounded by the occasional white picket fence. Although some of the more elegant homes were situated on lots as large as two or three acres, there were very few open spaces due to the well-established landscapes. Thick magnolia and willow trees with limbs that drape to the ground, along with plump fern shrubbery, cloaked the windows on the lower levels of many of the homes.

It was not a bitterly cold February night, but it was cold — too cold for the sounds of crickets or chirping birds and the other sounds of warmer nights. The silence was broken only by the occasional sound of barking dogs in the distance.

The eerie feeling that he would strike that night came with the first call at 3:50 a.m. Someone jammed the front doorbell button at a home on Carter Avenue. The bell was still ringing when police arrived. No one could be located in the area.

There were two alarms that night. The first one came at 5:15 a.m. With the cover of darkness, cloaked by surrounding shrubbery, he entered a basement window. He opened cabinet drawers and closets. Then he climbed the stairs towards the living quarters of the home. At the top of the stairs he found a locked door. Peering through the skeletal keyhole he saw that the key was inserted in the door on the other side. He slid a piece of paper under the door and then pushed the key out the other side, hoping it would drop on the paper which he could retrieve from under the door. The key missed and did not land on the paper. He went back down the stairs and climbed back out the basement window. None of this activated the alarm.

It was the Illges' residence again — the home burglarized on New Year's Day. After the first burglary, police had installed a C.A.R.E.S. alarm. It was a program that had existed in the department before the stranglings began. Named the Columbus

198

Armed Robbery Enforcement System, it was an alarm connected directly to the police department radio system. When activated it would immediately broadcast an alarm code on the radio. Dispatchers would then broadcast the address the code represented. It was the quickest possible way for an alarm to summon police.

He found a ladder on the back of the Illges' pool house. He carried it to the north side of the house, climbed to the window and pried it open. The C.A.R.E.S. alarm was not connected to this window either. He entered the second floor of the residence, walked across the floor and stepped on a rug at the door. Under the rug was a pad which *was* connected to the alarm. Police arrived to find the two windows open on the north side of the house, but the intruder was gone. As they surveyed the scene of the Illges' burglary a call came over the radio — the second alarm.

It was 5:44 a.m. The address was 1800 Carter Ave. It was just around the corner. Detectives Lynn and Matthews jumped into their blue Ford LTD II and drove the block and a half to the alarm call. They both had become extensively familiar with the neighborhood and its potential victims. They knew exactly which house they should go to. It was the home of Ruth Schwob.

It was a neat, well-constructed brick home which appeared modest compared to others nearby. Despite the darkness they could see the open window. It was not the kind of window that raised up or down but one that swung out when opened. The design was intended to allow the maximum flow of cool morning air, but not the coldness of that early February morning. There was an air-conditioning unit under the window that, when stood on, provided an easy entrance.

During night after night of endless surveillance, Matthews and Lynn had encountered several open windows that meant nothing. Initially they were not aware that it was important or urgent.

Then suddenly, the urgency was immediately obvious. Their first sensation was apprehension...maybe even a moment of fright — not for themselves because they knew they were okay — but for her. Then there was quick excitement. The silence had been broken by a muffled scream and then a gasping of breath, followed by a gurgling sound coming from inside the home. Ronald Lynn thought to himself, "He's in there; he's strangling Mrs. Schwob."

Lynn motioned for officers running up the driveway to surround the house. "Don't let him get out!" he told them. He stepped up on the air-conditioner and went through the window, quickly followed by Matthews. Once inside the dark house they pulled their guns and began to make their way towards the screams which by now had been reduced to moans. First through the kitchen, then down the hallway checking the bedrooms, not wanting to let him slip by them. Wanting to be quick, but needing to be careful.

"We moved as quickly as we could, but we didn't want to round a corner in the dark and have him stick a knife in us," Lynn remembered. "We really thought we had him. I remember thinking we were probably going to have to kill him, and it was going to be over — this was going to be it." They were wrong. He was gone. Officers had failed to surround the home quickly enough.

They found Ruth Schwob in a bedroom on the front of the house, in her bed with a stocking around her neck. Lynn reached down and loosened the stocking. As soon as the stocking was loose she rolled over and began vomiting. She had survived.

"This joker was moving around at will." Lynn later recalled. "It seemed the more we did to catch him the easier it was for him to move around." The officers surrounding the house saw nothing but a neighbor who reported seeing a man run through his yard. The ambulance which was called for Mrs. Schwob reported that a man had run across the road in front of the ambulance a little more than a block from the residence. Both witnesses that night reported the fleeing man they saw was black.

200

Ruth Schwob did not have a C.A.R.E.S. alarm. Her alarm system did not connect to the police radio dispatch and alert all officers of its activation. It was a simple button attached to the side of her bed — connected with one simple wire led to the bedroom of her next-door neighbor, Dr. Fred Burdette. A homemade alarm had saved her life.

Dr. Burdette told police that as soon as the alarm sounded he called Mrs. Schwob and when she did not immediately answer he called the police, then dressed himself and went outside. The police were so close that they arrived as he exited his home barefooted to check on his neighbor. The press reported the following day that radio logs showed that police response time had been two minutes.

After realizing that the intruder was no longer in the Schwob home, police had summoned tracking bloodhounds and a helicopter. An extensive search of the Wynnton area was conducted with no success.

Mrs. Schwob told the police, and later the press, her chilling story of survival. "I just awakened and he was there," she explained. "He was on the bed and had his hand on my throat and then he wrapped pantyhose all around...He never uttered a sound."

The press reported that Ruth Schwob, 74, walked or jogged daily. Her physical fitness, which was no doubt intended to extend her life, had done so in a way she never expected. The fitness level which she enjoyed, and other victims had not, had allowed her to fight off her attacker until police arrived.

———————————————

Police continued to be frustrated over their inability to protect the women of Wynnton. The survival of Ruth Schwob was seen as a moderate success amidst what had been, up to this point, total failure. But the strangler was still out there. Task Force Director Ronald Jones told the press the task force was "trying to outguess [the strangler]." "We're on the defense and he's on the offense," Jones told the hounding press.

Just days before the early morning attack on Ruth Schwob, 10 additional two-person patrol units had been added in the area. The following week was to have been the first week since Christmas that investigators would receive one day off. After the Schwob attack the planned off-days were canceled. An entire police force of dedicated men and women were struggling to defend a neighborhood from a seemingly unstoppable nightmare.

The latest attack at the Schwob residence, which happened early Saturday morning, was just one block from the first attack at the home of Ferne Jackson. That Saturday night, just one block further south, he struck again. The press speculated he was frustrated at having failed to claim a sixth victim. Within 24 hours he *had* claimed his sixth victim.

It was Sunday morning, February 12, 1978. Most of the members of the task force were gathered at their headquarters in the basement of the Columbus Government Center. At 11:55 a.m., they burst out the doors and headed for their cars.

Their destination was 1612 Forrest Ave., the home of a 78-year-old widow named Mildred Dismukes Borom. Relatives had reported that they were unable to reach Mrs. Borom, who lived alone in the Wynnton neighborhood. Jones, director of the task force, forced entry into the brick home. He found her in the hallway. Wrapped around her neck was a Venetian-blind cord. It had been cut from a window inside the home. There were obvious signs that she had fought back, including a broken lamp near her feet.

Investigators were baffled at how he had entered the home. The only sign of attempted entry was a broken window on the front of the home, but the hole did not appear large enough for a person to fit through. Investigators first believed the window had been broken to allow it to be unlocked and opened, but further examination revealed the window was secured shut by screws that were undisturbed.

The screws had been installed by a workman sent to the home by Mrs. Borom's son, Perry Borom, Jr. He had that very morning discussed his mother's safety with his boss, George Woodruff Jr. "I'm worried about your mama," Woodruff had told Borom. No one understood the need to protect a parent on that morning more than Woodruff. His own mother Kathleen, had been the fifth victim of the strangler.

It was an ironic twist of fate. George Woodruff Jr., was the chairman of the board of the Woodruff-Brown Company. Perry Borom Jr., was vice president of the company. Both men lost their mothers to the strangler.

Ronald Jones had been the task force director since its inception. Before the stranglings he had been the director of the robbery/homicide squad. Since September, he had lived and breathed the strangler case. After looking at Mildred Borom's body, the months of pressure, personal responsibility, and constant failure, all came crashing down on him. He walked to another room in the house and began openly sobbing. Luther Miller, an officer serving since 1966, also had been on the task force since it was first formed. He was in the Borom home when Ronald Jones viewed Mrs. Borom's molested body for the first time. "Ronald had begun to take it personally. He felt like it was his responsibility to stop the strangler," Miller later remembered. "He had... we all had been working day and night trying to protect these women. He started thinking it was his fault each time one was found dead. He was just taking it all too personal. It was just an emotional breakdown — Chief McClung decided he needed a break." The Columbus police chief ordered that Jones be transported to the hospital for an examination. The press reported that Jones was suffering from exhaustion. Chief McClung told the Columbus Enquirer, "He's been working real hard and long hours since September." Miller took over supervision of the task force during Jones' absence.

It was obvious the city was in trouble. The Columbus Enquirer made a desperate plea to the people to protect the women in the Wynnton area. They even raised the possibility of calling in the National Guard. The editorial, printed February 13, 1978, read as follows:

TIME TO ACT

The strangler must not be invited to strike again.

If Columbus cannot outwit the strangler or stranglers, at least we can protect our elderly women. We can take measures to see that no women live alone in the Wynnton area as long as this threat hangs over our city.

It will not be easy or convenient, but it can be done. It must be done, if we are to avoid more tragedies.

Many women who live alone have relatives who can temporarily take them in or who can live with them or stay with them at night. Others have friends and fellow church members who can see that they are

204

not alone.

For women who cannot leave their homes or do not have relatives or friends to stay with them, there are churches, civic groups and individuals who stand ready to extend that service. If their numbers are insufficient, we believe the City of Columbus and the State of Georgia should provide whatever guards are needed to see that no woman is left alone in the target area.

If necessary, the National Guard should be used.

The Ledger and Enquirer newspapers stand ready to assist the city and state in publicizing and coordinating an effort to provide protection for every woman who needs it.

The other major objective, of course, is to find and apprehend the killer or killers.

Any bits of information which could relate to the tragedies should be shared with police without delay. Special numbers for the task force are being published regularly, and there is a reward for information leading to arrest of the strangler.

If anyone has information, but is hesitant to contact police directly, the Ledger and Enquirer will relay it to police. Information may be mailed to Investigation Desk, P.O. Box 711, Columbus, or called to 322-8831.

The first priority, though, is to protect our live-alone women — beginning now.

The same issue of The Columbus Enquirer reported on a series of burglaries which had taken place in the Wynnton area during the same time period as the stranglings. The article speculated on whether there was a connection between the crimes.

In a case which seemingly couldn't get more complicated, in early February of 1978 it suddenly, frustratingly, became more complicated for Police Chief Curtis McClung. He received a letter claiming to be from a group calling themselves the "Forces of Evil."

The letter claimed that the "Forces of Evil" was a vigilante group of seven persons, originating in Chicago, who intended to seek revenge for the what the letter referred to as the "S-Strangler."

The letter stated a belief that the killer was black and gave police a deadline of June 1, or as the letter put it, 1 June, to catch the strangler. The letter threatened to kill a black woman in retaliation. The letter claimed that a woman named Gail Jackson already had been kidnaped and was being held for just such a purpose.

Gail Jackson, a black female, was reportedly a prostitute from the bar district which catered to the military personnel of nearby Fort Benning. Police learned more about her as they began to investigate the letters, but the most notable thing they learned was that she was missing.

Subsequent "Forces of Evil" letters to police demanded a $10,000 ransom. A police force already stretched thin by the strangler investigation became stretched even further as they now were working the strangler cases and the "Forces of Evil" case simultaneously. In late March they turned to the Federal Bureau of

Investigation for help on the new twist in the case.

Through the Georgia Bureau of Investigation, the Columbus Police Department sought the assistance of an F.B.I. unit that was just finding its niche in the fight against serial crimes in America. It was the Behavioral Science Unit located at the F.B.I. training facility in Quantico, Virginia. They had begun a program they called profiling. The unit was run by F.B.I. Agent John Douglas, who later co-authored the best-selling book, *Mindhunter,* in which Douglas summarizes the Columbus "Forces of Evil" case.

On March 31, 1978, the Behavioral Sciences Unit at Quantico received the official request to examine the case and came to some startling conclusions. They felt the author, or authors, of the "Forces of Evil" letters was not seven white men, but more likely one black man. The profilers believed he probably already killed Gail Jackson and that the letters were intended to divert attention away from the real killer. The profile predicted him to be an artilleryman or military policeman. An excerpt in the letter which stated, "the victims will double" led profilers to believe that he may already have also killed two other women. The profilers believed he would be 25 to 30 years old and, because of the poorly written letters, probably not an officer. They also believed that he might be the stocking strangler.

After the profile was distributed in the Fort Benning area a suspect was developed with an eerie resemblance to the profile — William H. Hance, a black, 26-year-old artilleryman at Fort Benning. Hance eventually confessed to having written the "Forces of Evil" letter. He also confessed to being a serial killer. His victims had been Gail Jackson, Irene Thirkield, and Karen Hickman. All were killed in the Fort Benning area — none were considered to be victims of the stocking strangler. Nothing implicated Hance in the Wynnton area stranglings.

As obviously precarious as pull-overs are to police patrolmen, they inevitably become mundane to the average veteran officer. Even though every police officer is aware that with each traffic stop one never knows who one may come in contact with, pullovers still become monotonous after so many are performed uneventfully. It was April 10, 1978. It was just another routine pullover. The orange Volkswagen had committed a minor traffic infraction. Columbus Police Officer Larry Mitchell walked up to the vehicle, and the driver identified himself as Michael David, but that was a lie. Mitchell wrote the man a ticket and let him go. He didn't know at the time that he had what every policeman in the City of Columbus wanted. He had the Columbus Stocking Strangler.

Sixty-seven days went by with no stranglings. Radio stations would announce each morning — 61 days with no stranglings, 62, then 63. It was as if he was being challenged to return.

Sixty-one-year-old Janet Cofer was a first grade school teacher at Dimon Elementary School. She was not afraid to live alone. She didn't live in the Wynnton area, but a mile and a half further away on Steam Mill Road in south Columbus. She had her dog, Buffy, a dachshund that always slept under her bed, and her son, Mike, who stayed with her on and off, so she did not feel quite as threatened as many of her friends. There was one other reason for Janet Cofer to feel a little safer. She lived directly across the street from Sgt. Charles Golden, a Columbus police officer.

She did, however, attend church in the Wynnton area and was well aware of the plight of her friends at Wynnton United Methodist Church. In October, the church held a prayer vigil and more than 100 people attended, including many elderly women.

Her courage notwithstanding, her neighbor, veterinarian F. T. Sutton, and his son still felt it necessary to run a buzzer into her kitchen which would sound in the Sutton home. They had intended to run it into her bedroom but never got around to it.

Her bedroom is where he found her and made her his next victim. On April 20, 1978, Chief McClung told The Columbus Enquirer that Janet Cofer was found on her bed strangled with some sort of cloth. McClung described the slaying as having followed "the exact method of operation of the other six stranglings." He had forced entry to the home through a window on the front of the home. There were no signs of a struggle. She had apparently not been alerted to his presence until it was too late. Her dog, Buffy, had been struck and killed by a car two weeks earlier. Her son, Mike, had stayed with family in Dallas, Ga, that night. The buzzer in Dr. Sutton's home had never sounded.

When she failed to show up for work at Dimon Elementary School, Sally Mitchell, a youth aid officer for the Columbus Police Department, went to her home to investigate. She climbed through the open window and discovered the body.

Mrs. Cofer had attended choir practice at her church the night before. She had been preparing the music for an upcoming talent show. She went home alone at around 9:30 p.m. She had refused friends' offers to follow her home.

Jackson: 9/15/77   Dimenstein: 9/25/77   Scheible: 10/21/77

Thurmond: 10/25/77   Woodruff: 12/27/77   Cofer: 4/20/78

Columbus Ledger-Enquirer. Reprinted with permission.

By 1978 Celestine Sibley had been a reporter for The Atlanta Constitution and later The Atlanta Journal-Constitution for 37 years. She went to Columbus to cover the strangling story and interview some of the women of the Wynnton area. On April 24, 1978, she wrote a column that captured the plight of the detectives working on the task force:

A FEELING OF
FRUSTRATION IN COLUMBUS

As an old murder mystery fan I may have more sympathy than some for detectives. Police officers caught up in a hideous life-and-death puzzle like the one which is driving law enforcement officers in Columbus crazy these days, are sometimes very appealing to me. Women, kind, good women, the mothers and grandmothers of some fine citizens, have been brutally killed — killings which have been repeated six times in the last eight months.

The detectives, local officers and the state's GBI officers, have set up a fantastic network for gathering information and catching the murderer. Some of them work night and day. Some haven't seen their wives and children except for a few minutes every week or so. All of them are bombarded with questions, a few impatient jibes and nut calls and now snide accusations that a police officer might be the murderer.

Plodding Along

And they plod along patiently, watching the rising cost of trying — but not succeeding — to protect innocent citizens. They know a lot but not enough, and if they fail, another woman may die.

The other morning in a snack shop

211

in the tall, government building in downtown Columbus we had a cup of coffee with a young GBI agent named Horace Waters, a hollow-eyed fellow who had been up most of the night with his senior, Agent Jimmy Davis, investigating the death of Janet Cofer, a 61-year old school teacher.

He drank his coffee and talked very little about the case, but shot through everything he said was a thread of sadness for the victim and her family, a humble awareness that he and his fellow officers had not been wise enough or quick enough or lucky enough to get to the killer before he got to Mrs. Cofer.

Later, in a little conference room, Chief Curtis McClung held his regular mid-morning session with the press. He entered the room flanked by the department's public information officer, David Hopkins, and Assistant Chief R.H. Matthews. An amiable looking gentleman with gray hair and a gray moustache, the chief smiled and nodded at the reporters he knew and sat down. He said there were "no new significant developments" in the Cofer case but wearily added that "all characteristics are the same...there are many similarities."

Unanswerable Questions

And then he invited questions. There were a lot of them and the chief frequently replied that he didn't know the answers or that he couldn't give out information about evidence. But he was polite and patient, even when some of the questions got waspish and hostile — the if-you-don't-protect-us-why-not? type.

He said money from the governor and new contingents of state officers would help widen the perimeter around the Wynnton neighborhood, where all but the last killing took place. In answer to questions about the reward for the strangler's arrest, he said it now totals around $100,000, but this case is one which apparently does not turn on money. So far as the officers will say, the murderer takes nothing and the people who might know him have not shown that they are interested to try for the reward.

"This killer is careful," the chief said tiredly. "He's very careful."

The only hope Columbus citizens have is that the law enforcement authorities are careful, too. They have devised many new methods and they

213

have called on all the scientific
resources available, but Chief
McClung still believes that plodding,
unglamourous, routine policing will
get him yet.

As with every murder that does not find quick resolution, rumors began to permeate the population. Another column written by Sibley addressed one of the rumors floating around at the time:

Fear in Columbus

COLUMBUS — The brutal killing
of four elderly Columbus women
which has turned this city on the
Chattahoochee into an armed camp "is
the greatest test of our women since
the bitter days of the Civil War," a
female civic leader said Thursday.

"We are called upon to be brave —
and that's all right. They have asked
us to contribute a dollar each to the
reward fund — and that's little enough.
But now they are saying that the killer
could be a woman — and that's
unbelievable."

The basis for the rumor that the
killer of four Columbus women is
another woman lies in some details
which many members of the media
regard as too terrible to publish.

214

> Although the stories repeatedly say the
> women were "sexually assaulted"
> police have said the attacks have been
> particularly brutal.

The speculation that a killer might be a woman was ignited after reports were released that the women had been tortured sexually with some sort of "inflexible object". This combined with a statement made by a civic leader that "This is rape without lust," caused the rumor that the killer might not be male.

Detective Lynn never gave any consideration to the speculation that the killer could be a woman. "Women don't leave semen stains behind," Lynn said. "We were trying not to let the press know everything. It was one of the details we had withheld. Semen had been found on some of the women."

Lynn also never believed the speculation about torture with an inflexible object. "There was a lot of speculation about the injuries and damage done to some of the ladies in their vaginal area," he said. "Some people speculated that they were being tortured, violently penetrated, with foreign objects."

"We were hearing everything from broom sticks to screw drivers to axe handles. I never believed any of that. Some of us believed that it was just the act of rape itself, violently committed by a young man against elderly women, that was causing the damage."

The last portion of one of Sibley's columns addressed the self-imposed curfew the people of Wynnton were observing:

> Although Columbus has not
> declared a curfew, most citizens, both
> male and female, find it expedient to
> get home early. A steak restaurant in
> the shopping center near the places of

the murders had the slowest night of
its history this week. The dining room
was quiet. A young couple with a
young baby in an infant carrier ate
quietly and listened to the
conversation of a middle-aged couple
at the next table.

"You see all these women have
been strangled to death with nylon
stockings," the husband was saying
accusingly. "That ought to make you
stop washing yours and hanging them
in the bathroom. You are just making
murder weapons handy for somebody,
and I'm going out of town."

"Not without me, you ain't," the
wife said. "I'm going with you and
taking my stockings too."

Ms. Sibley sat at a table in the Hungry Hunter Restaurant
listening and observing the fear of the people. As she sat there she
had no idea just how warranted those fears were. Not just for the
elderly women in Wynnton but the patrons and employees of its
restaurants.

Georgia has a law which forbids the wearing of masks or hoods
in public places. The law's intent was to prevent members of the Ku
Klux Klan from concealing their identity in public. But he wasn't
with the Klan. The white pillow case he wore over his head hid the
face of the strangler as he entered the rear of the Burger King just up
the road from the steakhouse where Sibley ate. Witnesses told police
he pulled a .38-caliber blue steel revolver and took $1,879 from

employees and customers of the fast food restaurant.

Three weeks later, at 9:30 p.m., he entered the steakhouse Sibley had written about – the Hungry Hunter on Midtown Drive. This time he was wearing a white paper bag over his head. Witnesses said he was armed with a blue steel .38. Even if they could have seen him they would not have known he was the strangler. He took $4,900 from the restaurant. The strangler had a new job. He was robbing restaurants.

There was no clue for police that the robberies and stranglings in the neighborhood were being committed by the same person. They suspected the strangler had a gun. A .9mm Luger had been taken in one of the burglaries in the Wynnton neighborhood, and police believed that burglary was committed by the strangler. Witnesses in the robberies identified the weapon used in the robberies as a .38 revolver and not a Luger.

When Theda Cartwright reported her .357 Magnum Hi Standard revolver missing they did not suspect the strangler as the thief because she did not live in the Wynnton neighborhood. If she suspected her boyfriend, Carlton Gary, of having taken the gun, she did not tell police.

When summer comes, along about the month of June, many Georgians head for the Florida sun. The Columbus stocking strangler was no exception. On June 19, 1978, he robbed the Wendy's on Archer Road in Gainesville, Fla. of $2,405. He wore a bandana across his face with sunglasses and carried a sawed-off shotgun. On June 27 he robbed the Brown Derby Restaurant on W. 13th St. in the

217

same city. It was 1:24 a.m. and again he covered his face. This time he got $4,633. Again he used a sawed-off shotgun.

Meanwhile back in Columbus the countdown of days had begun again since the strangler struck. It had again been more than 60 days but the people of Wynnton had learned not to trust or enjoy the lulls of peace. With every day that passed the women of Wynnton became sure that the risk increased that he would strike again soon. But he would not. Although he did return to Columbus, he did not stay there long.

―――――――――――

Hapeville, Ga. was and is a sleepy suburb of Atlanta, Ga. Central Avenue serves as the main street through town. North and South Central Avenue are separated by a railroad track which runs through the middle of town to the Ford Motor Company plant on the east side of the small town.

The automobile manufacturing plant had been the center of Hapeville's economy for decades — overlooking Interstate 75 just 10 minutes south of Atlanta — directly across from the Royal Inn Hotel. The Royal Inn was a 200-room hotel with plush royal blue carpeting and a glass elevator. The size of the hotel was moderate by Atlanta standards, but the decor was luxurious for the times.

Both the glass elevator and south balconies overlooked the Ford Plant and southbound lanes of the interstate leading towards Macon, Ga. The north balconies overlooked the interstate leading to Atlanta and little else — except on the date of June 29, 1978. On that date — in the early morning hours after 4 a.m.— it also overlooked the

Columbus Stocking Strangler as he scaled its north balconies. He was captured by the Hapeville Police Department climbing from room to room by way of the balconies with a gold bag over his shoulder containing $1,478.25 in U.S. currency. He gave them the name Michael A. David and told them he was born in Indiana. But gave a current address of Rochester, N.Y.

Hapeville, which supported a population of less than 10,000, was approximately 100 miles northeast of Columbus. Members of the Hapeville police department likely had heard of the Columbus stranglings, but since even Columbus police did not yet know his identity or aliases, they had no way of knowing who they had in their custody. Hapeville police filed a misdemeanor charge of criminal trespass. He was allowed to post a small bond and left before they discovered his true identity. Again he was free.

In the following months, he traveled the states of Georgia, Florida, and South Carolina participating in a string of restaurant robberies. Restaurants like Wendy's, McDonald's, Western Sizzler, Ryan's, and Po' Folks. Many of the robberies involved more than one masked man — he sometimes did not act alone. In some of the robberies in which he admitted involvement, waitresses were raped.

The neighborhood of Wynnton sat still and quiet through the nights. Weracoba Park in the Wynnton area, usually scattered with joggers even after sunset, was now being abandoned long before dark. It was a strange, silent summer of 1978 as the people of Columbus continued to count the days since the strangler last struck.

The scars of the tragedies were left all around the neighborhood of Wynnton. Once fine shrubberies were chopped short because they blocked the view of windows on lower floors exposing burglar bars on many of the windows. The once bustling neighborhood saw its streets abandoned each night when the sun set.

On July 24, 1978, police released a photo of a Ruger semi-automatic .22 caliber pistol taken during one of the burglaries in the

Wynnton area. Chief McClung told the media he did not know if the strangler took the gun but they were releasing the information in hopes that it would shake loose a clue that would give them the break they desperately needed. It would — but it would not happen soon.

Riverdale, like Hapeville, is a suburb south of Atlanta which, in the late 1970s, began experiencing a population boom. It was a neat community of moderately priced homes just minutes from Atlanta's Hartsfield Airport. There were numerous restaurants popping up on the main street through town which was Georgia State Highway 85. Employees from the busy airport were finding the usually sleepy suburb to be a convenient commute. The Stocking Strangler found it to be just another convenient target.

It was midnight, November 29, 1978, at the Shoney's Restaurant in the center of Riverdale, less than two miles from the police department. A masked man and an accomplice entered through the kitchen door. Both wore handkerchiefs as masks. There were 13 employees present. The robbers stuffed $3,000 into a bag and escaped into the night. The people of Riverdale were left shaken by the robbery in the small town. The people of Columbus were safe because, for now, he was gone. But they had no way of knowing when he might return.

Riverdale is located in Clayton County. By the late 1970s Clayton was a metropolitan Atlanta county which soon would be home to a portion of Atlanta's Hartsfield International Airport. There is nothing to indicate the Stocking Strangler ever traveled by plane. Every witness related his mode of travel as being by car. But something caused him to return to Clayton County several times. On January 27, 1979, he returned there to rob the McDonald's at the Georgia Highway 139 exit of Interstate 285, the perimeter highway that circles Atlanta. The McDonald's employees were left unharmed but it was not the last time they would see him. His luck, however, was about to run out.

Donna Blackwell was a waitress for the Po' Folk's restaurant in Gaffney, S.C. On February 15, 1979, she was surprised by an abductor as she exited the back door of the restaurant. It was dark — 9:50 p.m. He pulled a blue steel revolver, put it to her head and escorted her back into the business. He was a black man, wearing blue jeans, a gray wool cap with a bill and a turtleneck pulled up to cover the lower portion of his face. Once inside, the robber confronted the manager, Bob Harris, forcing Harris to take him to the cash register and then the safe, emptying both. Allison Randolph was a young waitress who worked in the restaurant and was inside when the robbery began. As she watched in fear, her fellow employee, Karen Harris ran from the restaurant and crossed the street catching the eye of Richard Weaver, an on-duty police officer with the Gaffney Police Department. Weaver was on the way to police headquarters with prisoners but stopped to investigate anyway.

When Weaver pulled to the rear of the store, he immediately became aware of the danger of the situation. He observed a black man bolting from the rear of the store carrying a pistol. Still not knowing the circumstances, Weaver did not fire at the fleeing armed man as he watched him run into the woods. He investigated and found that the restaurant had been robbed and immediately radioed for assistance.

Luck, on that night, continued to reign on the side of law and order. There was a team of bloodhounds and their handlers nearby searching for another suspect. They canceled that search and responded to the robbery.

Police dog handlers have a unique relationship with their bloodhounds. They train from the time the hounds are pups, teaching them to trace pre-set tracks. The handlers learn to read the dogs' habits and tendencies. A good handler can read his dog so well that he knows if the hound is tracking a human or an animal that has taken his interest. Handlers pay close attention to the dogs body language, the arc of his tail, his pattern of breathing, to know if the bloodhound is on the trail he should be on. A good handler frequently "checks" the animal for confidence that it is, indeed, a person he is tracking. A reassured demeanor tells the handler the dog is on his track.

These bloodhounds were on a good scent and their handlers knew it. They chased the man for three hours. At 2:30 in the morning the dogs caught their suspect: a 28-year-old man who identified himself as Michael David. The man calling himself David was wearing three sets of jogging clothing. He told police he had an accomplice named Malvin Crittenden. He claimed Crittenden had done the actual robbery and then had driven off with the getaway car – a white Pontiac Firebird with Ohio tags – leaving David to be captured by the tracking dogs. This story, however, was quickly discounted by numerous witnesses in the restaurant who all identified this man known as Michael David as the robber. Police later found the true getaway car – a blue Firebird with a Georgia license plate – still parked at an apartment complex previously described by David as the location of the supposed white Firebird.

Gaffney police learned that their suspect had lied to them about several things, including some very significant events in his past. The man calling himself Michael David was the same man who identified himself as Carl Michaels when his fingerprints were found in the home of Nellie Farmer after she was strangled in Albany, N.Y. in 1970. He was also the same man found in possession of Jean Frost's watch the day after she was attacked, and the same man who had escaped from the Janesville Correctional Facility in Onondaga, N.Y. — just weeks before the first strangling occurred in Columbus, Ga.

On March 10, 1979, Columbus detectives Richard A. Smith and Bruce Berreth interviewed the suspect in prison in South Carolina and he confessed — to five armed robberies of restaurants, including some in the Wynnton area. The stranglings were never mentioned. The

222

Columbus detectives had been summoned there by South Carolina authorities who told them he was a restaurant robbery suspect with ties to Columbus, so they only questioned him about those robberies. His name had not been given as a suspect in the stranglings.

The man known at the time as David Michaels — also known as Carl Michaels — was sentenced to 21 years for the robbery in South Carolina. In August of 1979, he was taken to New York and sentenced to two to four years for his escape from the Onondaga County Penitentiary, and then returned to South Carolina to serve out his sentence.

Back in Columbus, police were as baffled as ever — using every investigative technique known to modern day law enforcement to no avail. The task force had a new leader, Luther Miller, the man who would later be named the city's chief of police. Although police were declaring they had not given up on the case, the press was reporting they were no closer to solving the case than they were the first week.

As more time passed without another strangling, it began to seem as though Columbus would never be the same again. Even though tensions had eased noticeably there were still few women found outdoors after dark. Several male family members were living in Wynnton for the sole purpose of protecting mothers, aunts, and grandmothers.

Just as things began to relax, in the summer of 1980, another violent death occurred in Wynnton. On June 7 of that year, Mary Sue Ogletree was stabbed more than 30 times. Mrs. Ogletree lived alone, not far from where Mrs. Borom was killed. Coroner Don Kilgore told the press the murder was the act of "a damn madman." She was younger than the other victims — only 54. There were no signs of strangulation. Police concluded that the murder was probably not the work of the strangler, but that did not soothe fears. The Columbus Enquirer quoted one 68-year-old woman from Wynnton as saying, "Oh God....here we go again."

223

The strain of the case affected every part of the city and threatened the stability of peaceful co-existence among the races. William "Billy" Winn, a reporter for The Columbus Ledger/Enquirer wrote about one of the complications of the case in a column in the Nov. 9, 1980, Sunday section titled Perspective:

Had race relations in Columbus been otherwise ideal at the time, which they were not, this situation would have been difficult enough. As it was, police and city officials found themselves simultaneously faced with both a rampaging sex murderer who had terrified the city's white female population, and a large and growing group of irate black residents who were sick and tired of being hassled by police every time they walked out to get a pack of cigarettes or a Coca-Cola.

That the confrontation between the primarily white police involved in the Strangler investigation and young blacks in Columbus has not escalated beyond the rhetoric is attributable to many factors, including the good will of black citizens of the town and especially the parents of black teenagers, most of whom understand the necessity of the police investigation and have cooperated fully with the members of the Strangler Task Force.

The years continued to pass without resolution to the strangler case. No one in Columbus knew he was sitting in prison in South Carolina. The pressure and stress on the careers of the different police detectives assigned to resolve the case did not wane. The list of investigators who resigned under pressure, were run out by politics, or just walked away out of frustration, was long. Each new chief would be asked the inevitable question by the press of what priority the Stocking Strangler case would have in their administration. In 1982, the chief was Jim Wetherington, former commander of the uniform division that patrolled the Wynnton area during the times of the stranglings. Wetherington offered the same assurances that the case would remain a top priority. He displayed the same frustrations as previous police chiefs, telling the press, "I hope I'll see the day when this case is cleared." But Wetherington offered another opinion when speaking of the possibilities of solving the case that proved almost prophetic: "It can be done, when the right lead or right piece of evidence comes along." Two years later, it did.

It was 1984. The president of the nation was Ronald Reagan, the governor of Georgia was Joe Frank Harris. The chief of police of Columbus was still Jim Wetherington; the sheriff of Muscogee County was Gene Hodge.

Famine in Ethiopia had sparked a world-wide aid effort while in

America a company by the name of Apple introduced the Macintosh sparking the evolution of personal computers.

The May 3, 1984, edition of The Columbus Ledger reported that Chief Jim Wetherington was announcing that the "strongest lead ever" had developed in the Columbus Stocking Strangler case. A suspect had been developed, and a man was being sought for questioning. His name had surfaced in a lead that police had been following for more than a month. Chief Wetherington did not release the suspect's name nor did he release the details of the lead.

By now the man arrested in 1979 for the robbery of the Po' Folks in South Carolina under the name of Michael David had escaped. He had served five years of his sentence at Kirkland Correctional Institution, a high-security prison in Columbia, S.C. On March 1, 1984, he was transferred to Goodman Correctional Institution, a minimum-security facility where he was made a trusty. Fifteen days later he escaped. On March 24, 1984, he again returned to Clayton County, Ga. and again robbed the McDonald's at Interstate 285 and Highway 139. Then he returned to Columbus.

On April 18, 1984, Columbus Police Department Vice Squad Detective J.R. McMichael was working undercover watching Smitty's Lounge on Benning Drive. He saw a man sitting in a Ford LTD in the parking lot smoking a marijuana cigarette. McMichael approached the man and attempted to place him into custody. The suspect shoved him and ran into a wooded area. McMichael pursued him into the woods and caught him in a foot chase. Another struggle ensued and this time, McMichael was slightly injured when the suspect fell on top of him. The man was eventually taken into custody and arrested on a misdemeanor drug charge and for obstruction of an officer, also a misdemeanor in 1984. He was the escapee from South Carolina. He identified himself to police as Michael Anthony David, the same name he had used while serving time in South Carolina. He was, in fact, the Stocking Strangler, but police still did not know it was him. He was released on a misdemeanor bond. But, again, his luck was about to run out — this time for the final time.

He began traveling with three others — Ernest Mitchell, Phyllis Green and Alonzo Williams. On April 29, 1984, they checked into room 209 of the Holiday Inn on the 280 Bypass in Phenix City, Al. — just across the Chattahoochee River from Columbus. They were driving a 1984 Lincoln.

A Phenix City detective named Boyd Battles was investigating a series of robberies in his city. Detective Battles was pursuing a theory that the robberies were being committed by a group traveling in the area of Gainesville, Florida, Phenix City, and Columbus, transporting cocaine between the cities. Someone in the group, Battles believed, also was robbing restaurants as the group traveled those cities. Battles discovered this group's mode of transportation was a 1984 Lincoln.

Meanwhile, Columbus police were furiously pursuing their new lead — a handgun which had been stolen in the Wynnton area during the time of the stranglings. The initial inquiries about the stolen handgun were sparked by a mysterious phone call. Someone — no one knows who — called Henry Sanderson and said, "The police have the gun you had stolen from you." Sanderson then called the Columbus police and asked if they had his weapon. They did not. When Lt. Charlie Rowe and Detective Mike Sellers began discussing the weapon they suddenly realized the significance of it. "That's the gun stolen at Callye East's house." Callye East was one of the theft victims in Wynnton during the time of the stranglings. It was believed for years that this .22 Luger handgun, stolen in the Wynnton area during the time of the stranglings, could be the key to solving the case. Police knew the serial numbers to the gun, 13-70073, and had hoped it would one day surface. Detectives Rowe and Sellers realized that if that gun was in police custody somewhere they desperately needed to know where.

Sellers sent out a nationwide teletype inquiring if anyone had the weapon. Frequently, the problem with a nationwide teletype is that agencies are too busy to follow up on them or don't take them seriously if they are from an agency several states away. In Kalamazoo, Michigan two clerks took the teletype very seriously and began checking their records of registered handguns. Their search virtually solved the case. The gun was not in police custody but it had been registered there in 1981. Michigan Police Captain Tom Bartlett tracked down the gun and its current owner and also tracked down how he came into possession of the gun. Bartlett reportedly called police in Columbus and asked, "Do you know where Phenix City, Alabama is?"

Bartlett had learned that the gun owner in Michigan had gotten the gun from a man named Jim Gary in Phenix City. Gary told police he had gotten the gun from his nephew — a nephew named Carlton Gary.

When the lead surfaced on the weapon, Chief Wetherington created a five man team to follow up: Lt. Charlie Rowe, Detective Ricky Boren, Detective Lem Miller, Detective Mike Sellers and Detective Jim Warren. Sellers was given the assignment of trying to find fingerprints on Gary to match against prints found at some of the stranglings. He soon learned they had missed him by less than two months — just 46 days earlier Gary had escaped from prison in South Carolina where he had been serving time under the name Michael David for armed robbery. Sellers asked the South Carolina prison to send him a copy of Gary's fingerprints. It took more than 10 days to receive the prints due to misdirected mail. Through family and informants police found that Gary had been seen in the Columbus/Phenix City area. The detectives were nervous and anxious. If Gary was their man, then they knew their task was urgent: the strangler was probably back in Columbus.

On April 30, 1984, Sellers received the fingerprints of Carlton Gary. He and Detective Lem Miller took the prints to Identification Technician Doug Shafer and asked that they be compared to one of the latent (unknown) fingerprints found at Kathleen Woodruff's home, more than six years earlier, after she was found dead there. Sellers went to a phone to call South Carolina to cancel a second set of prints he had ordered when the first did not arrive. He put that call on hold to take a call from Shafer who was checking Gary's fingerprints. Shafer spoke the two words into the phone receiver that every policeman in Columbus had wanted to hear for nine years — "They match." Seller's heart was pounding as he and Miller raced to find Lt. Rowe, Boren, and Warren. They didn't have their man, but they now knew who he was.

Phenix City Detective Battles contacted Columbus police and told them about the group of suspected robbers and cocaine runners he was investigating, one of which used the name Michael David. This time the Columbus police knew — Michael David was Carlton Gary. Battles told them Gary was in the Phenix City area driving a 1984 Lincoln.

On the same night that Gary's fingerprint was matched to one found in Kathleen Woodruff's home, Columbus police detectives went to Phenix City to look for Gary. At 1:30 a.m. a Phenix City patrolman found the Lincoln parked at an apartment complex. The patrolman shined his spotlight at the apartment building and the light penetrated the bedroom window of one of the apartments — the one Carlton Gary was in with Anita Walker. Walker later told police that as soon as Gary saw the light he looked out the window and saw the police car. He then went out the back door and over the second floor railing — naked with clothes in hand. Once again he got away.

On the afternoon of May 1, 1984, Detective Battles and other Phenix City officers raided room 209 of the Holiday Inn at the 280 Bypass. Located in the room and arrested for possession of cocaine

229

were Ernest Mitchell, Phyllis Green, and Alonzo Williams. They had not arrested Carlton Gary. He was gone. He had again slipped through their fingers.

Police began to put enormous pressure on everyone associated with Gary. For some of them it was easier to give him up rather than take the heat themselves. Gary had left some cocaine in Phenix City. Police attempted to use that cocaine to lure him back. It did not work. But after two days of working with associates of Gary, police found out where he was — Albany, Ga. It was the beginning of the end for The Columbus Stocking Strangler.

———————

It was the Holiday Inn at 422 Oglethorpe Blvd. in Albany, Ga. It was May 3, 1984. At 8:30 that morning Carlton Gary and †Rachael Adams had checked in to a second-floor room there. Fourteen years later, in 1998, James Paulk remembered it as though it were last week. "A strong storm had come through that day. There were sticks and limbs all over the streets." Paulk was a corporal with the Albany Police Department at the time and a member of the Albany P.D. S.W.A.T. Team. "It was a S.W.A.T. call out," Paulk continued. "We gathered at the muster room. They told us they thought the strangler was holed up at the Holiday Inn, that they had him under surveillance and that we would probably have to go in and get him out."

The S.W.A.T. team assembled and began to plan their entry into the room. The first S.W.A.T. members to enter the room would be Corporal David Noel, Corporal Paulk, Max Carver and Jiles Lovejoy,

230

followed by two or three other Albany S.W.A.T. team members. Rachael Adams came out of the room and headed for the ice machine. S.W.A.T. team members intercepted her and took her to a room for questioning. She told police that Gary was in the room alone but that he had a .357 magnum handgun on the night stand and would probably shoot anyone who entered. Adams told the officers that Gary would not open the door for anyone but her.

S.W.A.T. team members took her to the hotel room door. Her instructions were to knock on the door, wait for Gary to begin to open the door, and then she could leave. She did not follow her instructions.

S.W.A.T. team members led her to the door with a bucket of ice in her hand. She knocked on the door and then dropped the bucket of ice, turned, and ran before police could stop her. Gary opened the door anyway. Paulk described what happened next. David Noel and Paulk attempted to enter the room. When Gary saw that it was police he tried to slam the door shut. Noel and Paulk put their shoulders to the door to keep it open. Gary reached out and grabbed Noel's .45 caliber service weapon. "When we saw him struggling with David for his gun we put our shoulders to the door and forced it open. He went towards the night stand and we tackled him," Paulk remembered. "He really didn't have a chance — there were too many of us." Albany S.W.A.T. members handcuffed Carlton Gary and placed him under arrest. The Stocking Strangler finally was caught.

Columbus police were notified that Carlton Gary was in custody. Columbus Detectives Rowe, Boren, Sellers, Miller, and Warren all rushed to Albany. Boren recalled that when they arrived he was met in the parking lot of the Albany Police Department by the supervisor in the Albany Crime Scene Unit, Sgt. Robert Lamar "Butch" Windam. Boren recalls Windam saying, "It's him." Boren asked, "What do you mean Butch?" Windam responded, "It's the strangler.

I've already matched the print." Boren then remembered they had distributed the unknown print found on Mrs. Woodruff's window screen to all of the larger police agencies in the state. Windam had compared the print while awaiting their arrival, unaware that it had already been compared. It reaffirmed, in Boren's mind, that the match was a good one.

Boren drove Carlton Gary back to Columbus with Rowe in the front seat of his 1979 Chevrolet Impala and Sellers riding in back with Gary. Warren and Miller followed in Warren's police issued Dodge Diplomat. Sellers later spoke of that ride to Columbus Ledger-Enquirer columnist Richard Hyatt. "He had been a ghost. Now I was sitting in the back seat with him. He was a human being. A couple of times I leaned over and brushed against him just to see if he was real."

When they arrived in Columbus they were met at police headquarters with lights, cameras, and a flood of media which they avoided while they led Gary upstairs and began to hear his story. In the following days Carlton Gary gave police what Boren remembers as "a very factual" accounting of crimes he had committed or was involved in over the past nine years, but not the stranglings. When confronted with the matching of his fingerprint he admitted to being at the Woodruff home but claimed that someone else had done the strangling.

Gary claimed that the strangler was actually Malvin Alamichael Crittenden. Gary called him Michael. Gary told police during the first few days of questioning, "I did the burglaries and Michael killed the old ladies."

Two nights after his arrest Detectives Rowe, Boren, and Sellers rode Gary around the Wynnton neighborhood while Gary accurately pointed out the homes of the strangling victims and described details of the homes. Detective Boren later recalled Carlton had a phenomenal memory.

232

Columbus police quickly located and questioned Crittenden. They set out to find out everything they could about the man Gary claimed was the strangler. They also began to find out more about Carlton Gary.

Crittenden denied any involvement in the serial killings, and none of his fingerprints were found in any of the homes. On the other hand, Gary's fingerprints and palm prints matched with unknown prints found at the homes of Florence Scheible, Martha Thurmond and Kathleen Woodruff.

Police then began to learn of Gary's past and his various aliases. They learned that in 1970 his fingerprints were found in Nellie Farmer's home after she had been raped and strangled. When he was arrested he claimed an associate had done the strangling while he burglarized the home. They learned that in January of 1977, he was found in possession of property taken from the home of Jean Frost after she was assaulted, strangled and left for dead. When he was arrested, he once again claimed that an associate did the attack and that he was simply handling the stolen property.

Carlton Gary had established a pattern of being connected to homes where elderly women were strangled and consistently blamed the acts on others when the evidence was always strongest against him. Police also learned a seemingly trivial, potentially revealing piece of information about Carlton Gary's past. According to press reports, while Carlton Gary was growing up in Columbus his mother helped make ends meet by cleaning houses. She was a maid for the rich women of Wynnton. Police released Crittenden and charged Carlton Gary as the strangler.

233

On May 4, 1984, the citizens of Columbus first learned that a suspect had been arrested in the strangling case. The article told of Gary's past arrest and the fact that he was an escapee from South Carolina. Reporters had learned that Gary's fingerprint had been matched to one found in one of the strangling victim's homes, but Columbus Police Chief Jim Wetherington would not confirm it during a press conference held just after the arrest.

Chief Wetherington described Gary as "an extremely brilliant young man who played the game well." Chief Wetherington also announced that the district attorney would be presenting Carlton Gary's case to the grand jury that same day, less than 24 hours after his arrest. The press seemed confused about why the district attorney was rushing the case to the grand jury. It was probably done to avoid revealing too much information in preliminary hearings. Georgia law in 1984 did not afford a suspect a preliminary hearing after an indictment by a grand jury. Prosecutors often sought quick indictments to avoid revealing the substance of their case too soon.

Columbus attorney John Allen represented Gary immediately following his arrest. Allen complained to Superior Court Judge John Land that police were interviewing Gary without having his attorney present. Allen later testified at a hearing that Judge Land spoke with Chief Wetherington and reported back to Allen that it was Gary who was initiating the interviews. Allen testified that Judge Land told him "The boy (Gary) might not be telling the truth."

Gary eventually was arraigned on July 10, 1984, and pleaded innocent to his charges. On Aug. 29 of that year, Gary selected the attorney who eventually became his lead defense counsel through the course of his trial, August F. "Bud" Siemon III, a decorated Vietnam War veteran who specialized in handling capital cases and blocking death penalty sentences. He was assisted, for a while, by Atlanta attorney Bruce Harvey. Together they inundated the court with a multitude of pre-trial defense motions which delayed the trial for two years. People in Columbus were becoming irritated that the trial was taking so long. Lawyers and jurists did not want to go on record criticizing other lawyers and judges, but privately some were complaining to the press that the case was taking too long to come to trial.

One lawyer with extensive experience in capital cases, who asked not to be identified, told The Columbus Ledger, "That is how you fight a death penalty case. The more motions you file the longer it takes. Since the end of the process may mean the death of your client, the longer you can delay the trial the longer you can keep your client alive."

As a result of the motions, Judge Land was removed as the trial judge as was Judge E. Mullins Whisnant. The trial judge eventually selected to hear the Carlton Gary trial was Muscogee County Superior Court Judge Kenneth Followill. He was described by the press as a patient and careful jurist.

The defense tactics also involved accusations of "prosecutorial impropriety" on the part of the district attorney, William Smith. There were also motions claiming mistreatment of Gary and requests for public funds to interview out-of-state witnesses. Judge Followill eventually ruled that there had been no prosecutorial impropriety and that Gary had not been mistreated. The defense's request for public funds to seek expert assistance was also denied. During one of the motion hearings Attorney Siemon told Judge Followill, "The real delay is that this is all going to be reversed. This is a practice trial."

At an October 7, 1985, hearing Judge Followill scolded Gary's attorneys for not questioning a sufficient number of witnesses. The attorneys said they had questioned only 10 to 15 witnesses from a list of about 400 submitted by the prosecutors. In subsequent appeals the prosecution team accused Gary's attorneys of feigning incompetence hoping to give Gary an issue to argue on appeal. In July of the following year, Bruce Harvey withdrew from the case citing lack of funding.

The delays in bringing Carlton Gary to trial only served to further deepen the wounds he caused to the City. There was fear in the community that he may one night prowl their streets again as the press reported that sheriff's deputies uncovered an attempted escape by Gary. City officials hoped a public trial which revealed all of the evidence against Gary would allow the citizens to rest easy, secure in the knowledge that the strangler was finally off of the street. It would take years for this to occur. Some in the Wynnton neighborhood of Columbus would never rest easy again.

It was 1986. The president of the nation and the governor of the state had not changed. The U.S. had bombed Libya for its complicity with terrorists. Americans were learning that their government had been less than honest about Irangate while the Soviets learned their government had been equally elusive about a nuclear accident at Chernobyl.

There were further delays in the trial in March when Judge Followill ordered a postponement to allow a psychiatric evaluation of Gary. In April, a jury determined Gary mentally fit to stand trial.

The trial of Carlton Gary finally took place in August of that year in Columbus, Ga. One of the many motions filed by Gary's attorneys was a request for change of venue. A change of venue motion is a request to move the trial to a different community and is common in a case of this magnitude. The defense predictably asserted that, due to the overwhelming publicity, it would not be possible to seat a fair and impartial jury in Columbus. Judge Followill's ruling, however, was not so typical. He agreed that seating an impartial Columbus jury would be difficult, but he would not deny the city of Columbus their long-awaited public trial.

Judge Followill was well aware that in December of the previous year, the 11th U.S. Circuit Court of Appeals had ordered a new trial for the accused killers of six members of the Ned Alday family, who were slain at their Seminole County mobile home in 1973. The appeals panel ruled that allowing the trial to take place in Seminole County, with a Seminole County jury where there may have been a "presumption" of prejudice, made the convictions unfair.

In the Gary case, Judge Followill ruled that the proceedings in the Carlton Gary trial would be moved northeasterly 75 miles to the city of Griffin, Ga. long enough for the two sides to choose a jury from the pool of Spalding County voters in and around Griffin. Once the jury was chosen, the proceedings and the new jury pool were moved back to Columbus for the trial.

The prosecutor for the trial was Muscogee County District Attorney William J. Smith, a former F.B.I. Agent who was appointed district attorney the year the stranglings ended. Smith had already successfully prosecuted the "Forces of Evil" killings of 1978.

Prosecutor Smith began the trial by telling the jury, and the city of Columbus, what he believed the state's evidence would be against Carlton Gary. Smith told the jury that although Gary was only charged in three of the slayings, he intended to introduce evidence linking Gary to all seven. Smith told the jury how Gary had admitted to being present at six of the seven slayings, but claimed he only burglarized the women's homes and that an accomplice did the stranglings. He then told the jury that the alleged accomplice will testify that he was never with Gary during the slayings. Smith also

237

told the jury that hundreds of fingerprints found in the victims' homes were examined and none were found to match those of the alleged accomplice, but Gary's fingerprints were found in all three of the homes of the victims he was charged with killing.

The nine-man, three-woman jury heard for the first time from prosecutor Smith that this was not the first time Carlton Gary had been accused of raping and strangling elderly women. Smith told the jury that he expected to introduce evidence of the murder of Nellie Farmer in Albany, New York and how Gary claimed the crime was committed by an accomplice after his fingerprints were found there.

During Smith's opening remarks jurors and spectators learned for the first time that there was a witness to one of the attacks — an eye witness — one of the survivors. Just five days before the first victim, Ferne Jackson, was raped and murdered in her home, a 64-year-old woman was attacked in her home and "got a good clear look" at her assailant's face. Smith told the jury she would testify it was the face of Carlton Gary. Smith told the listening jurors and press, "The evidence will show that he did rape her, he did strangle her, but she did not die." Smith continued, "The evidence will show that she was left for dead, but by the grace of God she survived the hell she went through."

The jury was then told the story of Ruth Schwob and the night she survived her attack. Prosecutor Smith told the jury that, sadly, Mrs. Schwob would not be testifying against her attacker. She had passed away three years after the attack.

Next came the account of the attack on Jean Frost in 1977 in Syracuse, New York, and how Gary was found the following day in possession of property taken from her apartment. While telling the jury what Gary's explanation to police was regarding his possession of the stolen property, Smith remarked, "You probably know the answer he gave better than I do... 'Yes, I was there but a friend was with me. He went into the house while I was the lookout.'"

238

By Allen Horne/Ledger-Enquirer
Carlton Gary wears suit at trial this morning.

Columbus Ledger-Enquirer photo. Reprinted with permission.

Tuesday August 12, 1986

MURDERS GARY IS CHARGED WITH

● MURDERS GARY IS CHARGED WITH

● THE OTHER MURDERS ALLEGEDLY CONNECTED TO THE CASE

○ BURGLARIES ALLEGEDLY CONNECTED TO THE CASE

RAPE-BURGLARY ALLEGEDLY CONNECTED TO THE CASE

MURDERS GARY IS CHARGED WITH
1. FLORENCE G. SCHEIBLE, 89, 941 DIMON ST., OCT. 21, 1977.
2. MARTHA B. THURMOND, 69, 2614 MARION ST., OCT. 25, 1977.
3. KATHLEEN WOODRUFF, 74, 1811 BUENA VISTA RD., DEC. 28, 1977.
THE OTHER MURDERS ALLEGEDLY CONNECTED TO THE CASE
4. FERNE JACKSON, 60, 2505 17TH ST., SEPT. 16, 1977.
5. JEAN DIMENSTEIN, 71, 3027 21ST. ST., SEPT. 25, 1977.
6. MILDRED BOROM, 78, 1612 FOREST AVE., FEB. 12, 1978.
7. JANET COFER, 61, 3783 STEAM MILL ROAD, APRIL 20, 1978.
BURGLARIES ALLEGEDLY CONNECTED TO THE CASE
8. CALLYE EAST, 1427 EBERHARDT AVE., OCT. 8, 1977.
9. WILLIAM SWIFT, 1710 BUENA VISTA RD., DEC. 20, 1977.
10. ABRAHAM ILLGES, 2021 BROOKSIDE DR., JAN. 1, 1978 AND AGAIN ON FEB 11, 1978.
11. RUTH SCHWOB, 1800 CARTER AVE., BURGLARY AND ATTEMPTED STRANGLING, FEB. 11, 1978.

By Don Coker/Ledger-Enquirer

Columbus Ledger-Enquirer photo. Reprinted with permission.

239

Smith's opening remarks effectively painted a picture of Gary's custom of accusing others whenever he was linked to the rape and strangulation of elderly women which, for Carlton, had been a reoccurring event through the decade of the 1970s.

Bud Siemon's opening remarks to the jury were not quite so clear and very probably were not meant to be. In regards to Gary's fingerprints being found on the scene of several of the murders, Siemon told the jury, "Fingerprints prove nothing except that a person was at a location. They don't prove that he was the murderer. If they can't connect Carlton with those crimes, the fingerprints are no good." It was an attempt at planting the thought in some jurors' minds that placing Gary at the scene of the crime was not a way of connecting him to the murders.

Siemon told the jury that the state's case against Gary rested on statements Gary gave police that "the state admits are not true." He was acknowledging to the jury that Gary had lied to police to make it sound as though it was somehow the lawmen's fault. Siemon told the jury "The evidence will be and the police will admit — because I will make them admit — that the statements contain material inaccuracies."

Seimon also told the jury, "They had officers in trees, they had officers hiding in the bushes with night-vision devices, they had stake-out houses with police inside. All this and they didn't catch the killer when he was committing all these crimes. It had to be someone with an intimate knowledge of Columbus, and Carlton didn't have it." The jury would later hear through testimony that Gary not only admitted being at six of the seven stranglings, but had also ridden around with police and shown them most of the crime scenes.

The American Justice system's rules for attorneys on opposite sides of a criminal trial are often inconsistent with the search for the truth. While the prosecutor is bound, by a code of conduct, to the truth, even if the truth hurts their case, the rules for the defense are different.   If a defense attorney learns that the truth will hurt their client's case, the nature of their mission is to avoid it.

The defense counsel will, if his client demands it, stand before juries and declare his client's innocence — often proclaiming honest men to be liars and their clients as innocent victims of society. Many times their arguments to the normal observer seem ludicrous but their objective, particularly in a more difficult case, is not necessarily to plant the seed of doubt in 12 jurors' minds. They need only to cloud the judgement of one. The nature of the system makes the truth seem only important to the defense when it is in their best interest.

Gary told Judge Followill at the start of the trial that he was sick and asked to be excused from "this circus or whatever you call it." Followill denied the request and ordered that he remain in court.

The prosecution's first witness was Doris Lausenberg. She testified she saw Carlton Gary quickly walk by her home on the day Florence Scheible was killed. Mrs. Lausenberg, who lived four blocks from the Scheible strangling, testified that he walked quickly, glancing repeatedly over his shoulder. "He turned and looked at me as he passed my house." She testified of having picked him out of a photo line-up in 1984 after his arrest. "He had a very distinctive face — a high forehead and an unusual nose." When asked if she could identify the man she saw walking, Mrs. Lausenberg looked at Gary and replied, "Yes I can. He's sitting right there at that table." She was visibly nervous during her testimony. Defense attorney Siemon queried, "Why were you looking into your purse, for your glasses?" "No, I was reaching for my nitroglycerin," she replied.

The next witness was Muscogee County Medical Examiner Joe Webber who described the rape and murder of Florence Scheible. Fingerprint experts testified next that Carlton Gary's thumb print was found on her bedroom door.

Throughout the day the jury heard of Gary's past, his involvement in steakhouse robberies, his eventual arrest and statements claiming

241

he was at the scene of most of the murders, but that someone else did the rapes and stranglings. That someone else then took the stand in the form of Malvin Crittenden and reputed those statements.

The defense objected to Crittenden testifying, declaring to the court that the defense no longer maintained that Crittenden was involved. Judge Followill allowed the testimony. Crittenden testified he had been the getaway driver for Gary during a series of robberies in South Carolina, but that he knew nothing about the stranglings.

More of Gary's past followed when 64-year-old Jean Frost took the stand and told the jury about the vicious attack and rape she suffered on her 55th birthday in Syracuse, N.Y. Albany detective Anthony Sedotti took the stand next and testified that Carlton Gary's fingerprints also were found in the home of Nellie Farmer after she was raped and murdered in 1970 in Albany. Detective Sedotti testified that Carlton Gary later claimed he was at the scene of that attack but that someone else, John Lee Mitchell, had committed the rape and strangling. John Lee Mitchell testified next.

Sixteen years earlier, Carlton Gary had testified that John Mitchell was a murderer and rapist. Mitchell took the stand, looked Gary in the eye and did the same. He testified of having spent a year in jail awaiting trial for a rape and murder that Gary had committed. Mitchell, now owner of a heating store, testified that he had met Gary in a bar but was only a casual acquaintance when Gary fingered him for a crime which he did not commit.

Detective Mike Sellers testified of his interviews with Gary after his arrest. Sellers testified that Gary said he would hide in the bushes in the Wynnton neighborhood to avoid patrol cars riding the neighborhood. Jurors heard testimony that Gary had shown police six of the seven homes of the victims and that his fingerprints were also found in the homes of Martha Thurmond and Kathleen Woodruff, the other two women whom he was charged with having murdered.

Sheila Dean, Gary's former common-law wife, testified of having lived with Gary in Albany, N. Y. in 1970 — placing him in that city at the time of the murder of Nellie Farmer.

Dollie Crittenden, the mother of Malvin Crittenden, who Gary first claimed was the strangler, also testified against Gary and showed open hostility towards him. She told the jury that she lived next door to Alma Williams, Gary's great-aunt, on Fisk Avenue in the East Wynnton area of Columbus. Ms. Crittenden testified that Gary came to stay with his great-aunt in August of 1977, which would place him in Columbus shortly before the stranglings began. Adding to Mrs. Crittenden's credibility as a witness was her testimony that Gary came to Columbus at that time walking funny, "hopping like a duck." This testimony was consistent with earlier testimony that Gary injured his ankle in a 20-foot jump made while escaping from prison in Syracuse, N.Y., in August of 1977.

Alma Williams' son, Gary Williams, testified that he didn't like Carlton Gary staying with his mother and asked him to move. Louise Vaughn, another great-aunt of Gary's who also lived with the elderly Alma Williams, testified that she didn't like Carlton staying there either because he would stay out late at night and she would have to get up to let him in.

A-8   The Columbus, Ga., Ledger, Wednesday August 27, 1986

Carlton Gary returns to seat before hearing the jury's verdict Tuesday. By Larry Cutchall/Ledger-Enquirer

Columbus Ledger-Enquirer photo. Reprinted with permission.

243

By Allen Horne/Ledger-Enquirer
Robert Westervelt of the Albany, N.Y., police force testifies while flanked by Judge Followill and District Attorney Smith (r).

Columbus Ledger-Enquirer photo. Reprinted with permission.

The press was reporting the trial was expected to last three months. It lasted less than three weeks. The state rested on Friday, Aug, 22, after two weeks of testimony by more than 100 witnesses. On Monday, Aug. 25, 1986, the defense began presenting its case. The presentation for the defense took less than two hours using only five witnesses — Jerome Livas, the man who confessed to some of the stranglings early in the investigation, and four former task force investigators including former director Ronald Jones. The entire defense took less than half the time prosecutor Smith took in his opening arguments to the jury.

Defense attorney Bud Siemon attempted to convince the jury that police had molded the evidence to fit Gary. The jury didn't buy it. Deliberations took even less time than the defense's presentation of evidence. After only one hour the jury found Carlton Gary guilty on all nine counts. Three were for murder, a charge for which there can only be two possible sentences — life in prison or death by electrocution.

On Aug. 27, the jury began listening to the arguments of prosecutor Smith as to why Carlton Gary should die in Georgia's electric chair. Smith told the jury a death sentence for Gary would "set the tone for justice in our state." Smith also told the jury, "I didn't say vengeance or revenge, I said justice." Smith continued by telling the jury that if death in the electric chair is not appropriate for Gary, "it isn't appropriate for anyone." Smith ended with the statement, "appropriate punishment is what separates civilization from savagery, civilization from barbarism."

Arguing on Gary's behalf, Bud Siemon told the jury again that Gary was framed. Gary sat and listened, dressed in a caftan and wearing dark sunglasses. Siemon told the jury that police had driven Gary through the neighborhoods, planting suggestions in his mind. Siemon said to the jurors, "Do you believe that the same Columbus Police Department that tried to frame Jerome Livas couldn't try to frame Carlton Gary?" But Siemon's arguments were in vain. The jury's quick finding of guilt indicated there was little doubt in their minds that Gary was the strangler. Prosecutor Smith had done an effective job of portraying Gary's pattern through the years of blaming others when the evidence weighed more heavily against him. This time, this jury didn't buy it. After three hours of deliberation the jury brought back the sentence of the extreme penalty — death.

The historic river district of Columbus is just a few miles from the Wynnton neighborhood. The district lies on the banks of the Chattahoochee River near the Dillingham Street Bridge which connects Columbus with Phenix City and the State of Alabama. The Historic Columbus Hilton hotel is where the 12 jurors from Griffin, Ga. lived for three weeks at night, while by day they listened to the evidence and then deliberated the fate of Carlton Gary. It is a large brick building renovated into a hotel, but maintaining the historical flavor of the old grist mill it was. It overlooks the Chattahoochee River just two blocks from the Government Center, home to the Stocking Strangler trial.

A train trestle bridge crosses just a little further south on the river. The tracks attached to the trestle carry the Southern Railway trains into Georgia from Alabama and back. The train is actually in Georgia territory as soon as it leaves land on the Alabama side.

As it reaches land on the Columbus side it travels up 9th Street —not across 9th Street — up 9th Street — in the right lane of traffic —sometimes even parallel to those traveling in the left-hand lane.

There are no guard rails or blinking lights to warn motorists of the train, just a rotating light and a blaring horn to alert motorist of a trains approach. Eric Bellamy works in the river district. "It's a strange thing to see in your rearview mirror — a train coming up behind you. "You could just change lanes and ride along side of it, but they don't recommend it," said the long-time Columbus resident.

James "Rick" Howard, a lifetime Columbus resident, also works in the district at the riverside Columbus Hilton, serving drinks in the downstairs bar. He laughs about the train tracks that run up 9th Street in front of the historic hotel in which he works. "The strange thing is you never hear of any wrecks with the train here. You hear about all the wrecks at train crossings where there are guard rails and blinking lights but not here. We listen to the train coming and all the

246

lights will turn red as it comes through and there's never a problem."

Howard also listened to those at his bar who speculated about the trial of Carlton Gary. In 1998, 20 years after the stranglings and a dozen years after the trial, the people of Columbus still share varying opinions of Gary's guilt. One particular couple who came in every afternoon and sat at the bar to await the daily lottery drawings on TV, gossip and wonder about stories that flurried at the time about other rumored suspects.

Tending bar alongside of Howard is Donte Smith. Donte has something in common with Carlton Gary. He is also a black man who has lived in both Syracuse, N.Y., and Columbus, Ga. In 1998, he explained the differences he observed, "The police pay more attention in Georgia, they check you more carefully and ask you more questions when they stop you." Both he and Howard were curious as to how Gary prowled the Wynnton Road area without constant confrontation.

Benjamin Harrow is a Columbus police officer —a beat cop who patrols the river district. On his beat they call him Ben. He is large, friendly, and non-intimidating even in the gray and blue uniform. He has one thing in common with Carlton Gary — he is also black.

Harrow is one of the rare policemen who does not believe in the death penalty. Not because he's a liberal but because he's a Christian, raised on the beliefs taught him in a black Baptist church in Michigan. Ben was reared in a family with strong ties to the church and taught to believe that "thou shall not kill" applied to everyone. He never found any exemptions in the Bible for government killings.

He also has strong convictions about doing right and punishing wrong. He believes life without parole for those who kill, but wishes for a way to achieve it without burden to the taxpayer. Ben Harrow knows he doesn't have all the answers and is thankful that, so far, few people have asked him to provide them.

He was living in the North at the time of the stranglings. All he knows is what he has heard, mostly from the African-American community, various people's opinions about Carlton Gary. "Most folks in the African-American community say he was just a petty thief and had never been known to be violent. There's still a lot of doubt in people's minds about whether or not they got the right guy," he says. Ben, however, maintains faith in the department for which he works.

The evidence against Carlton Gary was strong. To believe he is innocent, jurors would have to have believed that police had been planting evidence against him since 1970. It would have to have involved a collaboration between police in Albany, N.Y.; Syracuse, N.Y.; Albany, Ga.; and Columbus, Ga. The strongest evidence that this is not the case is whenever Carlton Gary was confronted with the fact that his fingerprints were in the home of strangled women, he never claimed they had been planted. He always acknowledged his presence and pointed the finger at other men — other black men. The loyalty that many African-Americans display in each other apparently did not extend to Carlton Gary.

Most of the people of Columbus weren't aware of the violence in Gary's past. It had all occurred far away from Columbus. When 12 jurors from an unaffected area of Georgia were presented with the evidence, it took them less than one hour to conclude that the Columbus Stocking Strangler was Carlton Gary.

Gary continues to wait on death row for higher courts to decide his fate. He has, as of this writing, been on death row for more than a dozen years. Even though his case has been upheld through all state appellate courts, including the Georgia Supreme Court, Gary now has the option of appealing his case through the entire federal appellate court system, which could delay his final destiny as much as another decade. Making matters worse for those who are waiting for his sentence to be carried out is that if, at any point during the process any of the courts find reversible error, Gary could be sent back to Columbus to be tried again.

Even with Gary's conviction, the people of Columbus continue to be denied the justice most feel they deserve more than two decades after his reign of terror. The families of nine women who didn't deserve to die still know the pain of their loss. A race not wanting to believe the worst of one of their own struggle for the truth amidst their own distrust. A city that did not deserve the tragedy, having suffered through eight years of fear and frustration, now suffers with a generation of doubt and wonder. At this writing, Carlton Gary sits on Georgia's death row, seemingly as deserving as anyone who ever sat there.

8

MURDER ON TROUBLESOME CREEK
Griffin, Georgia 1991

He stood shivering in the cold December rain. Twelve-year-old Matthew Huey stared at the small wooden shack he was too afraid to enter. It was the home in which he lived with his six-year-old brother Jacob and their parents, Steve and Barbara Huey.

The shack was constructed from plywood, four uninsulated walls and a black felt roof covering the one-room structure. The majority of the wood was unpainted except for the green screened door that closely matched the garden hose — the structure's only source of running water — hanging from the rope clothesline outside. It was constructed on a wooden platform which allowed Matthew or Jacob to see any loose balls or stray cats hiding under the shack or, for that matter, the other side of the yard beyond the structure. But Matthew wasn't looking for loose balls, or stray cats, in the pouring rain. He was listening to his parents as they argued inside.

Suddenly — gunshots! Matthew took off running through the woods, sure that the sound of gunfire meant that his mother was dead. When the boy reached their neighbor's home through the woods, Kerry Sampler found a frightened and crying 12-year-old Matthew. The boy told his neighbor, "I think my mother has been murdered."

Sheriff's deputies arrived to find that neither Barbara nor Steve Huey had been murdered. Steve denied that shots had been fired, but they had.

District Attorney case file photo.

The deputies listened to Matthew's tale of the violence the two boys had witnessed and notified the state's Department of Family and Children Services known by the acronym DFACS

DFACS was called in to review the children's situation. State worker Mary Ann Lyons talked to the boys and decided the appropriate action would be relative placement — placing the boys with a relative who could provide a more appropriate atmosphere until the parents could insure a non-violent home.

That was the function of DFACS, providing a temporary safe haven for children, preferably a home familiar to them. When the children's home atmosphere was deemed appropriate, DFACS would counsel the parents hoping to persuade them to maintain the proper, nurturing home to which the children could return.

The DFACS worker eventually assigned the task of following through with the Huey case was Gloria Boyer. Upon her first home visit after receiving the case, Boyer was shocked at the living conditions in the plywood shack with its lack of running water and indoor plumbing.

For Steve and Barbara Huey, a proper atmosphere would require radical improvements to the one-room shack they called home. Until that could be achieved, the children were sent to live with their grandparents, and then later with Steve's brother.

Boyer developed a plan which Steve and Barbara would have to follow, including adding an indoor bathroom and other improvements, in order to have their children returned to them. Those improvements would never come.

He laid drunk in the misting rain. Sleeping off his second night of celebrating his inheritance — a whopping $3,200 — his share of the proceeds from the sale of his deceased mother's home. For Carol Baggett it was a fortune which couldn't have come at a better time. As he lay there he had not yet realized he had already been relieved of his windfall, enjoying only freedom from jail and a couple of nights of drunk celebration before the loss.

He had been sitting in jail unable to post bail when the money came through. He was serving time for a probation violation after he failed to pay his fines on a driving under the influence charge. His nephew Kim, who delivered him his money, used a portion of it to post the bond of $388. Carol once again was free.

After securing Carol's release from jail, Kim drove his uncle to his current place of residence, 129 Green Valley Road, in Griffin. His home was not the residence at that address but a junk car which sat in the front yard. The house there belonged to Carol's friend, David Jones, and his mother. But Carol didn't have to sleep in the car that first night out of jail. Thanks to his new-found wealth he would be able to stay in a motel room.

Before he went to find a room he sat and drank beer with his friend, David. David tried to talk Carol into putting his money in the bank but Carol wouldn't hear of it. Buddy Imes came by and took Carol to the Capri Motel where he could spend the night in a comfortable bed instead of the back seat of a junk car or in a jail cell.

They stopped at the liquor store on the way and Carol brought a quart of Canadian Hunter whiskey. He spent that Friday night alone with his whiskey.

The following morning, Buddy Imes came back to pick him up because the motel would not let Carol stay another night. The Atlanta Motor Speedway was just north of Griffin and it was Saturday, March 16, a race weekend. A motel room would be hard to find, and the price for a room would be expensive. The motel operators would be profiteering in response to the heavy demand for rooms due to the upcoming race.

Buddy took Carol back to David's house where the junk car awaited him, but this time there was a problem. David's mother had grown tired of Carol hanging around and sleeping in the car. She told David to get rid of him.

By that time, Steve Huey and Tim Kent had stopped by in Steve's truck. David told Carol he would need to find somewhere else to sleep. Carol got in the truck and left with Steve, Tim, and David to look for a motel room.

They tried Baker's Motel but it was full. After leaving Baker's, David asked to borrow $150 of Carol's inheritance to buy some marijuana. Carol agreed and pulled out his wad of fifties and hundreds. It was the first time Steve and Tim saw the money. They took David to buy his marijuana, then took him home.

Steve offered to let Carol sleep at his place. The three planned to drink by a campfire. Steve and Tim saw this as an opportunity to be one step closer to the wad of money they now knew to be in Carol's wallet. They stopped and bought a half gallon of liquor and some beer and headed for Steve Huey's shack, but not before stopping for gas, which Carol paid for, as he had the beer and liquor.

They drank by the fire at Steve's until they all became sleepy. Steve went inside the shack to sleep. Carol slept in the truck and Tim slept by the campfire. The following morning Steve and Tim woke Carol and told him they were taking him back to David's house. It was there they put him out. He was "about half rum dumb" as he would later put it and couldn't get the car door open so he simply lay on the ground. That's where David found him lying in misting rain and told him to get up and get in the car.

"Do you still have your money?" David asked. Carol checked for his wallet in his back pocket and it wasn't there. He found his wallet in his coat pocket and to his horror, his money was gone.

When Carol sobered up, David called the sheriff's department to come to the Green Valley Road home to take a report of Carol's stolen money. It was Sunday, March 17. Carol named Tim Kent and Steve Huey as suspects in the theft.

Tim Kent's mother was worried about him. He hadn't called her as he always did. She began calling friends and family inquiring about him. He had, however, called his half brother, Todd.

On Sunday, March 17, Tim called Todd Blanton and told him he had checked into the Scottish Inn Motel in Locust Grove and wanted Todd to come see him. When Todd asked why, Tim said he wanted Todd to get him some marijuana. Todd went by his half brother's motel room and collected $200 from Tim to be used for the purchase of marijuana. Todd returned to the motel room later in the day with a friend named Keith and the marijuana. Todd saw that Tim had a wad of money, fifties and hundreds. Todd thought it was about a thousand dollars. Tim told Todd that he and Steve Huey had gotten a guy drunk then taken his money. Tim said Steve had the same amount of money. Tim asked Todd to call their mother and tell her he was all right but not to tell her where he was.

On Tuesday, March 19, Todd and Keith decided to go by and see how Tim was doing. They found him in the motel room drinking liquor and attempting to put together a tent in his motel room. He told them Steve Huey had just left. Tim told Todd and Keith that he wanted to go camping and fishing and showed them a Zebco 33 rod and reel he had also purchased.

Todd leaned back on the bed and drank a shot of liquor while Keith showed Tim how to put the tent together. Tim told them that he had to leave the motel on Wednesday. That was when he planned to go on his camping and fishing expedition. Todd and Keith left Tim alone with his liquor and his tent. Todd never saw his brother again.

———————————

Maurice Foster operated two grocery stores in the Griffin area with the help of his two sons. One store was in the downtown Griffin area and the other, Foster's Supermarket, was at the corner of McIntosh Road and Hill Street. On Thursday, March 21 Maurice's son, Kenneth was working at the Hill Street market when a familiar customer entered the store.

Steve Huey had been a customer at the Foster's Supermarket for almost 16 years. Kenneth knew him as a rather loud customer whom he often heard before he saw. He was also a customer who seldom purchased more than $10 in groceries at a time. That Thursday was different. Steve gathered more than $60 in groceries, including numerous expensive meat items: a whole ham, whole chicken fryers, ground beef, etc.

Kenneth asked Steve what all the groceries were for. Steve told Kenneth they were going camping on Troublesome Creek to live like mountain men. The "they" that Steve spoke of was the other oddity in Steve's shopping habits that day. Steve usually came into the store alone, but that day he was with a friend. Kenneth saw Steve go out to his pickup truck where his friend was waiting. Kenneth saw the friend give him money. Steve reentered the store and purchased a case of Budweiser.

Kenneth was so surprised to see Steve with someone he turned to Sheila Cochran and asked, "Who was that guy with Steve?" Sheila replied, "He's a guy that used to work for my father." Sheila would later identify him from a photograph as Tim Kent. Cathy Reece knew Tim Kent well. She also saw him with Steve that Thursday, later in the evening, between 8:00 p.m. and 9:00 p.m., at the Kangaroo Nite Owl convenience store next to Mason's Grocery. Tim was sitting on the passenger side of a white pickup truck parked at the gas pumps.

Cathy knew Tim's mother was worried about him and looking for him. Tim's mother had called Cathy asking her to go to Steve Huey's shack with her and look for Tim. She went up to Tim and told him he needed to get in touch with his mother because she was worried. He looked at her and just gave a sort of laugh. At that point, Huey approached the truck and told Tim that he was flat broke and asked Tim for money to pay for the gas and beer.

"I'm not giving you any goddamn money!" Tim snapped. "You had just as much money as I had. What the hell did you do with it?" Steve replied, "If you don't give me the money to pay the man, he's going to call the law and we're gonna go to jail." Tim reluctantly gave Steve the money. Cathy's encounter was the last time anyone would ever admit seeing Tim Kent alive.

Thirty-three-year-old Amos Surrett was a salesman for Bob Evans Farms. For the past seven years he had lived in a rural area of Spalding County on Bar H Road. When the weather became hot, Amos would run his hunting dogs up Troublesome Creek to cool off.

It was hot that Saturday, March 23. Amos had been running his dogs for a little over two hours. They were in a densely wooded area of the creek when he decided to stop and smoke a cigarette. As he watched his dogs, he noticed one dog began sniffing in the air. When Amos looked in the direction that had drawn the dogs attention, he saw one of the worst sights he would ever have to endure. There was a body in Troublesome Creek. As Amos approached closer he saw that the body had been horribly mutilated.

Amos hurried home and called the sheriff's department. When the operator answered the phone Amos told her, "I just found a body in Troublesome Creek with no head and no hands!"

Lieutenant Laurie Littlejohn had been with the Spalding County sheriff's department for eight years. She was currently assigned to the Detective Division working crimes involving children.

She was working that Saturday in the lobby of the sheriff's office with Sheriff Richard Cantrell. They were collecting money for the junior deputy program, hoping to send some of the junior deputies to Washington, D.C.

Brenda Collins, the sheriff's receptionist, had just received the shocking phone call. She knocked on the glass to get the Sheriff's attention in the lobby. "I've got a man on the phone who says he's just found a body in Troublesome Creek with no head and no hands."

The sheriff turned to Detective Littlejohn, knowing her county-issued vehicle was a sport utility and instructed her. "Go to my house and get my trailer and four-wheeler and meet me at the Wolf Creek Baptist Church."

The sheriff also summoned the on-call detective, Ted Godard, a 17-year veteran in the department. He told Godard to meet him at the Wolf Creek Baptist Church on Smoak Road.

Godard arrived and met with uniformed officers who informed him of the direction of the discovery. Godard traversed the five or six hundred yards of thick forest and came to an open pasture with a fence along the creek bank. When he looked down into the creek, he saw the body.

Godard, known as a keen observer and a master of understatement, later testified of this moment; "I noticed that the head and the hands were missing." Godard also saw what he believed to be bloodstains on a tree and on the ground at the top of the creek bank.

Sheriff Cantrell and Detective Littlejohn arrived, and the three went into the water to retrieve the body. Littlejohn stood at the head of the body, Godard at the feet. Sheriff Cantrell stood beside the body and rolled it over. He began to look for some type of identification. He noticed two packs of Marlboro cigarettes in the back pocket of the victim. As he removed them he noticed one of them had a fishing license tucked down into it. As valuable as the fishing license was, the cigarette packs would prove to be just as important to the case.

Littlejohn, known to all of her co-workers as Laurie, watched her boss unfold and read the fishing license and then give her a solemn look. "I'm sorry, Laurie," he said. With those words fear struck Laurie as she ran through her mind a list of possibilities of who it might be. "It's Tim," said the sheriff. He didn't need to say "It's Tim Kent" and he didn't bother. The simple words, "It's Tim," told her exactly who the victim was. The hairs arose on the back of her neck and she rocked her head back thinking of the worried phone call she had received from her Aunt Tillie, knowing what this would do to her.

Searches for the head and hands of the victim that Saturday evening were futile. Rain-swollen tributaries to the creek were deeper than usual and difficult to search.

With nothing more than a fishing license to rely on as identification Sheriff Cantrell opted not to attempt to notify Tim's next of kin until a more reliable identification could be made. On the following day the waters on the creek's branches shallowed with the drier weather. Tim's hands were found a short distance up the creek. The finding of the hands would allow for a positive identification of Tim by fingerprints. By then investigators also had identified him by a distinctive tattoo on his right shoulder — a symbol of his outlook on life. It was a tattoo of a hand giving the sign universally recognized as "the bird." The time had come for the family to be notified — Laurie's family.

Laurie's immediate supervisor was the chief investigator for the sheriff's department, Lieutenant Clint Phillips. On that Sunday he came to her and said, "Laurie I think you should tell Tim's mother what has happened." Laurie's response was immediate. "I really don't want to! If I do that she will think of it every time she sees me. It's not fair to her and it's not fair to me!" Phillips told her. "Well, I think you should do it."

Laurie's uncle was Tim's step-father, Bob Brown. His wife Phyllis is the aunt Laurie calls Tillie. Bob worked for a local phone system company and Lieutenant Phillips devised a plan Laurie would summon her uncle to the sheriff's department under the pretense that a phone was in need of repair. "God, I hated doing it that way!" she later recalled.

There had been rumors all over town that a mutilated body had been found the day before. When Bob arrived he had heard the rumors and only needed to be told that the body was indeed Tim. Lieutenant Phillips instructed Laurie to go with her uncle to inform his wife that she had lost her oldest son.

Bob Brown pulled into the driveway of his middle class brick home in his black Ford Courier pickup with his niece, Laurie, following in her sheriff's department Chevy Blazer. Laurie was in uniform. When her Aunt Tillie came to the door and saw them approaching she immediately knew this visit was official. She, too, had heard the rumors going around town. Her son was missing, and any parent would have been running those worst fears through their mind.

She spoke before either Laurie or Bob could even approach her. "Noooo! Noooo! Noooo!" She backed her way into the dining room. Throwing up her arms she kneeled down in the corner blocking her ears from the news she could not endure. She eventually raised a tearful look at Laurie and asked, "It's Tim, isn't it?" Laurie painfully acknowledged it was.

Tim Kent in happier days. District Attorney case file photo.

It was 1991. The President of the nation was George Bush; Zell Miller was serving his first year as Georgia's governor. It was the year of the Gulf War — Desert Storm — and the year Civil War broke out in Yugoslavia.

Bob and Tillie arranged for Tim's burial. Tillie had wanted to delay the burial while police looked for his head. Laurie later recalled, "The hardest thing for her was burying Tim without his head but she couldn't wait any longer." Sheriff's investigators continued to search for Tim's head as well as the identity of his killer. The Georgia Bureau of Investigation was invited into the case and assigned Special Agent Doug Carter to join the investigation.

There was no smoking gun leading investigators to Tim's killer. The investigators and prosecutors would have to piece their case together bit by bit. They began tracing the last few days of the life of Tim Kent. They theorized that the reason for cutting Tim's head and hands off was to hinder his identification. Therefore, they believed that finding out who he was with the last few days of his life would lead them to their suspect. This would eventually lead them straight to Steve Huey.

Plaster casts of tire impressions on the ground, photographs and samples of the blood, and tool marks on the ground were the only physical evidence gathered from the crime scene.

That Saturday night, March 23, a crucial witness approached a deputy who had been left to guard the crime scene. Clint Davis, a local school teacher, told the deputy that he had confronted a man camping in that same wooded area Thursday afternoon between five and six p.m. The man had identified himself to Davis as Steve Huey and had pretended to be the caretaker of the property.

The following day investigators gathered at the campsite where Davis indicated he had seen Steve Huey. One of the investigators present was Chuck Hudson, an 11 year veteran of the Spalding

County Sheriff's Department. Hudson knew Steve Huey and told the other investigators that Huey lived only a quarter-of-a-mile away.

Hudson and Agent Doug Carter drove to Huey's shack with the intention of merely turning around in the driveway so Carter could observe the shack. When they attempted to turn around in the driveway, Huey was at the top of the hill talking to two other men and waved at the car to come up the driveway.

Huey recognized Hudson and began talking to him about the discovery of his friend Tim Kent's body. Hudson asked Huey about his whereabouts that week. Huey gave an accounting which did not include him being in the area of Troublesome Creek or Smoak Road on the Thursday Davis had reported seeing him. Hudson specifically asked him if he had been fishing or camping in the area. On that initial interview, Huey answered no. When Hudson attempted to question him further Huey said he was tired and wanted to rest before answering any more questions.

Later in the evening, Huey voluntarily came to the sheriff's office where he was again interviewed by Chuck Hudson. This time he gave a story which conflicted with the one he told Hudson earlier in the day. He still denied being in the woods off Smoak Road on Thursday afternoon and denied having been with Tim Kent at all on that day.

The investigators considered Huey a good suspect. The following day they decided to arrest him — not for murder but for his role in the theft of Carol Baggett's inheritance. Investigators began to build their case. Numerous discrepancies were found in all of his statements, and numerous witnesses were found who could swear they saw Huey with Tim on Thursday — the last day he was seen alive. A significant circumstantial case was prepared by Agent Carter and Spalding County sheriff's investigators. On March 26, 1991, Gerald Steve Huey was charged with the murder of Tim Kent.

On April 2, 1991, the skull portion of Tim's head was found. A dog owned by Mrs. Tilman Blakely ran up in the yard of her Smoak Road residence with the skull. Missing from the skull was the lower mandible. Mrs. Blakely's dog was locked up, and cadaver dogs from Columbus, Ga., were brought in to search for the mandible, to no avail. On the following day, April 3, sheriff's investigator Ron Buchanan went back to the Blakely residence and released the dog that had found the skull. The dog ran to an open field and came back with the missing mandible. The yard dog had done what the trained cadaver dogs could not. Finally all of Tim's remains had been located. But Tillie Brown could still not bury all of her son. Prosecutor Bill McBroom wanted to use the skull in the trial. Not until after the trial would she be able to complete the burial.

Gerald Stephen Huey shortly after his arrest.
District Attorney case file photo.

Gerald Stephen Huey was indicted by the Spalding County grand jury for felony murder, malice murder and theft by taking. The trial judge was Chief Superior Court Judge Andrew Whalen, recognized by that time as a legal legend in the state. The District Attorney for the Griffin Judicial Circuit was W. Fletcher Sams. Sams was in the middle of a re-election campaign and was unable to properly prepare the case for trial. He assigned it to one of his assistants.

D.A. Sams assigned Assistant District Attorney William T. "Bill" McBroom, III to prosecute the case, with his assistance. McBroom was a sharp trial lawyer with a hard-driving courtroom presence.

Huey was represented by public defender Johnny B. Mostiler. In many court circuits there is a common belief that the use of a public defender is an inferior or less than competent defense — a defense of last resort. That was not the case in Griffin. Johnny Mostiler was a recognized, competent defense attorney and a worthy adversary for the state. He possessed subtle craftiness combined with a gentlemanly courtroom presence. Whether he believed it or not, Huey was well represented.

In pretrial proceedings Mostiler filed a motion for a change in venue. Judge Whalen ruled that the jury would be chosen in Cobb County north of Atlanta, but the trial would be conducted in the Spalding County courthouse in Griffin.

The Cobb County jurors got their first hints of some of the peculiarities of the case they would hear during a process known as the *voir dire*, where attorneys ask potential jurors questions in an attempt to determine if they will be suitable. Mostiler had asked the jury pool during *voir dire* if they would hold prejudices towards a person simply because that person lived a lifestyle alternative to that of their own. Mostiler was obviously worried about what the jury might think of Steve and Barbara Huey's lifestyle.

The trial began May 25, 1992 — Memorial Day. Some expected

a spectacular trial due to such a gruesome and horrific murder. The two-week trial was actually a tedious affair for prosecutors. McBroom and Sams laid out a circumstantial case against Gerald Stephen Huey, who was not only the last person to see Tim Kent alive but also was the last person seen arguing with him.

On the morning the trial was to begin, defense attorney Mostiler asked Judge Whalen to prohibit the state from mentioning the words dismemberment or disfigurement during the guilt/innocence phase of the trial since the autopsy proved that disfigurement was not the cause of death. Mostiler argued, "We would submit that it is not relevant to the issue of Tim Kent's death." Judge Whalen responded, "The fact of death is not the only fact the state has got to prove." Judge Whalen overruled the motion but told Mostiler he could renew the motion later if testimony did not appear relevant.

Before the trial began Judge Whalen gave Huey the opportunity to comment on his satisfaction with his defense attorney.

> **Judge Whalen:** Mr. Huey, at this time I want to give you an opportunity to state any objections that you might have to Mr. Mostiler as your defense counsel, or to the manner in which he is conducting or has conducted your defense.

> **Steve Huey:** Your Honor, I only want to say that I am well satisfied with my representation, and having never had to face anything like this before, I am well satisfied.

The trial proceeded with the state's opening argument presented by prosecutor McBroom. McBroom outlined the circumstantial case G.B.I. and sheriff's investigators had built against Gerald Steven Huey. McBroom also warned the jury that some of his own witnesses lived what some would consider alternative lifestyles — like that of

266

one his key witnesses, Carol Baggett. Prosecutor McBroom told the jury, "Carol Baggett is a drunk. Now, there's just no nice way of putting it, he's a drunk."

McBroom went on to explain to the jury his belief that the theft of Carol Baggett's short-lived wealth by inheritance was the beginning of the end for Tim Kent. McBroom laid out for the jury the foundation of his case — his belief that Huey killed Tim Kent for his remaining portion of the stolen Bagget money so that he could make the improvements to his shack that would allow his children to return home. (Evidence in the trial would show that Huey did not spend the money on those improvements but spent most of the money on himself.)

Public defender Johnny Mostiler gave the opening argument for the defense. He, too, warned the jury of his witnesses' alternative lifestyles including his client, Steve Huey. Mostiler told the jury:

> When Mr. McBroom mentioned mountain men, in some respects, that describes Steve's lifestyle. Steve was a man — and you all were asked if it would — you were asked about — on *voir dire,* about alternative lifestyles and the fact that Steve drank pretty heavily, which we will not deny, and the fact that he was sporadically employed. And Steve was an unusual individual in that he cherished his freedom, his right to be on the land, to do what he wanted to do, and not to have to work every day for his money.

Mostiler went on to portray Steve as Tim's best friend — acknowledging that they had spent much of Tim's final week together and that they had camped on Troublesome Creek. Mostiler told the jury that Tim had stolen Carol Bagget's money alone and that Steve had not killed him for it. Of Huey's need of money Mostiler told the

267

jury, "Steve had the skills and he had scraps of lumber around the house to make the room addition without any major expenditure of money. So Steve did not need money, was not seeking money, and had no use for it."

The first witness of the trial was Amos Surrett who testified about having discovered Tim's body. The next witness was Deputy Sheriff William Jenkins who testified that he escorted the ambulance to the crime lab. Jenkins was the first of several "chain of custody" witnesses that established the necessary legal requirements of accounting for the custody of certain evidence that would be presented in the trial.

Spalding County Sheriff's Chief Investigator Clint Phillips testified that he lifted plaster casts of tire impressions on the crime scene. He also testified that he responded to the call on Smoak Road where a woman reported finding Tim's head.

The next witness was Don Robertson, the Special Agent in Charge of the Thomaston Office of the Georgia Bureau of Investigation. Agent Robertson testified that he interviewed Phyllis Brown, Tim's mother, early in the investigation about the clothing worn by Tim the last time she saw him. According to Robertson, Tim was last seen by her wearing a pair of blue jeans, a pair of older, high-topped white athletic shoes and an aqua blue long-sleeved pullover-shirt. At this point Prosecutor McBroom attempted to introduce a photograph of Tim's body lying in Troublesome Creek.

Defense attorney Mostiler objected to the admissibility of the photograph and also argued, "Its prejudicial value outweighs its probative value, and I would request — or I would object — to its admission."

Judge Whalen responded, "I'm going to admit it on the grounds that it is the highest and best evidence of what it shows insofar as the identity of the clothing is concerned. And even though it might collaterally show other things, the *voir dire* in this case, as well as the testimony which has been introduced up to this point, has already informed the jury as to the condition of the corpse at the time that it was found."

Agent Robertson testified that the clothing Tim was wearing in the photograph was consistent with the clothing Tim's mother had last seen him wearing. Robertson also testified as to how Tim's mandible, the upper jaw portion of the skull, was later found by the same dog that found the head. The next witness, Spalding Sheriff's Investigator Ron Buchanan said the same.

Sheriff's Investigator Franklin Allen testified next that he arrested Huey after learning that a theft warrant had been issued for his arrest. He also testified of having observed what he believed was smeared blood on Huey's truck.

The next witness was Investigator Charles "Ted" Godard. Godard was one of the initial Spalding County sheriff's investigators who responded to the crime scene when the body was found. He testified to what he observed before the body was removed from the creek, and to witnessing Sheriff Cantrell finding the fishing license in Tim's back pocket tucked inside the wrapper of one of two packs of Marlboro cigarettes. He also testified about seeing bloodstains on a tree near the body and a tool mark in the ground as though someone had dropped an axe.

Godard also testified that he attended Tim's autopsy the following day, and that a motel key was found in his pocket with a plastic tag displaying the numbers 221. He then testified that he returned to the crime scene after the autopsy in the afternoon and found Tim's hands in a stream up the creek.

Godard testified that he found a campsite on the Fontaine property where a witness named Clint Davis had reported seeing Steve Huey camping. He also testified the camping area had been burned but that he found a whole roasted chicken just outside the burned area. He also found a piece of cellophane that looked like it came from a snack cake. Additionally he testified that he found a piece of red and white, heavy gauge paper which Godard thought came from a Marlboro cigarette pack.

Prosecutor McBroom asked Godard if he knew how far Steve Huey's shack was from the campsite. Godard answered, "approximately a quarter of a mile."

Prosecutor McBroom introduced aerial photographs and had Detective Godard show the jury the proximity of where the body was found relative to where the head and hands were recovered, and to the campsite. He also had Godard show the jury where Mason's Grocery and the Nite Owl were in relation to Troublesome Creek.

Godard's testimony was some of the most lengthy in the trial. He testified about search warrants that were conducted at Huey's home and about items found during those searches — cutting tools, axes, mauls, hatchets, and knives. He also testified that a Zebco 33 Classic Feather Touch rod and reel were found under Huey's house.

The prosecution believed the Zebco rod and reel to be a significant piece of evidence. Godard and other witnesses would testify that Tim had purchased a rod and reel identical to this one at Wal-Mart. Clint Davis would later testify that he saw Steve Huey camping at the campsite and saw a rod and reel identical to the one presented at the trial in the back of Steve Huey's truck.

Detective Godard testified that in addition to the burned-out area found at the campsite he discovered there had been a woods fire at Huey's shack. A tool shed had ignited and axe heads and other cutting tools were found to have been burned in the fire.

During cross-examination of Detective Godard, defense Attorney Mostiler made the point to Godard that Tim Kent was a frequent visitor of Huey's and suggested that he might have placed the rod and reel under Huey's shack. He also had Godard testify that no cash was found during any of the searches of Huey's shack.

Mostiler used Godard and other investigating officers to make the

270

point that no murder weapon was ever found anywhere and that no blood was ever found on any of the cutting tools. He also made the point that no evidence was found to place Steve Huey at the site on Troublesome Creek where the body was located. However Godard's testimony indicated that the campsite, where Clint Davis would later testify he saw Huey camping, was walking distance from Troublesome Creek.

The next witness presented by the state was Chris Sperry, the deputy chief medical examiner for the Fulton County medical examiner's office. It was with this witness that prosecutor McBroom introduced the skull into the trial to show the path a bullet had taken. Sperry also testified that the cause of death was a bullet to the brain.

Another key witness was Georgia Bureau of Investigation Special Agent Doug Carter. He was an intelligent, well-liked investigator in his sixth year with the G.B.I. He and Godard had been the main investigators on this case.

Johnny Mostiler, Chris Sperry, Bill McBroom, Debbie Bailey and Judge Andrew Whalen (left to right). Reprinted with the permission of the Griffin Daily News.

271

Carter had interviewed Huey's 12-year-old son Matthew. Matthew had told Agent Carter that his father had owned two .22 caliber weapons, a rifle and a handgun. Carter testified that Matthew told him, "Daddy called it a Saturday night special."

Carter also testified that Matthew had met him at Huey's shack and pointed out a tree that Huey frequently used for target practice. Carter testified that he cut out a portion of that tree that contained several bullets previously fired into the tree. Many of those bullets were too damaged to identify and none were successfully matched to the bullet which killed Tim Kent.

During cross examination, Mostiler again pointed out with Carter's testimony that no firearm was ever found that could be linked to Steve Huey.

On re-direct examination by prosecutor McBroom Agent Carter testified to the significance of the rod and reel. He also restated the significance of a piece of torn paper found at the campsite that matched one of the cigarette packages in the victim's pocket, placing Tim at the campsite where Huey had been seen camping.

After Carter's testimony, prosecutor McBroom began a series of witnesses to outline the remainder of his circumstantial case against Huey. More than 40 witnesses testified for the state. McBroom's case was based mainly on testimony showing that Huey was the last person to be seen with the victim; that they were arguing when seen together; that both the campsite and the Huey's yard had conveniently burned in the days following Tim's disappearance, and that Steve Huey had been seen at the campsite. McBroom also focused on Huey's conduct in the days following Tim's disappearance.

Keith Vining testified that on Friday, March 22, he saw Barbara and Huey at Wal-Mart. According to Vining, Steve said to him: "Tim is in town. He needs to get out of town. Somebody is looking for him." Vining testified that when he asked Steve who was looking, Steve changed the subject.

Eugene Roland testified he was working a night job at the Kangaroo Market on Saturday, March 23, when Steve Huey came in and tried to buy beer after midnight. Roland stated he would not sell Huey the beer and eventually had to call the sheriff about Huey. Roland testified he saw Huey in possession of two $50 dollar bills that night.

Cathy Reece had testified earlier about hearing Huey tell Tim Kent on Thursday night that he was broke. With Roland's testimony, prosecutor McBroom had established that by Saturday night Huey had money again — $50 bills like the ones taken from Carol Baggett.

Tommy Whitehead testified that Steve came by his business on Friday, March 22 and made the statement, "Tim has a bad enemy in Stanley Jones." Whitehead also said that after Steve was arrested he called Whitehead and refreshed his memory about the visit saying, "Do you remember I was at your business Friday?" Huey also told Whitehead during that conversation that he had not killed Tim Kent but that a police officer had. That allegation was never made at the trial.

To solidify in the jury's minds the chain of events that led to Tim's death, prosecutor McBroom effectively illustrated them by using a chart outlining his case. By the time he rested his case McBroom had successfully organized the last week of Tim Kent's life and presented a convincing string of circumstances pointing to Steve Huey having murdered Kent.

It was then defense attorney Mostiler's turn. His strategy was to convince the jury that Tim Kent wasn't murdered until Friday, March 22 — a day Steve Huey had spent establishing alibis all around Griffin. He also wanted the jury to consider other state's witnesses as potential suspects.

When David Jones was interviewed by the G.B.I. early in the investigation, before Tim's head had been found and after Steve had been arrested, he was asked to speculate on how he thought Tim had been killed. He guessed that he probably had been shot in the back of the head. At the trial, Mostiler wanted to know how Jones could have known this. Jones testified that he had simply guessed and that he figured Steve for a "back shooter."

The second-to-last witness for the defense during the evidence portion of the trial was Huey. Some observers at the trial believed this was when the defense's case took a serious turn for the worse.

Huey dropped a bombshell during his testimony. Huey testified that he set up camp with Tim at the Fontaine Lake property and did spend Thursday night at the campsite with Tim. Huey testified that when he and Tim went to the Kangaroo Nite Owl for more beer and gas, Huey claimed he saw Buddy Imes, David Jones, and Carol Baggett drive by in a black Jeep. He testified that he and Tim went back to the campsite and that Tim was very nervous. Huey claimed he left his truck with Tim and walked back to his shack.

Huey claimed that after he got back to his shack someone pulled up to the shack looking for Tim. Huey was very vague with details about this encounter but managed to slip in the suggestion that it may have been David Jones. McBroom objected. The transcripts for that portion of Huey's testimony reads as follows:

Mostiler: Then what did you do?

Huey: Well, someone came up.

Mostiler: Do you know who came up?

Huey: They didn't stay around long enough. I don't know if it was David Jones or who, really.

Prosecutor McBroom: Judge, if he doesn't know

if it is David Jones, I ask the jury to disregard.

Judge Whalen: Well, I sustain the objection.

Mostiler: If you don't know who it was, don't say any names.

Huey: I told the — the person who got out of the car Tim wasn't there, and they left in a hurry.

Huey testified that on Friday morning he walked back to the campsite and saw David Jones driving his truck with Carol Baggett standing in the back of the truck. Huey claimed that after they saw him, Jones and Baggettt ran over to a black Jeep being driven by Buddy Imes and sped off. Huey testified that when he went back to the campsite the tent was gone and Tim was nowhere in sight. Huey claimed he found Tim's rod and reel leaning against a tree and took it back to his shack and put it under the structure. Huey tried to explain away every piece of evidence the state had produced.

Prosecutor McBroom had never heard this story before. He asked Huey on cross-examination why he had never told this story to police in any of his interviews with them. Huey claimed it was because his lawyer told him not to, but on cross McBroom pointed out that Huey was not yet represented by an attorney during any of his three interviews with police.

McBroom also pointed out that Huey also failed to mention during all three interviews that he had encountered Clint Davis while at the campsite on Friday, a point that Huey admitted during his direct testimony. Huey claimed that Tim was also present at the time but hid in the woods.

Much of the cross-examination of Huey by McBroom was tense, and Mostiler would complain in his closing that McBroom was often yelling at Huey. McBroom said after the trial that he wanted the exchanges to be intense to emphasize to the jury when he believed Huey to be lying, like the exchange with Huey about a conversation Huey had with Agent Doug Carter:

> **McBroom:** Mr. Huey, as a matter of fact when Agent Carter asked you who your best friend was, you looked at him kind of like you're looking at me now and you said, "well, Tim Kent was." Isn't that right? That's just how you did it, wasn't it?

> **Huey:** I wouldn't say that I used that tone of voice.

> **McBroom:** Are those the words you said, Mr. Huey, yes or no?

> **Huey:** I don't recall saying that.

> **McBroom:** Well, if you don't recall saying it, how in the hell do you remember what tone of voice you used?

Mostiler objected to what he called profanity and McBroom apologized. But he had achieved his intended effect.

McBroom was able to get Huey to admit that in his initial interviews he denied being on the Fontaine property until Investigator Chuck Hudson insinuated that tire prints found there might match those of his truck.

Huey had testified he had gone to Buddy Imes' house on the same day he was arrested and watched a video of the news broadcast about Tim's body having been found. McBroom asked Huey if he loved his

276

wife. Huey responded that he did. McBroom asked Huey: "Then why did you take her over to Buddy Imes' house if you thought he was a murderer?" Huey's response was insignificant. McBroom successfully established through his cross-examination that Huey's conduct immediately after Tim's death was inconsistent with his current testimony.

The last witness for the defense was Joey Gilbert, a person who had known Tim Kent for years but had only met Huey while in jail with him as Huey awaited his trial.

Gilbert testified that on either Thursday, March 21 or Friday, March 22 he saw Tim Kent at the Kangaroo Night Owl at 6:30 a.m. Gilbert testified that Kent was with two people Gilbert did not know in a vehicle Gilbert could not describe. Gilbert said he remembered the incident because Kent paid for his gas even though Gilbert protested and assured Tim he had his own money. Gilbert remembered Kent being very muddy and telling Gilbert he'd been fishing.

On cross-examination, McBroom alleged that Gilbert had earlier asked for a deal on his pending criminal charges in exchange for his testimony, but Gilbert denied having done so.

After Gilbert's testimony, defense attorney Mostiler rested his case. It was time for closing arguments. Because the state bears the burden of proof, the state would be allowed to be the last argument the jury would hear. The defense is allowed to go last only when no defense at all is offered and closing is the only defense.

Mostiler's closing argument was excellent. He concentrated on a charge in the law that he knew the jury would be given by Judge Whalen. The charge would instruct the jury that a circumstantial case against a defendant must be proven to a point where there is no other reasonable explanation.

Mostiler pointed out that David Jones had told police the method of how Tim had been killed before the police knew.

Bill McBroom in front of a color flow chart outlining the chain of events. Reprinted with the permission of The Griffin Daily News

Gerald Stephen Huey at trial seated with defense team Investigator Billy Howard.

He told the jury the argument that Huey killed Tim Kent was reasonable, but that there were two other reasonable scenarios. He argued that it was also feasible that David Jones, Carol Baggett and Buddy Imes had killed Tim Thursday night and put him in Troublesome Creek to avenge the theft of Carol Baggett's money.

Mostiler offered a third possibility to the jury that one of the men seen with Tim Kent by Joey Gilbert at the Nite Owl had killed Tim and placed him in Troublesome Creek.

Mostiler suggested to the jury that Tim might have told Todd Blanton that Huey helped steal Baggett's money to divert some of the blame from himself.

Mostiler told the jury that Tim's was a terrible murder, but that should not make them feel inclined to render a verdict of guilty. A not guilty verdict would not be declaring Huey innocent, but simply a statement that the state had not proven him guilty.

The closing argument for the state was by McBroom. Before he began he politely asked a newspaper photographer in the courtroom to stop taking pictures of him. He outlined for the jury the circumstantial case he had presented. McBroom told the jury that murder was a crime of passion. He told the jury, "I don't think he killed him *for* the money. I think they were arguing *about* the money."

McBroom also addressed the question of why the murderer had gone to all of the trouble of removing the head and hands of the body and left the fishing license in his pocket. "I didn't say Steve was a good murderer, I just said he was a murderer."

The jury began their deliberation on June 2, 1992, at 9 a.m. On June 5, 1992 at 12:55 p.m. they sent word to Judge Whalen that they had reached a verdict. The jury found Gerald Steven Huey guilty of malice murder and theft by taking.

It was now time for the sentencing phase of the trial. Prosecutors Sams and McBroom were asking for the death penalty. Before the sentencing phase Judge Whalen offered Huey an opportunity to offer any objections to his defense. "I have none, sir," Huey replied.

During the sentencing phase McBroom called a string of witnesses who portrayed Huey as a bad individual with a bad reputation. Mostiler attempted to portray a conscientious citizen who loved animals. A former chief investigator for the sheriff's office, Larry Campbell, testified that Huey had once helped him solve a murder case and testified for the state in that trial. However on cross-examination even Campbell confirmed that Huey's reputation was bad.

On June 5, 1992, at 5:30 p.m. the jury from Cobb County began deliberation on the fate of Steve Huey. At 7 p.m. they adjourned until the next day and on June 6 they began again. At 11 a.m. Judge Whalen called the jury into the courtroom.

Judge Whalen instructed the foreman not to indicate which way they were leaning but to simply tell the vote at that time. "Seven to five." The foreman responded. Judge Whalen asked the foreman, "Do you feel at this point that you are hopelessly deadlocked at seven to five," the foreman responded, "Yes, your honor."

There were those among the Cobb County jurors who could not bring themselves to the verdict of death for Gerald Stephen Huey. Judge Whalen sentenced Huey to the only other penalty allowed by law for murder — life in prison.

One of the most remarkable aspects of the Huey case was his intelligence. One reporter who covered the trial remembers him having a near photographic memory. Bill McBroom remembered, "Regardless of his lifestyle he's an intelligent guy. He has a vocabulary larger than mine. You could place him in a cosmopolitan atmosphere with intelligent people and he could pull it off. The group would never know he didn't belong there."

McBroom was later appointed and then elected district attorney. He would go on to try eight death penalty cases during his first term of office. Five of the defendants were sentenced to death, the remaining three received life without parole.

Fletcher Sams was elected as Fayette County's first State Court judge. In 1998 Chief Judge Andrew Whalen announced his retirement after nearly a half-century as both prosecutor and Superior Court judge. He continues to serve as a senior judge.

Doug Carter continues to serve as a Special Agent for the Georgia Bureau of Investigation. McBroom credits the success of the case to Carter and Ted Godard. Without their help both before and during the trial, Huey would have never been brought to justice.

Detective Godard served 17 distinguished years with the Spalding County Sheriff's Department and earned respect among his peers there and in surrounding counties. Sadly, on October 25, 1996, Ted's daughter Heather walked into his living room and found him in his recliner, dead of natural causes at the age of 44.

Ted Godard, Sheriff's Department photo.

281

On April 1, 2000, Huey's defense attorney, Johnny Mostiler, died suddenly at his home at the age of 53. He had enjoyed a long prominent career as a lawyer and public defender. Although Huey later criticized Mostiler's work, observers of the trial praised Mostiler's defense strategies as masterful considering what he had to work with.

Seven years after Matthew Huey stood trembling in the rain thinking his father had killed his mother he stood, most likely trembling, before a Superior Court judge in Lamar County. At the age of 19 he was pleading guilty but insane to charges of kidnapping, aggravated assault, armed robbery and hijacking a motor vehicle. Having followed his father's footsteps to crime, he was sentenced to 10 years in prison.

Postscript

It was raining the day I drove up to the 1800's cabins which comprised Celestine's home, Sweet Apple. She escorted me past her moody dog and we spent the day going over Georgia's infamous murders. It seemed she knew them all.

I left there with her and Jim Minter's list of the crimes that rocked the twentieth century in Georgia. This is not an all inclusive inventory of their remembrances of the state's worst crimes. You could write 10 books from the memories of Celestine Sibley and Jim Minter.

These are the murders they recalled, that most captured my attention. There are other big murder cases such as the Alday family, the missing and murdered children in Atlanta, but I chose the stories that fascinated me. Stories that remind me that life is not always fair for people like Mary Phagan. More often than not, life is never fair to the poor and downtrodden, but in the cases of Leo Frank and Mrs. Henry Heinz, wealth wasn't enough.

The plights of Leo Frank and the blacks on John Williams death farm taught me a lesson about hatred. Until now I don't think I fully comprehended how evil it can be. I am thankful there were men like Gov. John Slaton around early in the century. If we are to leave Tom Watson's statue on the State Capitol grounds we should build one next to it of Gov. Slaton.

I hope this book resolves doubt in the minds of those in Columbus who I think were deceived.

I found out while researching this story that I could have easily had an encounter with Carlton Gary, the Columbus Stocking Strangler. On our wedding night, my wife and I stayed at the Royal Inn in Hapeville. We were hiding from my family who had a history of showing up on honeymoon nights as a joke. Two months later Gary was caught scaling the balconies there.

I encountered other eerie coincidences while writing this book. While I was researching the Strangler story in Columbus my Aunt Sarah told me, "You know Bruce, you have an aunt who was involved in that case." "Who?" I asked. "Aunt Tamera," she answered. I didn't even know I had an Aunt Tamera. My aunts, Patricia and Sarah, went on to explain that Tamera was my great-aunt, my grandfather's sister. "Why don't I remember her?" I asked. Aunt Patricia answered, "Well, she used a kind of colorful language and she didn't spend a lot of time around the children."

I found out she still lived in Wynnton. My Aunt Patricia took my family and me to see her. She was bedridden and being cared for by a nurse. My children were apprehensive, the way kids often are around the elderly. They walked around the room nervously looking at her antiques and a picture on the wall of a gorgeous Tamera in her thirties.

It was a surreal experience to sit and talk to the aunt I had just met about what she and her friends went through in Wynnton. The visit was not long after my grandfathers death. As we spoke I noticed that

284

she had eyes similar to his. She was the daughter of Green Jefferson Jordan, the owner of Jordan's Meat Market which had delivered quality meats to the Wynnton area until the Depression put him out of business.

She spent the last day of Martha Thurmond's life shopping with her at Mathew's Department Store near Wynnton. Martha was the Strangler's fourth victim. Tamera remembered, "We both bought London Fog rain coats, She bought the yellow one and I bought the green one. When I drove her home she said, "Come on in here and let me show you what my two sons did for me!" Martha boasted of the locks and window security her sons had provided her and proclaimed, "That Strangler will never get me." But he did.

Tamera's apartment was burglarized that same week, probably by the Strangler. Tamera said, "G.J. wanted me out of there right that minute." (G.J. was my grandfather George Jefferson Jordan, founder of Jordan Sausage Company)

The day I talked with Aunt Tamera I had just finished writing the Mary Phagan story, but she had no way of knowing that. Toward the end of our conversation I asked her a question I frequently ask the elderly. What did she remember about her childhood? She began to sing the ballad of Mary Phagan just a week after I had learned and written about it. She knew it word for word.

The following year Aunt Tamera passed away. I found her just in time to record her memories.

My family has a boat we call the "Midnight Cruiser." We call it that because we enjoy going out on Lake Jackson at night when there is a full moon shining on the lake. We have one favorite spot where for years we have sat and enjoyed reflections on the moon-lit lake. I found out while researching this book that our spot was also the spot where John Williams threw two of his victims from his death farm in 1921.

That's what I like about history. Truth *is* stranger than fiction.

Acknowledgments

She was slightly frumpy, wearing a sweater that looked like she made it herself. She had gold wire-frame glasses with a chain that let them to hang from her neck when they weren't being used. At the time she was using them. It was the tattered cover of the book she was reading that first caught my attention.

She was sitting at a table at Hartsfield Airport eating a cup of ice cream or yogurt while she read. I guessed she was around 65. On the table were several magazines with clipped coupons protruding from the pages as book marks. It was obvious she was about to catch a plane and had carried reading material for the trip.

I had never met her, and she obviously didn't know me because she looked up only briefly from her ice cream and my book to notice I was watching her.

She represents, in my mind, the many people who I should thank. People who never met me and don't know me, yet took the time to sit and read *Death Unexpected.* If not for them you wouldn't be reading these words. I hope *Murder in the Peach State* did not disappoint you.

I should also thank those of you who knew me and bought *Death Unexpected* anyway. Bless your trusting (or forgiving) souls.

Murder in the Peach State came only as a result of many people who helped or endured me through my three years traveling the state gathering some of the more interesting murder stories of the century in Georgia.

To all of my family, thank you for your support and patience.

I can't find the words to express my gratitude to Bill McKenney for his friendship, advice, encouragement and financial support. What an anomaly, a Yankee from New York who spends his money publishing Southern writers.

To two experts in writing, Jim and Rick Minter, thanks for your editorial input. Thanks also to Linda Jones, Robin Smith, Todd Foster and Susan Campbell for the editorial assistance.

For those who were involved in these stories and assisted me, I hope the accurate portrayal of your involvement is sufficient acknowledgment.

Librarians possess a special brand of patience that I am very thankful for. If I fail to mention any individual who helped me research I apologize. I do remember and appreciate you all.

Trying to acknowledge everyone who helped me through the last three years makes me nervous. I'm sure I'll forget someone and for that I am truly sorry. I appreciate the support and assistance of everyone who helped me including the following:

Chris Snell and the staff of the Fayette County Library.

The staff of the W.C. Bradley Memorial Library including but not limited to: Connie Heller, Linda Parker (thanks for bringing me lunch), Terenda Tolbert, and Wanda Robinson.

Helen Matthews and the staff of the Georgia Department of

Archives.

The staff of the Special Collections Department at the Atlanta Fulton Public Library: Joyce Burns, Patrick Stolleis and Malik Grohse'.

Becky Jordan, for her awesome work on our website, www.bjordan.com

I would also like to mention the many other people who are due acknowledgment for their deeds, thoughts, ideas and encouragement that contributed to this writing:

Julie Jordan	Ashley Jordan
Hayden Jordan	Ken Rose
Anne Minter	Fay Early
Ralph Ellis	Patricia Cloud
Al and Sarah Worthington	Allison Cloud
Dan Jordan	Richard Jordan
Mike Hattaway	Mahlon Donald
Michelle Walker	Renee James
Keith McQuilkin	Thom McKennie
Judge Fletcher Sams	Jim Hardin
Judy Sanders	Cindy Norton
Tommy Pope	Wayne Michel
Steve Orser	Dave McNaughton
Keith Whiteside	Gwen Imberg
Beth Carrington	Leo Candeleria
Tray Powell	Claire Bone
Nicole Smucker	Mike Pruitt
Carolyn McKenney	Les Gillespie

And my mom, Annette Chambers.

The following is a reprint of a column written by me, printed in the Aug. 26, 1999 edition of The Atlanta Journal-Constitution.

March of 1998 was the first and only time I ever came home and announced to my wife that I loved another woman. The fact that I am still here today, after making such an announcement is a testament to how special that woman was.

I had just spent the day with Celestine Sibley at her beloved Sweet Apple cabin. It wasn't the first time I had met her, but it was the first time I had spent an entire day with her and the first time I had been to Sweet Apple.

Sweet Apple was her home near Roswell. It consisted of two cabins, both built in the early 1800s, which she had connected by a short hallway and done very little else to modernize. The hallway was a wall of pictures of her life with her husband, Jack Strong, whom she referred to as "my friend."

To use the word "rustic" to describe the cabins would be an understatement and would fall short of describing her life there. I saw no televisions, stereos or entertainment centers. All I saw was books everywhere you looked – especially by the fireplace, which was as tall as my chin and was where we sat by a fire and talked all day.

"You can't help but love her!" I told my wife later that day.

"I know," she replied. "She looks like a sweet old lady."

"Oh, no," I responded. "That's not how I would describe her." "Celestine was not just a sweet old

289

lady." She was kind and thoughtful, but with much more depth and grit to her personality than most sweet old ladies whom I've met in my lifetime.

I suspect if she ever heard herself described that way she would have wrinkled her nose the same way she did if you mentioned a politician she didn't like.

She thought that I inferred she was old once and quickly retorted, "I'm not that old, Bruce!"

It gave me the opportunity, so I asked, "Well since you brought it up, how old are you?" She replied, "Well I don't know, I've lied about it for so long I don't remember anymore."

The purpose of my visit with her that day was a new book project of mine. She heard I was considering it and invited me to her home to discuss the project. We ended up spending the day talking about her days as a court reporter covering the trials of Georgia's most infamous murders.

At lunch, her daughter Mary brought over hot chili, which Celestine served with a glass of sherry while her dog, Kazan, lay under the table and growled if my feet came too near. It was one of the most entertaining lunches I've ever had.

After that day, Celestine would call me and have long conversations about writing and murder. She would send me books she read with notes about what she liked about them.

I have no idea how I was honored with the friendship of such a special lady. Her perspective on everything was so unique and thought-provoking, it humbled me to the point of feeling not worthy of ever trying to write again.

I truly came to love the woman. I found myself
struggling with how I felt about her loss until I heard
Bill Emerson's eulogy of her.

His words expressed my thoughts exactly. "I have
a hard time referring to you in the past tense....I will
remember you forever. Goodbye.

Bruce Jordan

Celestine Sibley
May 23, 1914 - August 15, 1999

Reference Guide

Georgia Department of Archives and History
Encarta Encyclopedia 1997
The Atlanta Journal, 1913-1915
The Atlanta Constitution, 1913-1915
The New York Times, 1913-1915
The Madison Journal, 1915
Knickerbocker Press, 1915
The Jeffersonian, 1913-1915
The Leo Frank Case, 1966, 1987, Leonard Dinnerstein Brown
  Thrasher Books
The Atlanta Journal, 1921
The Atlanta Constitution, 1922
Lay This Body Down, 1999, Gregory Freeman, Lawrence Hill
Books, Chicago Review Press

Death Unexpected: The Violent Deaths of Fayette, 1997, Bruce
L. Jordan, Midtown Publishing
Murder In Atlanta! 1981, James S. Jenkins, Cherokee
Publishing Co.
The Atlanta Journal, 1943-1945
The Atlanta Constitution, 1943-1945
Time Magazine, 1946
ATLANTA AND ENVIRONS; *A Chronicle of Its People and
Events*, Frank N. Garrett, "The Best People in Town Won't
Talk" *The Moores Ford Lynching of 1946 and Its Cover-Up,*
Wallace H. Warren
The Jackson Herald, 1967-1968
Time Magazine, 1967-1968
The Winder News, 1967
Gwinett Daily News, 1967
The Atlanta Journal, 1967
Athens Banner Herald, 1967
Athens Daily News, 1967
The Atlanta Constitution, 1967
Griffin Daily News, 1967
The Macon Telegraph, 1967
Newsweek, Aug. 21, 1967
Alone Among the Living, 1994, G. Richard Hoard,
Brown Thrasher Books
The Atlanta Journal-Constitution, 1977-1998
Columbus Ledger-Enquirer 1977-1991

INDEX